# PAUL

# PAUL

## THE FOUNDER OF CHRISTIANITY

# GERD LÜDEMANN

 Prometheus Books

59 John Glenn Drive
Amherst, New York 14228-2197

Published 2002 by Prometheus Books

Inquiries should be addressed to
Prometheus Books
59 John Glenn Drive
Amherst, New York 14228–2197
VOICE: 716–691–0133, ext. 207
FAX: 716–564–2711
WWW.PROMETHEUSBOOKS.COM

06 05 04 03 02    5 4 3 2 1

Library of Congress Cataloging-in-Publication Data

Lüdemann, Gerd.
    Paul, the founder of Christianity / Gerd Lüdemann.
        p. cm.
    Includes bibliographical references and index.
    ISBN 1–59102–021–2 (pbk. : alk. paper)
    1. Paul, the Apostle, Saint. I. Title.

BS2506.3 .L83 2002
225.9'2—dc21

                                                        2002021304

Printed in the United States on acid-free paper

This book is dedicated to
## Dr. John Bowden

# CONTENTS

# CONTENTS

# PREFACE

The following book is based on studies in Paul which stretch over a period of more than twenty-five years. My own approach to Paul received a decisive impetus when, during my work for W. D. Davies at Duke University in 1974/75, I became acquainted with the new Pauline chronology by John Knox and, at the same time, thanks to Professor Davies, with the Jewish side of Paul. As Davies's assistant I was also introduced to how British scholars usually approach the Apostle of the Gentiles with due consideration given to the historical value of Acts. This supplemented my training in the Bultmann tradition during my student days at the University of Göttingen, during which more attention was paid to the Hellenistic side of Paul and the question of the historical value of Acts was neglected, if it was addressed at all.

So far my work on Paul has resulted in the following four books which deal with various aspects of the apostle: *Paul, Apostle to the Gentiles: Studies in Chronology* (Philadelphia: Fortress Press, 1984); *Opposition to Paul in Early Christianity* (Minneapolis: Fortress Press, 1989); *Early Christianity According to the Traditions in Acts: A Commentary* (Minneapolis: Fortress Press, 1989); *Heretics: The Other Side of Early Christianity* (Louisville: Westminster John Knox Press, 1996). In the present book I have tried to pull the various aspects and results of my previous work together by presenting them in a preliminary synthesis, a monograph on the apostle. For understandable reasons the discussion of secondary literature had to be kept to a minimum.[1]

When doing research on Paul I want to discover what he really did, wanted, thought, and felt. The present book is written in the conviction that both Christians and non-Christians must come to terms with Paul, the most important figure in primitive Christianity and in the Church in general until today, in order to be able to rede-fine their place within or outside Christianity in the light of any new insights into the apostle's life and thought.

Let me hasten to add that when I say "Paul" I mean the histor-ical Paul, not the Paul of interpretation. As is the case with Jesus, a great deal of later material has been integrated with the authentic information we have from Paul himself and others. It has to be removed before we can meet the historical Paul. Toward this end we shall have to move through more than one layer of tradition before we can ask whether Paul means anything to us.

Following Albert Schweitzer let me outline the principles of my investigation:

> My methods have remained old-fashioned, in that I aim at setting forth the ideas of Paul in their historically conditioned form. I believe that the mingling of our ways of regarding religion with those of former historical periods, which is now so much practiced, often with dazzling cleverness, is of no use as an aid to historical comprehension, and of not much use in the end for our religious life. The investigation of historical truth in itself I regard as the ideal for which scientific theology has to strive. I still hold fast to the opinion that the permanent spiritual importance that the religious thoughts of the Past has for ours makes itself most strongly felt when we come into touch with that form of piety as it really existed, not as we make the best of it for ourselves. A Christianity which does not dare to use historical truth for the service of what is spiritual is not sound within, even if it appear to be strong. Rev-erence for truth, as something that must be a factor in our faith if it is not to degenerate into superstition, includes in itself respect for the historical truth.[2]

I am quite aware that such an approach is increasingly questioned in some circles, whose leaders consider the method of historical reconstruction and the aim of objectivity that Schweitzer championed to be a modern survivalist gesture that must be recognized as such. Others who claim to defend historical criticism so emphasize the history of interpretation of Paul as to imply that we can understand him only if we ascertain and appreciate the later images of Paul.

Both objections, however, seem to me to be nothing but an avoidance of reality. (The same is true, by the way, for the reconstruction of both Mary and Jesus where the emphasis on the history of interpretation also muddles the historical question.)[3] In other words, though we will never know *completely* who the real Paul was, we must try to approach him as closely as possible, and therefore a critical work on Paul must remain focused on the historical question.

The title of the present book, *Paul, the Founder of Christianity*, contains my historical thesis. Should the assertion be correct, the truth claim of Christianity would depend on Paul and not on Jesus; Paul's message and not Jesus' proclamation would be the primary basis on which the Christian faith was built. Given the importance of the subject, this is one more reason to present Paul as impartially as possible, and strictly on the basis of the sources critically tested. In addition, I want to present Paul with the utmost empathy. Such an attitude is necessary for a truthful presentation of persons whether from the past or present, including, in the case of Paul, not only his Christian and Jewish opponents but also his Gentile critics. Empathy to Paul does not mean

> to make him the only hero of the drama. Paul's letters are part of an ongoing *process* of history in which *conflict and struggle* loom large. In this drama, *every* actor must in principle have the *same* right to sympathetic understanding. In practice, there are problems: we have only the arguments from the one party. Nevertheless, scholarship must be prepared to understand the silent side as fully and seriously as Paul. An interpreter of Paul must *also* reflect on how opponents and nonbelievers might have responded to his arguments. Otherwise our exegesis becomes naive or even propagandistic . . . Understanding, then, *is* the goal. But the ideal . . . is not to understand just one text or one author. Rather, the ideal is to understand the *process* of which all the relevant texts and authors, as well as their opponents and coactors, are a part.[4]

Not until all of the relevant texts have been presented historically and with empathy can one assess their importance for the present and the future.

In the book I present more original texts in English translation than you might expect to find in a work of this size. One intent of this procedure is to emphasize that the ancient texts are the basis for any further work, whatever its methodology. With a similar goal in mind, I have employed underlines, italics, and bold-faced type to stress key words and ideas, and thus foster a close and discerning reading of the text. And by careful analysis of these texts I hope to further encourage the reader to participate in the process of inquiry and thereby to gain confidence in the results. In other words, I want critical readers who understand why one step follows after the other and why the steps have to be taken in the order in which they are taken.

Unless otherwise indicated, the translations are my own and have been discussed throughout, as has the whole book, with my good friend Tom Hall. The English version of this book owes a great deal to his generous sharing of ideas and formulating of conclusions. He began as an editor, he ended as a collaborator.

Gerd Lüdemann
Göttingen, Germany
April 28, 2001

## NOTES

1. I have made free use of some of this already published material without indicating it each time but always revising it.

2. Albert Schweitzer, *The Mysticism of Paul the Apostle* (New York: Seabury Press, 1968), pp. ix–x (from the preface to the 1931 edition).

3. See my books *Jesus After Two Thousand Years: What He Really Said and Did* (Amherst, N.Y.: Prometheus Books, 2001), pp. 1–2; *Virgin Birth? The Real History of Mary and Her Son Jesus* (Harrisburg, Pa.: Trinity Press International, 1998), pp. 7–39.

4. Heikki Räisänen, *Paul and the Law*, 2d ed., rev. ed. (Tübingen: J. C. B. Mohr [Paul Siebeck], 1987), p. xv.

# THE SEARCH FOR THE HISTORICAL PAUL

M any Christians think of the apostle Paul as one of the foremost disciples of Jesus. Moreover, the church has assigned his writings a major role in the canon of the New Testament, and in Christian theology Paul's thought is the focal point of traditional formulations and further reflections. During the history of the church, the rediscovery of Paul has played a pivotal role for church life, as we can see in the great interpretations of the letter to the Romans by the church father Augustine (354–430),[1] the reformer Martin Luther (1483–1546),[2] and the greatest theologian of the twentieth century, Karl Barth (1886–1968).[3] "In fact, one can almost write the history of Christian theology by surveying the ways in which Romans has been interpreted."[4]

From the first, not only Paul but also his supporters and detractors played major roles in the formation of the church, the development of Christian doctrine, and the struggle for ecclesiastical power. Of the twenty-seven documents of the New Testament seven letters stem from Paul himself, six from later pupils, and one other (Hebrews) received an ending (13:23–25) which associated it with Paul[5] and thus assured its inclusion in the Christian canon.

## PAUL'S SECOND LETTER TO THE THESSALONIANS AS A TEST CASE

By way of further demonstration of Paul's tremendous impact on the development of Early Christianity, indeed on the shaping of divergent streams of Pauline schools, let me try to highlight the dynamics of the process by using 2 Thessalonians as a test case.

This document of only forty-seven verses deserves more attention for the issue of orthodoxy and heresy in primitive Christianity than has hitherto been recognized. Its similarities to 1 Thessalonians in structure and vocabulary are rather striking. They were demonstrated by William Wrede in 1903 and acutely and thoroughly investigated.[6] The result was the view that the authenticity of 2 Thessalonians cannot be maintained if it is supposed to have been sent to the same community shortly after 1 Thessalonians. This supposition is (and was) generally accepted by the defenders of the authenticity of 2 Thessalonians in order to give a plausible explanation of the agreement between the two letters, but in fact no expedient can get around the recognition that 2 Thessalonians has used 1 Thessalonians as a model. This follows both from the fact that the most striking formal characteristic of 1 Thessalonians, namely a second thanksgiving (2:13), also appears in 2 Thess. 2:13, and from the numerous verbal agreements.[7]

Further, the contradiction between what is said in the two letters about the beginning of the end should be noted. According to 1 Thess. 4:13–17, the Second Coming of Jesus[8] will occur in the immediate future; according to 2 Thessalonians, the day of the Lord is not immediately imminent, for the rebellion must come first, and the man of lawlessness must be revealed, "the son of lawlessness (4) who opposes and exalts himself against every so-called god or object of worship, so that he takes his seat in the temple of God, proclaiming that he himself is God" (2:3c–4).

This difference, too, speaks against the authenticity of 2 Thessalonians.

Two attempts to disprove the thesis that 2 Thessalonians uses 1 Thessalonians do not get us any further: the first argues that 2 Thessalonians is earlier than 1 Thessalonians;[9] the second contends that 1 Thessalonians, with its lack of explicit scriptural quotations, is addressed to the Gentile Christian part of the Thessalonian community, while 2 Thessalonians, which often cites the Old Testament, is addressed to the Jewish Christian part. The latter thesis is contradicted by the fact that Paul's predominantly Gentile Christian communities were instructed in scripture from the beginning. The former view fails to explain the difficulty of the different expectations of the Second Coming of Jesus. Moreover, it is faced with the clear evidence that 1 Thess. 2:1–3:5 is looking back at Paul's stay during which he founded the community, clearly a visit which is quite recent. How then can there be room for a letter in the meantime?

But if Paul did not compose 2 Thessalonians, and 1 Thessalonians remains the earliest extant letter, then the question arises when, by whom, and why, 2 Thessalonians was written.

The predominant thesis today, which goes back to William Wrede, runs in the following way: 2 Thessalonians seeks to correct the imminent expectation of 1 Thessalonians which has been refuted by the reality of death in the meantime. It is, so to speak, a commentary on the right way to understand 1 Thessalonians.

*Against this*, a thesis which was already put forward in the nineteenth century recommends itself, namely that 2 Thessalonians was intended not to comment on 1 Thessalonians but to *displace* it, because its author regarded the imminent expectation of 1 Thessalonians as heresy and thus declared it out of hand as inauthentic. Thus even measured by the criteria of antiquity, the author of 2 Thessalonians is the one who deliberately produced a forgery. Yet obviously he felt no qualms of conscience in this matter, for he himself warns against a forged letter of Paul (2 Thess. 2:2). 2 Thessalonians then must be considered a counterforgery. (The detailed demonstration of this is given in Appendix 1 below, pp. 247–52.)

## THE ACTS OF THE APOSTLES IN DEFENSE OF PAUL

The Acts of the Apostles, the second part of which deals chiefly with Paul, could be called a work on Paul with a lengthy introduction. As regards the apostle it has two purposes.[10]

*First*, it seeks to remove Paul from the Gnostic sphere.[11] Luke makes Paul himself say (in his speech to the elders of Ephesus in Miletus) that after he leaves wolves will come in sheep's clothing

(Acts 20:29) from their midst and will say perverse things (20:30).[12] In all probability the teachers who are attacked in verse 29 put forward their own interpretation of Paul and claimed to have a secret doctrine accessible only to the perfect Christians. But verses 20 and 27 opposed this with their statement that in his preaching of the gospel Paul did not fall short of anything. That means that a nominally Pauline Christian community in Asia Minor had fallen apart. Luke is the representative of one Pauline party, which is in hopeless opposition to that of the Christian "wolves" who should probably be labeled gnostics or enthusiasts. A dispute has begun over Paul, and it is being played out in places where the apostle himself had worked.

*Second*, the author of Acts is at pains to show Paul accepted by the leaders of the Jerusalem church. This normative account does two things: it serves as a preemptive rebuttal of the charge that Paul deprecated the Jewish Law, but its forced insistence on his collegial status—at considerable variance with his attack on Peter in Gal. 2:11–14—indicates the necessity of defending him on this issue. Furthermore, the Paul we meet in Acts is as faithful a Jew as the circumstances allow. His circumcision of Timothy (Acts 16:1–3) may be more an olive branch than a necessity, but it shows that his heart is in the right place. Later he cuts short his Asian itinerary so as to arrive in Jerusalem as a Pentecost pilgrim (Acts 20:16); and upon arriving there he carries out a scheme proposed by James, ostensibly aimed at demonstrating his loyalty to Judaism (Acts 21:17–26). Still later, at a hearing before the Sanhedrin, he is portrayed claiming that he is (not was) a Pharisee, and by thus making himself a defender of resurrection is able, in effect, to produce a mistrial (Acts 23:1–10). Granted that in each of these cases Paul may be seen to display mixed motives; it is clear that the author of Acts offers us a consistently favorable portrait of his hero's essential Jewishness. Apparently Acts is defending Paul against the charge of being a renegade.

## OTHER TEST CASES: MARCION AND POLYCARP

Marcion, a son of a bishop in Sinope, in Pontus on the Black Sea, owed his basic religious experience to a reading of Paul's letter to the Galatians. He learned from Paul that the gospel is exclusively a gift from God, and cannot be compared with anything in this world. Marcion set out to restore it, and organized the first collection of Paul's (seven) letters with Galatians at the top. In addition he accepted one Gospel—the Gospel of Luke that was purged of latter additions—into his canon, for his hero Paul had also only one Gospel (cf. Gal. 1:6–9). He rejected the Old Testament and added to the canon his main work, called *Antitheses*. The introduction to it runs:

> O fullness of wealth, folly, might, and ecstasy, that no one can say or think anything beyond it [the gospel] or compare anything with it.[13]

Tradition reports that on his way to Rome Marcion met Bishop Polycarp. Bishop Irenaeus, a pupil of Polycarp, tells the following story:

> When Marcion once met Polycarp and said to him, "Recognize us," Polycarp answered, "I do, I recognize the firstborn of Satan!"[14]

This tradition is particularly vivid, as hate-filled legends are at all times. However, it does reflect the historical knowledge that Polycarp of Smyrna was radically opposed to Marcion, who seemed to him to be a baneful reformer. As a reaction to Marcion, Polycarp or somebody from his circle composed the so-called pastoral letters (1 and 2 Timothy and Titus).[15] Indeed, a direct reference to Marcion's *Antitheses* may be found in one of them. 1 Tim. 6:20–21 reads thus:

> (20) O Timothy, guard what has been entrusted to you. Avoid the godless chatter and contradictions [*antitheseis*] of what is falsely called knowledge [*gnosis*], (21) for by professing it some have shot far wide from faith.

Thus a battle over Paul between a radical student of Paul (Marcion) and an orthodox bishop (Polycarp) is in full swing.

## CRITICISM OF PAUL FROM OTHER CHRISTIANS

There are other New Testament documents from outside the Pauline groups, *James* and *2 Peter*, which reflect criticism of the Apostle. James criticizes Paul's doctrine that salvation comes by faith alone, while 2 Peter reflects the use of Paul's letters by heretics and grapples with their use of Paul's imminent expectation of the end. (For further clarification of why Paul was a problem, see Appendix 2, pp. 253–57, in which I have translated and commented on the passages in which the authors of the two writings deal with Paul.)

In addition, it should not be forgotten that Paul provoked a hostile reaction among many Christian groups that had an ethnic Jewish origin. In fact, his name must have been such a curse in their ears that hostility to Paul was transmitted from one generation to the other. In order to degrade him, members of these groups composed anti-Pauline accounts of which only fragments survive. These stories, which imply among other things a gentile origin of Paul, have been partly rehabilitated by modern interpreters of Paul;[16] but this claim is clearly unjustified because his Jewish roots are certain (see chapter 4 below, pp. 88–112).

## ADMIRERS OF PAUL OUTSIDE THE NEW TESTAMENT

As we saw in the case of Marcion, the battle over Paul was not limited to the New Testament documents. The example of a second-century presbyter is worth mentioning at this point.[17] Out of admiration for Paul he composed the so-called *Acts of Paul*, which relate that according to the apostle, women were permitted teaching and baptizing roles. The detection of this falsification—for he was not a companion of Paul, and Paul never allowed women to teach or to baptize—led to his removal from office as a presbyter. Fate was not as kind to our unfortunate elder as it had been to those who preceded him: his dealings were soon disclosed and thus discredited. Many similar activities, and even some of yet more dubious warrant, were accorded official sanction.

## ORTHODOX FOLLOWERS OF PAUL
## IN THE SECOND CENTURY: 3 CORINTHIANS

Another interesting document is the so-called *Third Letter of Paul to the Corinthians,* which is directed against Gnostic and Marcionite doctrines of the second century.[18] At one time it even belonged to the New Testament canon of the Syriac and Armenian churches. It claims to be Paul's answer to a letter from the Corinthians questioning the Resurrection and the almightiness of God, two tenets challenged by the two heretics Simon and Cleobius. By affirming both doctrines Paul becomes the defender of the confession of the Catholic church, the virgin birth being included.

## THE FICTION OF SENECA CONDUCTING
## A DIALOGUE WITH PAUL

Last but not least, there are fourteen letters purporting to be a private correspondence between Paul and the philosopher Seneca.[19] The two hold each other in high esteem, but Seneca criticizes the style of Paul's letters. Although this correspondence was regarded as authentic until the Renaissance, it was certainly forged by somebody interested in claiming favorable recognition for Paul by the leading Stoic philosopher, the brother of Gallio, whom according to Acts 18:12–17 he met at Corinth.

## RESULT

In view of the many diverse reactions to the Apostle, it is quite obvious how difficult it will be to discover the real Paul. How should we proceed in light of these difficulties?

The following procedure recommends itself. First, a chronology, which I regard as the eye of history, has to be established (chapter 2). It should include a reconstruction of the main events of Paul's life and therefore requires more space than the other chapters. After that I shall turn to Philemon, one of Paul's letters, which affords a unique insight into his personality *and* thinking. The letter to Philemon is the shortest of Paul's writings and will be presented in the context of a running commentary (chapter 3). It will be followed by a thematic study of the theological topics of Philemon, which can also be found in the other extant letters. Thereby I hope to provide a basis for the following chapters which deal with "Paul the Jew" (chapter 4), "Paul the Greco-Roman" (chapter 5), "Paul the Christian" (chapter 6), "Paul the Apostle of Jesus Christ" (chapter 7), "Paul and Jesus" (chapter 8), and "Paul the Founder of Christianity" (chapter 9). The final chapter, entitled "Paul's Relevance for Today," deals with a thorny but crucial question: If the ground of Paul's faith, Jesus' resurrection, was a canard, what profit is there in studying Paul today? A brief epilogue seeks to highlight both Paul's personal topography and the historical and cultural landscape of the era so as to enable a compendious assessment of the man and his accomplishment. In view of the complementary functions of thesis statement and conclusion, some may find it helpful to read this piece first as a way into the detailed argument of the book. Three appendices present material which, though it would have interrupted the flow of thought in the text, is necessary as a basis for the argument in various chapters of the book.


## NOTES

1. To be sure, Augustine's great commentary on Romans remained unfinished. We do have an exposition of selected statements from Romans, and a detailed exegesis of Rom. 1:1–7. On Augustine and other interpreters of Paul in the patristic period see Maurice Wiles, *The Divine Apostle: The Interpretation of St. Paul's Epistles in the Early Church* (Cambridge: University Press, 1967).

2. Martin Luther, *Lectures on Romans*, newly translated and edited by Wilhelm Pauck (Philadelphia: Westminster Press, 1961).

3. Karl Barth, *The Epistle to the Romans* (London: Oxford University Press, 1933). The English translation is from the sixth German edition. (The first German edition of Barth's commentary on Romans was published in 1919.)

4. John A. Fitzmyer, *Romans: A New Translation with Introduction and Commentary* (Anchor Bible, vol. 33, New York: Doubleday, 1993), p. xiii.

5. One hundred seventy-eight pages of the 680 pages of the Greek text of the twenty-sixth edition of Nestle-Aland claim to originate from Paul.

6. William Wrede, *Die Echtheit des zweiten Thessalonicherbriefs untersucht* (Leipzig: J. C. Hinrich'sche Buchhandlung, 1903).

7. Cf. 1 Thess. 1:1 with 2 Thess. 1:1–2; 1 Thess. 3:11 with 2 Thess. 2:16; 1 Thess. 5:23 with 2 Thess. 3:16; 1 Thess. 5:28 with 2 Thess. 3:18.

8. Note that the expression "Second Coming of Jesus," which for the sake of convenience I am using throughout the book, does not occur in Paul, who prefers to speak of the coming (in Greek, *parousia*) of Jesus.

9. Cf. John C. Hurd, *The Earlier Letters of Paul—and Other Studies* (Frankfurt: Peter Lang, 1998), pp. 135–61.

10. See the recent monograph by Stanley E. Porter, *The Paul of Acts: Essays in Literary Criticism, Rhetoric, and Theology* (Tübingen: J. C. B. Mohr [Paul Siebeck], 1999).

11. Note that in some gnostic circles Paul was simply called "the Apostle" (*Letter to Rheginus*. NHC I. 4; p. 45.24f.) or "the Great Apostle" (*Hypostasis of the Archons*. NHC II. 4; p. 86.21).

12. In the following I shall use the traditional name "Luke" as the author of Luke-Acts, though the name of the real author of these two writings remains unknown.

13. See the reconstructed text in my *Heretics: The Other Side of Early Christianity* (Louisville: Westminster John Knox Press, 1996), p. 162.

14. Eusebius *Ecclesiastical History* 4.14.7.

15. See the discussion in my *Heretics*, pp. 135–42.

16. Cf. Hyam Maccoby, *The Mythmaker: Paul and the Invention of Christianity* (New York: Harper & Row, 1986), and his *Paul and Hellenism* (Philadelphia: Trinity Press International, 1991). See similarly A. N. Wilson, *Paul: The Mind of the Apostle* (New York: W. W. Norton & Company, 1997). There is an assessment of Wilson's book by N. T. Wright, *What Saint Paul Really Said: Was Paul of Tarsus the Real Founder of Christianity?* (Grand Rapids, Mich.: Wm. B. Eerdmans Publishing Co., 1997), pp. 167–83. Like so many of my German and American collegues in the field of New Testament Studies today the author writes for a church audience.

17. See my *Heretics*, p. 142.

18. See my *Heretics*, pp. 143–46 and pp. 223–24 (English translation).

19. See Montague Rhodes James, *The Apocryphal New Testament, Being the Apocryphal Gospels, Acts, Epistles, and Apocalypses* (Oxford: Clarendon Press, 1924), pp. 480–84 ("The correspondence of Paul and Seneca"); J. N. Sevenster, *Paul and Seneca* (Leiden: E. J. Brill, 1961), pp. 11–14 (the rest of this impressive book deals with the relationship between Paul's and Seneca's ideas).

# 2

# A LIFE AND
# A CHRONOLOGY
# OF PAUL[1]

## THE TRADITIONAL APPROACH

The conventional view of Paul's life may be broadly described as the result of attempts to effect the most ingenious combination of the statements in Acts with the information in the letters. Indeed, a consensus has arisen as to how these two sources may be brought into harmony: one proceeds on the basis of the sole absolute datum for the life of Paul, the Gallio inscription. Since Gallio, the brother of the philosopher Seneca, held office in 51–52, Acts 18:12 is taken as a sure indication that Paul stood trial before Gallio in that year. Further confirmation is then derived from Acts 18:2, which mentions the arrival of Priscilla and Aquila from Rome after the expulsion of the Jews (that year is assumed, on the basis of a later Christian source from the fifth century, to be 49). Since these two dates confirm each other, especially as Acts 18:11 relates that Paul stood trial before Gallio eighteen months after his arrival in Corinth, it is held that Luke's report of Paul's *first* Corinthian mission is historically accurate. With the date of the mission on European soil relatively secure, other dates are reckoned both before and after this period.

*After* the stay in Corinth, Paul travelled to Ephesus, then on to Palestine, and then back to Ephesus (see 1 Cor. 16:8; Acts 18:18–19:1). There and in Macedonia, where he had gone after the stay at Ephesus (see 2 Cor. 2:12; 7:5–7; Acts 20:1), Paul wrote the Corinthian letters or parts of them, later traveling back to Jerusalem in order to deliver the collection (cf. Rom. 15:25–26; Acts 21:15–17).

*Before* the stay at Corinth, Paul had worked as a missionary in Philippi, Thessalonica, and Athens (based on the agreement of 1 Thess. 2–3 with Acts 17). Prior to this mission Paul had traveled as a delegate of the Antiochene congregation to Jerusalem for the conference (Acts 15:2).

One determines the date of the conference, fourteen to seventeen years after Paul's conversion, on the basis of the number of years given in Gal. 1:18 ("after three years") and 2:1 ("after fourteen years"). Confirmation of this view is then found in the reference to the ensuing conflict between Paul and Barnabas in both Acts 15:36–39 and Gal. 2:11–14. For eleven to fourteen years prior to the Jerusalem conference, Paul had worked as a missionary of the Antiochene congregation, in Syria and Cilicia (combining Gal. 1:21 and Acts 13–14). It was not until conflict arose in Antioch subsequent to the conference that Paul initiated the independent mission that ultimately took him as far as Greece.

But a serious problem arises: if this view were correct, then all of Paul's letters would have been composed within a period of about five years. They would all have been written by a man who had already been a Christian for about nineteen years and who was a veteran missionary (cf. Philem. 9: Paul as an "elderly man" of around fifty-five years, see further below, pp. 75–77). Accordingly, one should expect the letters to be quite homogeneous; little room would be left for any theory regarding the development of Paul's thought reflected in the letters. The historian's exposition of the letters could rather proceed from the old theological principle, "scripture is its own interpreter" (*scriptura ipsius interpres*).

## VARIOUS OBJECTIONS

May I now raise some critical objections to such an approach to the chronology of Paul?

(a) Paul was not a delegate representing Antioch at the Jerusalem conference, nor was he a junior colleague of Barnabas. In Gal. 2:2 Paul writes that his reason for traveling to Jerusalem was a revelation. This seems to stand in tension with the Lukan view of Paul as a junior partner of Barnabas (Acts 11:25; 12:25). Further, in Gal. 2:2 Paul stresses his intention to present the gospel that *he* preaches among the Gentiles; this statement allows one to conclude that, at that time, Paul had been operating an independent mission. In Gal. 2:1 Paul notes that he had taken Titus with him to Jerusalem, an action which reflects Titus's inferiority to Paul, while the reference to Barnabas in the same verse reflects an equal status of Paul and Barnabas. The action of taking with him Titus—who is never mentioned in Acts—witnesses to a considerable self-consciousness on Paul's part. It accentuates the inclusion of Gentile believers in the eschatological people of God, all the more so since the dispute at Jerusalem was centered around the demand that Titus be circumcised. Moreover, as we know of Titus only from Paul's mission in Europe, it is indeed plausible that Paul had conducted a mission independent of Antioch *before* the conference.

(b) 49 c.e. as the date of the expulsion of the Jews from Rome is actually uncertain. This date derives from a later Christian source from the fifth century (Orosius) and is in conflict with earlier pagan sources: The combined witness of Suetonius (early second century) and Dio Cassius (late second century) points to 41 as the date of the expulsion (more on this below, p. 60).

(c) Luke's references to incidents in world history are often incorrect. I shall mention here only the following:

1. Acts 4:6 and Luke 3:2 incorrectly designate Annas, rather than Caiaphas, as the high priest during the ministry of Jesus and after his death.
2. Luke 2:1–2 incorrectly dates the census by at least a decade; the census was also confined to Judea and Syria and was not, as Luke reports, worldwide.
3. Acts 5:36–37 incorrectly dates Theudas and blunders grossly by placing Judas the Galilean *after* Theudas.
4. The assertion of a worldwide famine in Acts 11:28 contradicts both world history and Acts 11:29–30 itself, for there it is stated that the congregation in Antioch was able to send aid to Jerusalem.

(d) Luke strings together episodes in Acts by means of loose chronological indications (for example Acts 6:1: "in these days," 12:1: "about that time," 19:23: "about that time," etc.). We must therefore wonder if Luke is not presenting selected episodes rather than a continuous history. Further, one should note the difference between the space allotted to the first thirteen to fourteen years of Paul's life as a Christian (a little over four chapters: Acts 11:26–15:41) and that allotted to the last few years of his life (fourteen chapters: Acts 16–28).

(e) The chronological information offered by Luke is often conditioned by his theological intentions. Luke is concerned to demonstrate that Christianity is a politically safe religion; it is ready to be adopted as a world religion. Moreover, Luke thinks in terms of eras in the history of salvation. The last stage begins with the formulation and adoption of the apostolic decree at the Jerusalem conference. The decree, which James enunciates in Acts 15:19–20 (cf. later 15:29; 21:25), consisted of four requirements for Gentile Christians: to abstain from things sacrificed to idols, from blood, from things strangled, and from fornication. These are things which Jews considered to be the grossest abominations of the pagans (on this see further below, pp. 101–103). Paul is then free to operate his mission among the Gentiles. For Luke, this decree means that Paul stands in continuity with the primitive church. Placing the Pauline mission *after* the adoption of the decree thus primarily serves dogmatic rather than chronological interests.

(f) Another point worth emphasizing under this heading is one that has seldom been noticed. Though Luke several times reports on visits by Paul to a given locality, he presents detailed information about the apostle's activity there only in *one* report, while any other visit is described in rather general terms. In the list that follows I shall give the reports with the detailed information first and after that the reports which are rather general: Thessalonica (Acts 17:1–10; cf. 20:2); Philippi (16:12–40; cf. the two visits in 20:2, 3–6); Corinth (18:1–17; cf. 20:2–3); Ephesus (19:1–20:1; cf. 18:19–21). It is unlikely that Luke had access to local traditions that were related to *one specific visit* only. He seems rather to have gathered various reports stemming from Paul's several visits to a given locality and combined them into a single account.

*The Task and the Method*

These diverse objections reveal the dubious nature of the conventional harmonization of Acts with the letters. Historical investigation is showing us that we have been too gullible with respect to Luke's chronological references: Luke most often operates as a theologian and develops his chronology from proper dogma. The further observation that Luke differs from Paul at some basic points—both historically[2] and theologically[3]—renders it necessary to adopt a method for the establishment of Paul's chronology that proceeds solely on the basis of the letters and only afterward attempts a critical evaluation of Acts. On this point I am indebted to Ferdinand Christian Baur (1792–1860) and John Knox (1900–1990), who both acknowledge the vastly inferior value of Acts as a source for Paul's career in comparison to the apostle's own letters. In 1845 F. C. Baur wrote:

> It would appear natural to suppose that in all the cases where the account in Acts does not altogether agree with statements of the Apostle, the latter must have such a decided claim to be considered authentic truth that the contradictions would hardly be worth attention. . . . The comparison of these two sources leads us to the conclusion that, considering the great differences between the two statements, historical truth must be entirely on one side or entirely on the other. . . . For the history of the Apostolic Age the Pauline Epistles must in any case take precedence over all the other New Testament writings as an authentic source.[4]

John Knox holds that the barest hint in the Pauline epistles is worth more than even the most explicit statement in Acts. Any statement in Acts that conflicts with the letters should thus be deemed an error. Acts merits *full* credibility only where the letters provide a supporting statement; never, however, where the epistles do not confirm an assertion. Knox attaches particular suspicion to those statements in Acts that serve a special interest or purpose of the author. They have to be regarded as redactional features which reflect Luke's purpose and not the historical record.[5]

Another problem—one not dealt with by Knox—arises from

those passages which are related to a period not covered by Paul's letters and which show no particular tendency. Is the information in them to be dismissed out of hand? The more I have worked on Acts the more I have become inclined to take these passages seriously. When analyzing these passages I usually take a piecemeal approach. As a first step, I look at them from the standpoint of redaction criticism; i.e., I try to discover the author's intention in writing the account. Second, I attempt to reconstruct the tradition, and third, I address the issue of whether the tradition is historically accurate. Still the result never has the same degree of accuracy as the reports that can be corroborated by the Pauline letters. In fact, the concurrence of Lukan reports with those of the Pauline epistles provides a high degree of historical certainty. *What Mark is for Matthew and Luke, Paul is for Acts.*

## A RESPONSE TO OBJECTIONS

Some critics regard such an approach to Acts as outmoded.

Admitting that linguistic and stylistic considerations seldom allow for distinction between tradition and redaction in Acts, it allegedly falls back on another old standby: anything that might conceivably have served Luke's agenda may be assumed to have been introduced by him and must therefore be questioned historically. This is, to be sure, the minimalist old saw of redaction criticism that has been challenged by conservative critics for years. They ask, "Why is it so difficult to imagine that Luke found anything edifying or useful in the tradition he received?" and claim, "The assumption that only material irrelevant or contradictory to Luke's own theology can be considered traditional is patently ludicrous, and prejudices the analysis from the outset."

Against this I propose the following: No one can doubt that it is reasonable *first* to reconstruct the intention of a text which is identical with the intention of the author of that text, and *second* to try to determine the tradition that the author had used to compose a text. One of the chief tools for identifying the tradition remains the observation of contradictions or tensions between the redaction and the tradition. *Third,* along with the task of determining the historical value of the tradition thus reconstructed, the question of whether reliable historical information may stand behind redactional statements must also be asked from time to time, even though the results are not often promising. *Finally,* every text requires a method of analysis that does justice to its individual nature. Therefore I shall be open to new insights in the course of analyzing the text of Acts, while for the moment and due to the lack of a better method continuing to use an allegedly outmoded approach.

On the other hand, Paul did not write as a historian either. His statements require critical consideration, due weight being given to the circumstances in which he wrote, to the purpose that he was following, and to the epistolary genre he employed.

To avoid as many of these pitfalls as possible, we shall first subject Gal. 1–2 to a careful analysis, and next employ the collection for the Jerusalem church (Gal. 2:10; cf. 1 Cor. 16:1–4) as an external criterion for the arrangement of the chronological data. After that, a return to relevant passages in Acts not previously analyzed will be necessary to assess how well the information there comports with that of the letters, for by no means do I wish to deny *en masse* the reliability of all the traditions in Acts. My claim is that the answers to such issues as the existence of an itinerary and the actual chronological place of the traditions in Acts may be approached only *after* a careful evaluation of the letters.

## A Reconstruction of the Chronology of Paul

A reconstruction of the chronology of Paul must begin with an analysis of Gal. 1:6–2:10, the central pillar of every chronology of Paul. Here, due to the infiltration of the Galatian congregations by Jewish Christians from Jerusalem, Paul is forced to present a summary of his relations to the Jerusalem apostles.[6] The opponents maintain the inferiority of Paul's gospel to the gospel of circumcision. They probably claim that Paul's gospel is dependent on the gospel proclaimed in Jerusalem, and they say that Paul has fallen away from this true gospel: his gospel must be supplemented with observance of the Jewish law.

For the sake of clarity I shall divide the analysis of the long section Gal. 1:6–2:10 into various pieces, beginning with Gal. 1:6–10.

*Gal. 1:6–10*

> (6) I am astonished that you are so quickly deserting the one who called you by the grace of Christ and are turning to a different gospel—(7) which is really no gospel at all. Evidently some people are throwing you into confusion and are trying to pervert the gospel of Christ. (8) But even if we or an angel from heaven should **proclaim a gospel** other than the one we proclaimed to you, <u>let him be accursed!</u> (9) As we have already said, so now I say again:If anybody is **proclaiming** to you **a gospel** other than what you accepted, <u>let him be accursed.</u>
>
> (10) Am I now trying to win the approval of men, or of God? Or am I trying to please men? If I were still trying to please men, I would not be Christ's slave.

This section refers to anti-Pauline agitation in Galatia. Some troublemakers had proclaimed to the Galatians a gospel contradictory to that of Paul, and Paul considers their acceptance of this preaching no less than an apostasy (verses 6–7). He twice pronounces a conditional curse on everyone who preaches contrary to his gospel (verses 8–9). This conditional curse corresponds to the conditional wish for peace to those who walk according to the Pauline canon (6:15). Verse 10 contains various rhetorical questions and forms a kind of transition to the next section.

To be sure, Paul did not explicitly say that the opponents had attacked him directly, but that is surely the implication of what Paul writes here and later specifies in condemning their demands for circumcision (6:12) and the observance of special days, months, and years (4:10).

In order to counter his opponents' claim that he was dependent on Jerusalem, Paul had to be both precise and authoritative. Note that he underscores his independence by an oath later in verse 20.

It is the importance of this issue coupled with the sworn attestation that allows us to base our reconstruction on Paul's statements.

*Gal. 1:11–24*

> (11) For I would have you know, brothers, that the gospel I proclaimed is not man's gospel. (12) For I did not receive it from man, nor was I taught it, but it came through a revelation of Jesus Christ.
>
> (13) For you have heard of my former life in Judaism, how I persecuted the church of God violently and tried to destroy it; (14) and I advanced in Judaism beyond many of my own age among my people, so extremely zealous was I for the traditions of my fathers.
>
> (15) But when he who had set me apart from birth, and had called me through his grace, (16) chose to reveal his Son to (or, in) me, in order that I might proclaim him among the Gentiles, I did not confer with flesh and blood, (17) nor did I go up to Jerusalem to those who were apostles before me, but I went away into Arabia; and again I returned to Damascus.
>
> (18) **Then** after three years I went up to Jerusalem to get to know Cephas, and remained with him fifteen days. (19) But I saw none of the other apostles except James the Lord's brother. (20) In what I am writing to you, before God, I do not lie.
>
> (21) **Then** I went into the regions of Syria and Cilicia. (22) And I was still not known by sight to the churches in Christ in Judea; (23) they only heard it said, "He who once persecuted us is now proclaiming the faith he once tried to destroy." (24) And they praised God for me.

*Verses 11–12:* These verses, while echoing verses 1:1–2, are the headline for what follows: Paul asserts a factual basis for the independence of his apostleship.

*Verses 13–14:* Paul refers to the readers' knowledge of his pre-Christian life and emphasizes his zeal for Judaism, which not only made him surpass most of his contemporaries but also drove him to persecute the church (see verse 23). On the basis of other Pauline texts the following facts can be established: Paul was a Pharisee (Phil. 3:5; cf. Acts 23:6) and hence—since a Pharisaic education was available only in Jerusalem (see below, p. 94)—must have studied in

Jerusalem. However, he was born and brought up in a Hellenistic city, most likely Tarsus (see Acts 21:39; 22:3). The Jerusalem synagogue of the Cilicians and those from Asia Minor (cf. Acts 6:9b) is probably the one to which the young Paul from Cilicia was attached while staying in Jerusalem.

*Verses 15–16:* See below, p. 173.

*Verse 17:* Paul's statement allows us to conclude that he had persecuted Christians near or in Damascus. (You return to a place where you have been before.) This verse provides the further information that Paul, almost immediately after his conversion, spent some time in Arabia. (There is no information about this in Acts.) Since Paul does not write anything about his stay in Arabia, its purpose and duration are unknown. One can, though, assume two things: *first,* the action of the Nabataean governor of King Aretas referred to in 2 Cor. 11:32–33 (see below, pp. 37–38) was connected with Paul's stay in Arabia, all the more so since "Arabia" means the Nabataean territory. *Second,* Paul engaged in a mission among the Nabataeans who "appeared to be the 'closest' kinsfolk of the Jews who were still Gentiles"[7] and this in turn made him dangerous in the eyes of the Nabataeaen authorities. Let me hasten to add, however, that we should speak of tentative missionary activities only. Moreover, Paul must have been in company of other Christians because a "solitary" mission (as well as travel without company) can be excluded on other grounds.[8]

As for the duration of Paul's missionary activity in Arabia, it cannot have been long extended, because Paul was a convert and must have been in touch very soon with the church members whom he had persecuted. I assume one full year for the journey from Damascus to Arabia, the stay, and the journey back to Damascus.

*Verse 18:* The word "then" (in Greek: *epeita*) at the beginning of this verse and later in 2:1 has created some confusion in research. While all agree that here it refers to the conversion (and thus indicates a time three years after the conversion mentioned in 1:15), opinion differs as to whether in 2:1 it refers to the conversion or to the first trip to Jerusalem in order to visit Cephas (1:18). The fact is clear, however, that whenever Paul uses the word "then" in a temporal sense, he thereby ties what follows to what immediately preceded it (cf. 1 Cor. 15:5, 6, 7, 23, 46; 1 Thess. 4:17). Since this is certainly the sense of the word "then" in Gal. 1:21, the same meaning should be inferred for "then" in 1:18 and also in 2:1 (see below). This means that the first Jerusalem visit took place three years (really two years) after the conversion and the second one fourteen (really thirteen years) after the first visit. (One has to make the adjustment from three to two and from fourteen to thirteen years because in antiquity fractional parts of the first and the last year were counted as full years.)

Verse 18, then, recounts the first visit of Paul to Jerusalem during his Christian period. Its purpose was to get to know Cephas. But it lasted only fifteen days.

There are two additional traditions available on Paul's first visit to Jerusalem. One is in Gal. 2:7–8, the other in Acts 9:19b–30. I shall first turn to Gal. 2:7–8, after that to the text from Acts.

*Gal. 2:7–8—A Tradition Going Back to Paul's First Jerusalem Visit*

In order fully to evaluate verses 7–8 as a tradition that ultimately derives from Paul's first visit to Jerusalem,[9] I shall include Gal. 2:9 in the analysis since it represents the agreement reached by the Jerusalem Conference.

*Gal. 2:7–9*

> (7) On the contrary, when they saw that I had been entrusted with the gospel to the uncircumcised, just as Peter had been entrusted with the gospel to the circumcised (8)—for he who worked through Peter for the mission to the circumcised worked through me also for the Gentiles—(9) and when they perceived the grace that was given to me, James and Cephas and John, who were reputed to be the pillars, gave to me and Barnabas the right hand of fellowship, that we should go to the Gentiles and they to the circumcised;

*Verses 7–8* have often been taken as a direct statement about the conference. Research has reached an impasse in attempting to determine whether these verses represent part of the minutes of the conference or a Pauline interpretation. However, it has seldom been asked whether verses 7–8 might be a tradition which did not stem from the conference, but belongs to an earlier time. This actually seems to be the case, for there are great differences between verses 7–8 and verse 9. *First,* in verse 9 the opposition between Peter and Paul is no longer mentioned. *Second,* in verse 9 Paul returns to his usual designation of Simon [Peter] as Cephas. *Third,* Paul and Barnabas are mentioned together; *fourth,* James stands at the head of the list. These differences lead to the conclusion that verses 7–8 cannot derive from an agreement formulated at the conference. Since they do, however, contain traditional material—Peter as a name for Simon, the circumcized-uncircumcized dichotomy, and the un-Pauline notion of a division of the (one) gospel—we must ask if it is possible to date this tradition.

One indication that this tradition predated the conference is the aorist participle in verse 7: Paul's mission among the Gentiles is both presupposed and recognized. The fact that the aorist recurs in verse 8 shows that Peter and Paul had been entrusted with their respective missions at a moment which lay some time in the past. Further, both the particle *for* and the fact that verse 8 consists of a parenthesis recalling information to the minds of the Galatians allow the conclusion that verses 7–8 reflect a tradition current among Paul's Greek speaking communities—this alone would explain the unusual designation of Simon as Peter—and the corollary that this tradition stems from Paul's first visit with Cephas in Jerusalem (cf. Gal. 1:18). The presentation of Paul and Peter as equals in verses 7–8 is also best accounted for as a formulation of either Paul or his followers, for historically this would be unlikely at the time of the first visit when Paul was still a recent convert. Let me hasten to add that the personal contact between Paul and Peter could very well have been accompanied by an agreement like the one in Gal. 2:7. Certainly Paul and Peter talked about more than the weather when they became acquainted.

*Acts 9:26–30—A Parallel Version of Paul's First Visit to Jerusalem*

This text is all the more important because it agrees with Gal. 1:17 that the apostle went from Damascus to Jerusalem after escaping a plot in Damascus which forced him to leave that city. The persons who pose the threat are different, however: according to Acts, the Jews; according to Paul (2 Cor. 11:32–33), the governor of King Aretas.

I shall now analyze Acts 9:19b–30 in order to gain new information, if possible, about Paul's first visit to Jerusalem as a Christian, or at least to confirm Paul's visit and his whereabouts before this visit. I shall examine the texts in four steps: after a translation I will first give an outline; second I will reconstruct Luke's intention by investigating the editorial elements; third I will analyze the tradition that Luke used; and fourth, under the heading "Historical Elements," I will attempt to reconstruct what really happened by a close comparison of the traditional elements with the witness of Paul himself.

*Acts 9:19b–30:*

> (19b) *He stayed some time with the disciples in Damascus.* (20) *Soon he was proclaiming Jesus in the synagogues, saying, "This is the Son of God."* (21) *And all who heard were amazed, and said,* "Is not this the man who was in Jerusalem trying to destroy those who called on this name? Did he not come here for the sole purpose of arresting them and taking them bound before the chief priests?" (22) *But Saul increased all the more in strength, and confounded the Jews who lived in Damascus by demonstrating that Jesus is the Christ.* (23) *When many days had passed, the Jews plotted* **to murder** him, (24) *but their plot became known to Saul. They* were watching the gates day and night, **to murder him**; (25) but his disciples took him by night and let him down through the wall, lowering him in a basket.
>
>     (26) *And when he had reached Jerusalem he tried to join the disciples; and they were all afraid of him, for they did not believe that he was a disciple.* (27) *But Barnabas took, and brought him to the apostles, and related to them how on the road he (Saul) had seen the Lord, who spoke to him, and how at Damascus he had <u>preached boldly in the name of</u> Jesus.* (28) *So he went in and out among them in Jerusalem, <u>preaching boldly in the name of</u> the Lord.* (29) *And he spoke and disputed against*

the Hellenists; but they were seeking **to murder him.** (30) *And when the brothers learnt of it, they escorted him to Caesarea,* and sent him off to Tarsus.

*Outline*

Verses 19b–25: Saul in Damascus
19b–20: Saul's preaching in the synagogues of Damascus
21: Astonished reaction of the hearers (reference to Saul's activity as a persecutor)
22: More powerful preaching by Saul
23–25: Saul leaves Damascus because of the plans of the Jews to murder him

Verses 26–30: Saul in Jerusalem
26: Saul seeks in vain to make contact with the disciples in Jerusalem
27: The role of Barnabas as a mediator
28–29a: Saul's dealing with the disciples in Jerusalem; preaching and controversy with Hellenistic Jews
29b–30: Saul is brought by the brothers via Caesarea to Tarsus, because the Hellenistic Jews want to murder him

## LUKE'S INTENTION

*Verses 19b–25:* Verses 19b–20 may derive entirely from redaction. The note of time, "several days" in verse 19b, is indeterminate, and the initial approach to the Jews in verse 20 follows Luke's known pattern. The phrase that Saul proclaims that "Jesus is the Son of God" is a remote echo of Gal. 1:16. Either Luke is citing here what is known about Paul in the community tradition or—though probably this is not to be understood as an alternative—here he is showing his knowledge of Pauline tradition and has deliberately become Pauline (cf. similarly Acts 13:38f.; 20:28). Verse 21a is Lukan in language. Verse 21b puts what has already been said (Acts 8:1, 3; 9:1, 14) in direct speech as a question; here by using the verb "to destroy" (in Greek, *porthein*), which he has not used before, the writer is indicating that he knows Pauline tradition (cf. Gal. 1:13, 23). The end of verse 21 takes up Acts 9:2. Verse 22 is redactional describing the preaching of Paul (Jesus is the Christ—cf. Acts 18:5, 28) who, according to the Lukan pattern, turns to the Jews (of Damascus). In its description of the Jews' plan to act against Paul, verse 23 is redactional (cf. 20:3, 19). It is introduced by a Lukan note of time: "when many days had passed." Concerning verses 24b–25 see below, p. 37.

*Verses 26–30:* In verse 26 Paul is in Jerusalem, as though the basket which lowered him down from the city wall of Damascus touched ground in Jerusalem. As the crow flies, the distance between Jerusalem and Damascus is about 125 miles. Saul's determination to see the disciples in Jerusalem after his conversion is a requirement of the redaction because the Jerusalem community is the base of salvation history for Luke's church. Since the disciples' fear of Saul (like the fear of Ananias earlier) is all too understandable, in *narrative* terms it makes sense to insert a mediator at this point. In verse 27 Luke may have inferred from the later tradition of the collaboration between Paul and Barnabas (Acts 13–14) that Barnabas introduced Paul to the Jerusalem community (cf. the parallel instance Acts 11:25–26). This combination may well have arisen out of the interest to write a historical narrative, for in the next chapters Barnabas and Paul are missionary partners. This verse also casts Barnabas in the role of spokesman to sum up the conversion of Paul which was narrated previously (verses 3–9) and his preaching activity in Damascus (verse 20). Verse 28 has Saul conversing with the Jerusalem apostles, preaching in Jerusalem, and debating with the Hellenists. Paul is doing in Jerusalem, in company with the Twelve, precisely what he had already done in Damascus before he made their acquaintance. In verse 29 the apostle fills the gap which resulted from Stephen's death. Of course, the Hellenistic Jews want to murder Saul, as the Jews of Damascus had planned to murder him and as they had previously acted against Stephen (Acts 6:11–14: accusation on the basis of false witnesses to bring about Stephen's execution). The threat against Saul in verse 30 explains why he is sent to Tarsus.

## THE TRADITION REWORKED BY LUKE

*Verses 19b–25:* The report that Paul preached in Damascus is very probably part of the tradition. However, this assumption is only indirectly supported by the present text, which has a redactional stamp throughout, and it arises mainly out of historical considerations (see below, p. 38). The note about the flight from Damascus (verses 24b–25) is part of the tradition. That follows *first* from source-critical reasons: verses 23–24a are a kind of exposition which depicts the Jews plan to murder Paul. The seam between verse 24a and verse 24b is visible in the concreteness of what follows. *Second,* the reconstructed tradition has a striking parallelism with Paul's autobiographical statement in *2 Cor. 11:32–33:*

(32) At Damascus, the ethnarch of King Aretas guarded the city of Damascus in order to seize me, (33) but I was let down in a basket through a window in the wall, <u>and escaped his hands</u>.

The two texts, Acts 9:23–25 and 2 Cor. 11:32–33, have an amazing similarity and break off with the lowering of Paul down "through" the wall, leaving aside the Pauline note of success in verse 33b (underlined in the above translation), which has no parallel in Acts. It is clear that here Luke is using tradition. This must have been as brief as 2 Cor. 11:32–33. Had Luke had a longer story, he would hardly have been able to arrive at such a compact version even if he had wanted to. However, we still have to keep in mind that the Jews as persecutors of Paul in this story derive from Luke as redactor.

As to the origin of the tradition that Luke inserted here, there are two possibilities: a) It ultimately stems from Paul's own oral account; b) it is based on 2 Cor. 11:32–33.

*Verses 26–30:* The analysis of the redaction showed that Luke composed this passage without any support from tradition rooted in Paul's first visit to Jerusalem.

## HISTORICAL ELEMENTS

*Verses 19b–25:* The traditions contained in this section correspond with Paul's own testimony that he had to escape from Damascus. The real reason for his flight was the interference from the ethnarch of King Aretas IV of Damascus who reigned between 9 B.C.E. and 39 C.E. (The ethnarch is the head of the ethnic group of the Nabataeans in the city of Damascus and not the governor.) Robert Jewett notwithstanding, [10] the action cannot be connected with a political rule of the Nabataeans over Damascus between 37 and 39 C.E., for that control never existed. The reasons for the action against Paul are not clear. However, possibly Paul's preaching to the Gentile sympathizers of Judaism might have led to turbulence as it did in his later career. In addition consider Paul's earlier work in Nabataean territory in Arabia (Gal. 1:17) which preceded his stay in Damascus: the action of the ethnarch could have been a consequence of Paul's earlier work, because in all likelihood it included also the Nabataeans living in Damascus.

The action of the ethnarch against Paul should not be exploited as a historical rehabilitation of Luke's account (the Jews as Paul's persecutors) by attributing the interference by the Nabataean ethnarch to the prompting of the Jews.

*Verses 26–30:* Verses 26–29 are a pure fiction of Luke; however verse 30, with the information that after his stay in Jerusalem Paul traveled in the direction of Tarsus, is historical. It corresponds to what Paul himself says, namely that after visiting Cephas he went to the regions of Syria and Cilicia. Tarsus was situated in Cilicia, and after 44 C.E. Syria and Cilicia formed one province. In Gal. 1:21, written between 50 and 55 (see below, p. 62), Paul may simply have adopted the contemporary terminology.

## SUMMARY

In sum, the two additional traditions about Paul's first visit to Jerusalem, Gal. 2:7–8 and Acts 9:19b–30 greatly help us to sharpen our knowledge of this crucial event in the history of primitive Christianity.

## CONTINUATION OF THE ANALYSIS OF GAL. 1:11–24

*Verse 20:* Paul's solemn oath confirms the accuracy of his statements. For example, an additional visit between the first related in verse 18 and the one mentioned in 2:1 seems to be excluded.

*Verse 21:* Syria and Cilicia are mentioned as the place to which Paul journeyed after his first visit to Jerusalem (cf. Acts 9:30). Refuting his opponents' arguments, Paul stresses the fact that he *left* the immediate vicinity of Jerusalem. Nothing is said of how he got to Syria and Cilicia, how long he stayed there, or where he spent the fourteen years after the first Jerusalem trip. (On verses 23–24 see below, p. 151.)

*Gal. 2:1–10:*

> (1) Then after fourteen years I went up again to Jerusalem with Barnabas and took Titus along with me. (2) I went up as the result of a revelation; and I laid before them—but privately before those who were of repute—the gospel that I proclaim among the Gentiles, lest somehow I should be running or had run in vain. (3) Yet even Titus, who was with me, was not forced to be circumcised, though he was a Greek. (4) But because of false brothers secretly brought in, who slipped in to spy out our freedom which we have in Christ Jesus, that they might bring us into bondage—(5) to them we did not yield submission even for a moment, that the truth of the gospel might be preserved for you. (6) And from those who were *reputed* to be something—what they were makes no difference to me; God shows no partiality—those, I say, who were of *repute* added nothing to me; (7) but on the contrary, when they saw that I had been entrusted with the gospel to the uncircumcised, just as Peter had been entrusted with the gospel to the circumcised (8)—for he who worked through Peter for the mission to the circumcised worked through me also for the Gentiles—(9) and when they perceived the grace that was given to me, James and Cephas and John, who were *reputed* to be the pillars, gave to me and Barnabas the right hand of partnership, that we should go to the Gentiles and they to the circumcised; (10) only they would have us remember the poor, which was the very thing I made it my business to do.

This passage gives a report of the Jerusalem conference which took place fourteen years (really thirteen years) after the first visit related in verse 18. Because of a revelation Paul went to Jerusalem along with Barnabas but also took Titus with him (verses 1–2). I suggest that the real purpose of this meeting may be determined through an evaluation of the agreement of the conference as reflected in verse 9.

Verse 9 presents us with the agreement formulated at the conference: it establishes an ethnographic division of the world missions. The purpose of the agreement was to eliminate problems that arose from the commingling of the two Christian groups, Jews and Gentiles. Now, Paul never mentions that he had a mission to the Jews,[11] all his letters being directed to Gentiles. The fact that Paul never did have a mission to the Jews and that Titus is the representative of Paul's mission provide the best example for Paul's statement in verse 6: "those who were of repute added nothing to me."[12] The emphasis of the expression "to me" indicates, however, that something may well have been added to Barnabas. He was the representative of a mixed community and thus would have been greatly affected by such an ethnographic division. The most likely conclusion is that something similar to the apostolic decree (cf. Acts 15:19–20, 29; 21:25) was formulated for the existing mixed communities; Barnabas would have taken this decree back to Antioch.

What happened at the Jerusalem conference? The discussion concerned the requirement that Gentile Christians should be circumcised in order to be able to become members of the Christian community (Gal. 2:3). It was directed against the practice of accepting Gentiles into the community without circumcision, specifically in the community of Antioch, into which those whom Paul calls "false brothers" had crept in order "to spy out" the freedom of the Christians there.

Immediately after that, Paul goes to Jerusalem with Barnabas. In a provocative act, he also takes with him the Gentile Christian Titus, in order to obtain in principle the assent of the Jerusalem leaders and the community there to his own practice.

Two different sets of negotiations can be distinguished in Paul's account in Galatians: one within the framework of an assembly of the community (verse 2a), the other with the "pillars" in a small group (verses 2b, 6–10). The chronological relationship between the discussions is not clear.

After tough discussions and excited arguments, Paul is able to wring from the "pillars" an agreement that the Gentile Christians need not be circumcised. At any rate, Paul's Greek companion, Titus, was not forced to be circumcised (verse 3; cf. verse 14; 6:12). Nevertheless the agreement was fiercely fought for; indeed, it must be assumed that at least initially the "false brothers" had considerable support in the Jerusalem community for their demand that Titus be circumcised.[13] They probably also continued to have "the pillars" at least partly on their side.

Nevertheless, Paul had in principle the assent of the Jerusalem community to his mission to the Gentiles without circumcision. The reason for sealing the agreement with a solemn handshake as a sign of their equality was evidently the mission's *success*. To this the Jerusalem Christians could not close their eyes. Also the readiness of the Gentile Christian communities or their representatives, Paul and Barnabas, to seal the agreement with a gift of money may have carried a good deal of weight.

The Christians of Jerusalem probably adopted an ambivalent attitude toward Paul: on the one hand his action was obviously inadequate, since those who had been converted by him did not observe the Torah. Indeed, it was even dangerous, since their example constantly prompted Jews to transgress the law. On the other hand, it was better than nothing, since Christ was being preached (cf. Phil. 1:18) and centers were being founded in which the work could be continued—and perhaps corrected by delegates from Jerusalem.

Assuming that these reflections are accurate, the generous gesture on Paul's part was perhaps what won them over, all the more so since from the gift they might infer certain legal requirements. Certainly Paul is restrained in describing this aspect of the conference when he asserts, "Those who were of repute added nothing to me" (Gal. 2:6). But then follows another clause, "only they would have us remember the poor, which was the very thing I made it my business to do" (Gal. 2:10). Therefore—historically speaking—the most important resolution of the conference was the least apparent: the pledge of a collection for the Jerusalem community; and Paul's further efforts for this collection were among the most important of his activity.

Let me hasten to add that the successful organization of the collection in Macedonia and Achaia seems to prove the existence of Paul's mission in these provinces *before* the conference, since it would indeed be very strange if at the conference Paul had promised to raise money from communities which did not yet exist. Or should we assume that Paul concluded that the agreement made at the conference would also apply to churches that he founded later on? However, Gal. 2:10 suggests that Paul raised the money soon after the conference in order to comply with the agreement. There seems to be no room for a "development" of the collection over many years. Furthermore, it would be hard to reconcile with Paul's consciousness of himself as *the* apostle to the Gentiles (Rom. 11:13) the idea that he had begun the mission in Europe only toward the end of his life, and years after the conference.


## THE NATURE OF THE COLLECTION[14]

Scholars have puzzled a great deal over this collection. One group understands it in analogy to the temple tax, which every Jew had to pay annually,[15] while another group points out that with it the promise of the pilgrimage of the nations is fulfilled.[16] Still others claim that the collection had been insisted on by the Jerusalem leaders and organized in the Pauline communities so that these could adopt the traditional status of the god-fearers. And finally some suggest that the collection was a polite "bribe" on Paul's part.[17]

As we have no primary sources for the view of the Jerusalem community, all this must remain uncertain. One thing seems sure, however: the negotiating partners from Jerusalem and Paul seem to have understood the collection in different ways, or to put it more cautiously, the agreement allowed them to interpret the collection in different ways. The Jerusalem leaders considered the agreement to call for some degree of legal observance. Paul, on the other hand, *disguised* or even *ignored* any legal implications of the support.

*Rom. 15:25–26*

(25) At present, however, I am going to Jerusalem with aid for the saints. (26) For Macedonia and Achaia have decided to raise a gift of partnership for the poor among the saints at Jerusalem.

At any rate, even during the conference, considerable tension remained between Paul and the leaders of the Jerusalem community from whom he was able to extract an agreement. Furthermore, despite the concordat with the apostle to the Gentiles, the "false brothers" continued to belong to the Jerusalem community, and must have contested the agreement as much as they could. In any case, their open hostility to Paul is to be presupposed as an operative factor both during the council and afterward.

## THE IMPACT OF THE FALSE BROTHERS ON THE RESULT OF THE CONFERENCE

If these reflections are not too far from the historical truth, we may also assume that "the false brothers" indirectly influenced details of the results of the negotiations, despite their defeat over the question of circumcision. This assumption is confirmed by a close examination of the formula of the agreement in Gal. 2:9, which displays a *legal* character: "We to the Gentiles, they to the Jews." The mission field is divided. From now on the mission to the Gentiles is the task of Paul and Barnabas, and the mission to the Jews that of James, Cephas, and John, based in Jerusalem. The very wording of the phrases "to the Gentiles" or "to the Jews" points to an exclusive definition of the two groups. This implies that in either case *only* Gentiles or *exclusively* Jews are the focal point of the mission. But that means that the agreement on a *union* was at the same time an agreement on a *division* or even *separation* of the two churches, one bound to the law and one free from it. (Of course this distinction was hardly absolute, for the Gentile Christians were strictly speaking not free from all law; if they were, they would be libertinists.)[18] The unifying formula mentioned above certainly assured Paul the unqualified right to engage in mission to the Gentiles. But it could also be used to reverse a mission to Gentiles *and* Jews. That is, the regulation did not exclude the possibility that in the future nonobservant Jews living in a Gentile Christian congregation could be obliged to observe the (complete) law. Here we find a development which is by no means rare in history, namely that a concern for unity at almost any price (and therefore really of no use) revives the opposed forces which had first sparked off the conflict. This obviously became true in the Pauline communities, which were invaded by Jewish Christian missionaries after the conference.

Another event of which we have an eyewitness account should, however, be dated before the conference, although Paul places it after the conference report.

*Gal. 2:11–14:*

> (11) But when Cephas came to Antioch I opposed him to his face, because he stood condemned. (12) For until certain persons came from James, he was taking his meals with the Gentiles; but when they came, he drew back and separated himself, because he was afraid of the advocates of circumcision. (13) And with him the rest of the Jews acted *hypocritically,* so that even Barnabas was carried away by their *hypocrisy.* (14) But when I saw that they were not straightforward about the truth of the gospel, I said to Cephas in front of them all, "If you, though a Jew, live like a Gentile and not like a Jew, how can you force the Gentiles to live like Jews?"

There are several reasons for dating the controversy at Antioch *before* the conference.[19] *First,* the undiscriminating table fellowship pictured in the above text could have occurred only before the conference. *Second,* a fundamental challenge to table fellowship between Jewish and Gentile Christians is likely to have occurred before the conference which tried to solve such a problem. *Third,* the demands of the opponents in Antioch are similar to the demands of those who brought about the conference: Jewish Christians must separate themselves from Gentile Christians. *Fourth,* given the partial list of the persons involved in the incident at Antioch and at the conference at Jerusalem

(Paul, Barnabas, James, possibly Titus), one is entitled to wonder whether the incident at Antioch was not the immediate reason for the conference. I would stress, however, that the above reconstruction, far from depending on this last point, remains quite secure without it.

## WHAT REALLY HAPPENED AT ANTIOCH

As becomes clear from Paul's account, in a newly founded community, Christians who had been born Jews and Christians who had been born Gentiles regularly ate together. Paul had taken part in these meals, and so had Peter. But when "certain persons from James," i.e., messengers sent by him, arrived in Antioch, all this suddenly changed. Peter, Barnabas, and the other Jewish Christians who were present withdrew from table fellowship "afraid of the advocates of circumcision" and in so doing excited the wrath of Paul. In his view Peter was in this way compelling the previously acceptable Gentile Christians to be circumcised in order to restore table fellowship. Indeed, Paul further sharpens his criticism by saying that earlier Peter had lived like a Gentile (verse 14).

The question arises as to how "Gentile" the lifestyle of the community had become. Had roast pork, donkey, or hare come to the table? Had something been done which the laws on clean and unclean animals in Lev. 11 or Deut. 14:3–20 strictly forbade? Did people in Antioch even drink Gentile wine which had previously been offered to the gods? Were there foods on which no tithe had been paid? Or did people eat meat which had originally been sacrificed to the gods?

On the one hand, to raise these questions is to show how little we really know about the interlude at Antioch. On the other hand, from 1 Cor. 8–10 we are familiar with Paul's attitude toward meat offered to idols. In general he had no hesitations about eating it (cf. 1 Cor. 10:25–27). But if the attention of a Christian was drawn by a Gentile host to the origin of the meat, he advised against eating it—for the sake of the members of the community who were weak in the faith (1 Cor. 10:28–29). So Paul personally was very free about eating meat offered to idols. That seems not to have been the case with Barnabas and the other Jewish Christians; otherwise they would not have retreated so quickly in Antioch. For this reason it is improbable that the extreme cases mentioned above applied. Rather, the Torah must have been observed loosely; only James himself insisted on strict observance and evidently had good reason for that: the Jewish Christians in Jerusalem were no longer to be compromised. In other words, here in Antioch—just as at the Jerusalem conference—a division exists. Only in this exigency could James be driven to consider interim solutions (see the so-called apostolic decree: Acts 15:29; 21:25).

Paul saw Peter's behavior as a false understanding of the righteousness before God in which they had once stood together (Gal. 2:15), but then exaggerates in remarking that previously Peter had lived in Gentile fashion. Immediately, though, the general question arose as to what validity the law was still to have for the young church generally. At any rate, the charge leveled against Paul both previously and later could not simply be rejected: namely that in painting things so much in black and white, culminating in an either-or position, he had dealt the Jewish law a decisive blow, even if he claimed the opposite.

The Collection as an External Criterion for the
Establishment of a Chronological Framework

The past tense (aorist in Greek) in Gal. 2:10a makes it clear that immediately after—not before—the conference, Paul began an operation intended to provide continual support for the congregation in Jerusalem. The remark "which was the very thing I made it my business to do" in the second half of the verse further indicates that the collection was known to the Galatians and that it was still underway.

For the present, let us see what we can learn about the collection from 1 and 2 Corinthians and Romans, the only letters besides Galatians which mention it.

1. The earliest reference to the collection is 1 Cor. 16:1-4. The Corinthians had asked Paul *how* the collection should occur and receive instructions as to how to collect the money. They should

follow the example of the Galatian churches. The Corinthians' knowledge of the collection is clearly presupposed. The nature of their question shows, however, that they have learned about the collection only recently.

2. Since 1 Cor. 16:1 refers to the collection among the Galatians, we may ask whether the chronological place of the letter to the Galatians can be determined. The following points speak for the chronological priority of 1 Corinthians over Galatians. *First,* Rom. 15:26 does not mention the Galatians as participants in the collection; it thus seems possible that the collection had failed in Galatia. (If at some point the collection did fall through at Galatia, then at some later time Paul would hardly have mentioned the churches in Galatia—as he does in 1 Cor. 16:1—as a paradigm for the organization of the collection.) *Second,* if Galatians had been written before 1 Corinthians, one would have to assume that Paul, through his letter, succeeded in winning back the Galatian congregations. Otherwise 1 Cor. 16:1 would not make any sense. In this case, however, the absence of a reference to the Galatian churches in Rom. 15:26 is difficult to explain. In addition, the lack of any Pauline tradition in Galatia in the period after the life of Paul suggests that he was unable to win back the communities in these regions. *Third,* the noticeable similarity of Galatians to Romans is best explained if these letters were written in chronological proximity to one another. *Fourth,* Galatians shares a number of stylistic and linguistic features with 2 Cor. 10–12. Thus, there is more than one reason to assume that Galatians was written after 1 Corinthians

3. The remarks in 2 Cor. 8–9 allow us to assume that the Macedonian collection began around the same time as the Corinthian collection (cf. 2 Cor. 8:1–4; 9:2).


## TOPOGRAPHICAL AND CHRONOLOGICAL REFERENCES IN THE PASSAGES CONCERNING THE COLLECTION

From the occurrence of the Passover motif in 1 Cor. 5:7 it is likely that Paul wrote the letter in the spring. Due to the references to the past in 15:32 and given the time which must be allowed for the organization of the collection from Ephesus, where 1 Corinthians was written (cf. 1 Cor. 16:8: "I will stay in Ephesus until Pentecost"), Paul probably spent at least one winter in Ephesus.

Gal. 4:13 ("You know that it was because of an illness that I preached the gospel to you the first time") and the reference to the Galatian churches in 1 Cor. 16:1 make it probable that Paul had been in Galatia for a second visit during which he organized the collection.

The Corinthian correspondence (cf. 2 Cor. 1–2; 7:5–7) allows us to follow the apostle as he travels after the conference: first to Corinth for a short painful visit, then back to Ephesus, and finally back to Corinth again by way of Troas and Macedonia. Not only the numerous events that followed upon the composition of 1 Corinthians, but also the phrase in 2 Cor. 8:10 ("what you began a year ago") seem to be sure indications that a winter had elapsed between the beginning of the collection and the composition of 2 Cor. 8. Paul then stayed the next winter in Macedonia, traveled to Corinth in the spring, and remained through the following winter in Corinth, where he wrote the letter to the Romans. The entire period under consideration thus covered three to four years.

The Initial Mission in Macedonia and Achaia

From 1 Cor. 4:18 ("Some are arrogant, as though I were not coming to you") and the reference to a letter to the Corinthians prior to 1 Corinthians (1 Cor. 5:9: "I wrote you in my previous letter not to associate with immoral men") it is most probable that, when Paul composed 1 Corinthians, he had not been in Corinth for quite some time. Other passages also hint that the founding of the Corinthian congregation had not occurred in the recent past:

(a) Apollos's stay in Corinth (1 Cor. 3:6) after Paul had left the city, and his later presence in Ephesus with Paul (1 Cor. 16:12).

(b) The manifold problems that had arisen in Corinth (see especially the many questions that Paul had to answer in 1 Cor. 7).

(c) The fact that "many" had died since Paul's last visit (1 Cor. 11:30).

(d) The announcement of a *sudden* arrival (1 Cor. 4:19) and reasons proffered for the delay (1 Cor. 16:8).

(e) Paul's reference in 1 Cor. 15:32a to having fought with beasts in Ephesus in the past—he must have escaped that danger in the meantime—indicates a long stay in Ephesus, where 1 Corinthians was composed, and an even longer absence from Corinth.

## A CLEAR REFERENCE TO THE BEGINNING OF PAUL'S MISSION: PHIL. 4:15

Positively, Phil. 4:15 ("You . . . know that in the early days of my mission when I set out from Macedonia, no church entered into partnership with me . . .") specifies the time lapse between 1 Corinthians and the founding of the congregations in Macedonia and Achaia. Moreover, it suggests the chronological setting of the mission in Europe. Here Paul speaks of the "early days of my mission"[20] as following upon and including his mission in Macedonia. This phrase is most naturally understood as an indication of the beginning of Paul's missionary activity as a whole, though this does not fit in with the standard view that Paul preached in Greece only after the Jerusalem conference. 1 Thess. 2:2 and 3:1, 6 then indicate the cities along the route of Paul's initial mission to Europe: Philippi, Thessalonica, Athens, and Corinth.

The combination of all these facts renders it probable that Paul operated a mission in Greece *before* the Jerusalem conference and therefore was able to promise to raise money from these communities for the church in Jerusalem.

The Eschatological Statements in 1 Thessalonians as a Confirmation of the Early Macedonian Mission

In short, the hope that the vast majority of Christians would be living witnesses to Christ's return from heaven (1 Thess. 1:9–10 and 4:13–17) points to the likelihood of composition in the first decade of the Christian movement, when such imminent expectation ran high.

Let me illustrate this by comparing two texts which have a genetic relationship to each other: As we established previously, 1 Thess. 4:13–17 was written in Corinth during the founding of the community and reflects what Paul told the Corinthians about the future. 1 Cor. 15:51–52 addresses the same problem that 1 Thess. 4:13–17 had addressed, but introduces some significant changes.

In 1 Thess. 4:15 Paul makes the following remark about his expectations of the future:

> For this we say to you in a word of the Lord, that **we who are alive**, who are left until the Lord's coming shall by no means precede those who have fallen asleep.

He then goes on to elaborate the cosmic event: the Lord will come with a cry of command, with the call of the archangel and the sound of the trumpet of God from heaven. He continues:

> (16b) And the dead in Christ will rise first; (17) then **we who are alive**, who are left, shall be caught up together with them in the clouds to meet the Lord in the air; and so we shall always be with the Lord.

The expression "we who are alive" refers to Paul and the recipients of the letter—and only to them, though it seems to include all the other Christians of Paul's generation. This can mean only that Paul thought that he along with his fellow Christians in Thessalonica and elsewhere would experience the advent of the Lord from heaven during his own lifetime.

As is generally recognized, this expectation came to grief. Time went on, and as it did, more and more people died, until the majority of the first Christian generation were dead. So we may ask what then happened to Paul's expectation of an imminent end? What was the apostle's response to this manifest miscalculation?

In 1 Corinthians Paul deals with this problem a second time and formulates another solution while at the same time using the language and structure of his earlier model in 1 Thess. 4:13–17. He writes in 1 Cor. 15:51–52:

(51) Listen, I tell you a mystery. **We shall not all sleep**, but we shall all be changed, (52) in a moment, in the twinkling of an eye, at the last trumpet. For the trumpet will sound, and the dead will be raised imperishable, and we shall be changed.

First of all, it should be emphasized here that the expectation of Jesus' coming (on the clouds of heaven) has remained constant, and similarly that Paul continued to assume the survival of some Christians to that point. But precisely what does the statement "we shall not all sleep" mean? Paul clearly seems to indicate that not all shall die though the majority will. In 1 Corinthians, that is, survival represents the exception, whereas in 1 Thessalonians it is the rule. For the Corinthian community to have accepted both messages (1 Thessalonians was written from Corinth, remember) we would have to assume a chronological separation of some ten years and the cumulative effect on the Corinthians of the deaths that caused the change in Paul's statement. Hence the above chronology can very well gain additional support from the different ways of dealing with the problem of death in 1 Thess. 4 and 1 Cor. 15.

## THE TIME OF THE FOUNDING OF THE GALATIAN COMMUNITIES

While it is certain that the Galatian congregations were founded before the Jerusalem conference, it is uncertain whether these communities are to be located in the north or in the south of the Roman province of Galatia,[21] and whether they were founded before or after the mission in Greece. However, it seems likely that Paul did not plan to found the Galatian communities, for he himself reminds the Galatian Christians, "You know it was because of a bodily ailment that I proclaimed the gospel to you at first" (Gal. 4:13).

There are two more points in favor of the dating of the foundation of the Galatian communities after the mission in Greece. *First,* Phil. 4:15 clearly describes the mission in Greece as the beginning of Paul's missionary activity (see above). *Second,* the way Paul describes his founding preaching in Corinth in 1 Cor. 2:1–2 has an

analogy in Gal. 3:1. In other words, in both places the emphasis on
Jesus as the crucified one played a major role, whereas in Thessalonica things must have been different (see 1 Thess. 1:9–10 as a
summary of Paul's founding proclamation in Macedonia). The
reason for this change seems obvious: after the defeat at Athens (see
pp. 126–30) Paul placed increased stress upon the paradoxical foolishness of the cross and the crucified Jesus.

At the same time, the mission in Galatia which was due to an illness
must be distinguished from the stop in South Galatia during which Timothy was converted. This must have occurred before the founding of the
community in Corinth, for Timothy had part in it. See 2 Cor. 1:19: "For
the Son of God, Christ Jesus, whom we proclaimed among you, I, Silvanus, and Timothy, was not Yes and No; but in him it is Yes."

Yet Luke's story of Timothy's conversion is important in still
another respect. Should it be true that Paul really circumcised Timothy,
the question arises whether this action stands in contradiction to
everything that Paul tells his converts about salvation by faith and not
by works of the law. An analysis of the passage is therefore called for.[22]

*Acts 16:1–5:*

> (1a) He (Paul) went on to Derbe and to Lystra.
> (1b) *There* he found a disciple *called* Timothy, the son of a
> Jewish woman who was a believer and a Greek father. (2) He was
> *well spoken of* by the brothers at Lystra and Iconium. (3) Paul
> wanted to have him in his company when he left the place. So he
> took him and circumcised him, out of consideration for the Jews
> who lived in those parts; for they all knew that his father was
> Greek.
> (4) *As they went on their way through the towns they handed on the
> decisions taken by the apostles and the elders in Jerusalem.*
> (5) *So the churches were strengthened in the faith, and they
> increased in number daily.*

*Outline*

Verse 1a: Journey from Derbe to Lystra
Verses 1b–3: Timothy is circumcised and taken along (from Lystra)

Verse 4: The Apostolic Decree is handed over to the communities there

Verse 5: Short summary. Strengthening and growth of the communities

## LUKE'S INTENTION

*Verse 1a:* Paul's journey to Derbe and Lystra is a Lukan duplication of the same trip narrated in Acts 14:6f., 20f. After the Jerusalem conference Luke relates further journeys by Paul into these cities, since only at the beginning of Paul's independent mission does he want to report that Timothy was his companion.

*Verses 1b–3:* Luke's reason for the circumcision of Timothy is given explicitly in verse 3: Paul circumcises Timothy because of the Jews in those places; they know that his father was Greek. So Timothy is circumcised, because Paul wants to go on a mission with him among Jews and because the Jews had learned that Timothy's father was Gentile. Luke evidently assumes that Timothy was a Gentile because he had a Gentile father, and since now Luke's Paul can have only Jewish colleagues for the mission among the Jews, he has to make this colleague a Jew by circumcision.

*Verse 4:* This refers to the account of the Jerusalem conference, and indicates that the decisions made there in the interest of the continuity of the church were being promulgated and, by implication, implemented (note verse 5).

*Verse 5:* After the manner of Acts 6:7 and 9:31, this verse is a short summary and refers to the passages there.

## THE TRADITION REWORKED BY LUKE
## AND ITS HISTORICAL VALUE

*Verse 1a:* The visits to Derbe and Lystra seem to be part of the tradition and historical, though with the qualification that they have a genetic connection with those mentioned in Acts 14. In other words, Luke has duplicated them.

*Verses 1b–3:* Tradition most likely underlies the narrative about Timothy, first Lystra as his living place, second his origin from a mixed marriage, and third Paul circumcising him. But it should be stressed that Timothy was not a Christian when Paul met him, but that Paul converted him; see 1 Cor. 4:17a: "Therefore I have sent to you, Timothy, who is my faithful and beloved child in the Lord." In the context Paul calls the Corinthians like Timothy his beloved children (verse 14). He has given birth to them through the gospel. Therefore it is natural to assume this also for Timothy. Paul converted him, like the Corinthians, to faith in Christ. This took place on the way to Greece, where Timothy, along with Silvanus and Paul, participated in the founding of the church in Corinth (2 Cor. 1:19).

Scholars have long doubted the historicity of Paul's circumcising Timothy, for they point out that at the conference Paul had rejected any demands for Titus's circumcision. But that case was more complicated because Titus was a "pure" Gentile while Timothy came from a mixed marriage. Since he had a Jewish mother, by rabbinic law he was a Jew. (The status of a child in mixed marriages is determined by the mother.) According to Paul "every one should remain in the calling in which he was called" (1 Cor. 7:20). In the case of Timothy, all the more it was the Jewish state. Hence it is very likely that Paul circumcised Timothy all the more so since he could thereby ward off Jewish objections to his preaching.

## The Arrangement of the Traditions of Acts into the Framework Developed Solely on the Basis of the Letters

We may now turn back to Acts to consider how the information there fits in with the chronology developed solely on the basis of the letters. We shall limit ourselves to the passages that are related to the chronology constructed above.

## THE PUZZLE OF ACTS 18:22

By its very brevity, Acts 18:22 ("When he [Paul] had landed at Caesarea, he went up and greeted the church, and then went down to Antioch."—RSV) forms a puzzle for exegetes. The note is imbedded in a report of a journey from Ephesus to Caesarea, then to Jerusalem, and from there to Antioch, Phrygia, Galatia, and Ephesus. Julius Wellhausen once described the special character of this journey as follows:

> "From Ephesus, to Caesarea, up to greet the brothers, back down to Antioch, then back through Galatia and Phrygia." All in a rush and reported in telegraphic style. No American could do it better.[23]

The absence of a direct reference to Jerusalem in verse 22 is a sure sign that we are dealing with a tradition, and not redaction, for Luke usually expresses special interest in trips to Jerusalem (cf. especially Acts 11:27–30, which is a Lukan composition). The brevity of the whole report in 18:18–22 thus seems to indicate Luke's possession of an itinerary with the following stations: Corinth, Ephesus, Caesarea, Jerusalem, Antioch, Galatia, and Phrygia. While the work of Luke the editor is evident in the report of Paul's earlier trips to Jerusalem, the unaffected simplicity of 18:22 points toward its traditional nature: Luke demonstrates no particular interest in this visit.

We may therefore ask whether 18:22 originally represented Paul's second visit to Jerusalem and whether the visits postulated by Luke in 11:27–30 and 15:1–4 are not just Lukan creations formulated parallel to this visit. The linguistic evidence of these latter two passages points unmistakably to the hand of the redactor, though it is also clear that Luke is employing some traditional material: 11:27 mentions Barnabas together with Paul and also a collection; 15:1–4 also mentions Barnabas alongside Paul. There are, however, major differences between 15:1–4 and Paul's own statements: *First,* Acts fails to mention that Paul traveled to Jerusalem due to a revelation. *Second,* Acts overlooks Titus, an important person for Paul. *Third,* Paul himself does not state that he traveled to Jerusalem from Antioch.

These differences reveal an apologetic motive behind Luke's report and are related to his particular reasons for placing the Jerusalem conference in chapter 15. For him, the conference represents the pivotal juncture marking the transition from the mission by both the Jerusalem and the Antioch communities to Paul's world mission. After the continuity of salvation history between the earliest churches and Paul has been established, Paul steps to the center stage; James, Peter, and the representative of the Antiochene congregation, Barnabas, are left to one side and (except for James: Acts 21:18–25) never reappear in Acts. Here we see Luke developing the appropriate chronology on the basis of proper dogma: For him, Paul's world mission *cannot* have occurred before it was legitimated at the Jerusalem conference. Since Acts 11:27–30 is also Luke's work, I conclude that 18:22 represents Paul's second visit to Jerusalem while assuming at the same time that Luke has shifted the Jerusalem conference from there to Acts 15.

## PAUL'S ITINERARY IN ACTS COMPARED WITH THE STOPS IN HIS LETTERS

This last statement receives verification from the letters, for the itinerary listed by Luke after 15:1–29 agrees with those places mentioned by Paul as his stops *before* the conference. Compare the following lists:

   *Acts*: Antioch, Syria, Cilicia, Derbe, Lystra, Phrygia, Galatia, Philippi, Thessalonica, Athens, Corinth.
   *Paul*: Syria, Cilicia, Philippi, Thessalonica, Athens, Corinth.

The additional stops listed in Acts derive, for the most part, from the redactor. The visit to Antioch in 15:30–41 functions as a transition to Paul's independent mission (and also to Luke's new source of information regarding this mission in 15:40–41). This passage does, however, reflect the historical dissolution of Paul's relations with Antioch.

The visit to Derbe and Lystra (16:1–5) serves Luke *first* to introduce Timothy and *second* to represent the continuity of the church (the transmission of the apostolic decree to the communities that were founded before the Jerusalem conference).

The trip through Phrygia and Galatia (16:6–8) is a strange

account of a nonmissionary journey. Verse 6 ("And they went through the region of Phrygia and Galatia, having been forbidden by the Holy Spirit to speak the word in Asia") reflects the difficulties Paul encountered in Asia (cf. 1 Cor. 15:32; 2 Cor. 1:8). When Luke writes in verse 7 that "the Spirit of Jesus did not allow them (to go to Mysia and Bithynia)," he is consciously creating a contrast to the European mission (cf. verse 9). These strange notes do seem to indicate, however, that Luke is working here with certain traditions, the nature of which can no longer be determined.

The correspondence of the stops in Acts 16–18 with those contained in and to be reconstructed from Paul's letters for the period between the first and second visits to Jerusalem provides strong arguments for Acts 18:22 as the original chronological location of the second visit. Further support for this view is found in the stops mentioned after 18:22, for they correspond exactly with those reflected in the letters of Paul: Antioch, Galatia, Phrygia, Ephesus, Macedonia, Achaia.


## THE REPORT ON PAUL'S MISSION IN CORINTH—AN ASSEMBLAGE OF ELEMENTS FROM THE TRADITION

*Acts 18:1–17:*

(1) After this he left Athens and went to Corinth.

(2) And he met a Jew *called* Aquila, a native of Pontus, lately come from Italy with his wife Priscilla, because Claudius had issued an edict that *all* Jews should leave Rome. And he approached them; (3) and, because he was of the same trade, made his home with them, and they worked together, for by trade they were tentmakers.

(4) *And he argued in the synagogue every sabbath, and persuaded Jews and Greeks.*

(5) Then Silas and Timothy came down from Macedonia, and Paul devoted himself entirely to preaching, testifying to the Jews that the Christ was Jesus. (6) And when they opposed him and resorted to abuse, he shook out his garments and said to them, "Your blood be on your heads! I am innocent; from now on I shall go to the Gentiles." (7) With that he left and went to the house of

a worshipper of God, *called* Titius Justus; his house was next door to the synagogue. (8) Crispus, the ruler of the synagogue, now became a believer in the Lord, with all his household; and many of the Corinthians listened and believed, and were baptized.

(9) *One night in a vision the Lord said to Paul, "Do not be afraid, but speak and do not be silent; (10) for I am with you, and no one shall attempt to do you harm; for there are many in this city who are my people."*

(11) So he settled a year and six months, teaching the word of God among them.

(12) But when Gallio was proconsul of Achaia, the Jews made a concerted attack on Paul and brought him before the <u>tribunal</u>, (13) saying, "This man is persuading men to worship God in ways that are against the law." (14) Paul was about to open his mouth, when Gallio said to the Jews, "If it had been a question of wrong-doing or vicious crime, I would not hesitate to attend to you, Jews; (15) but since it is a matter of questions about words and names and your own law, you may see to it yourselves; I have no mind to be a judge of these matters." (16) And he drove them from the <u>tribunal</u>. (17) And they all seized Sosthenes, the ruler of the synagogue, and beat him in front of the <u>tribunal</u>. But Gallio paid no attention to this.

*Outline*

Verse 1: Journey from Athens to Corinth
Verses 2–3: Paul as tentmaker with Aquila and Priscilla
Verse 4: Paul preaches every sabbath in the synagogue (*Transition*)
Verses 5–8: Intensified mission work by Paul
Verses 9–10: Vision of Christ
Verse 11: Note of time (eighteen months)
Verses 12–17: Paul before Gallio

## LUKE'S INTENTION

*Verse 4:* This verse exemplifies Luke's motif of making Paul go to the Jews first. It is also redactional since in anticipation of the next unit, verses 5–8, it describes the two groups to which Paul's preaching is addressed: Jews and Gentiles. It further serves as a transition to verse

5, which in Lukan language describes Paul's intensified missionary activity, since it provides a necessary precondition for this further outreach by describing Paul's weekly preaching in the local synagogue.

*Verses 9–10:* "Vision" (cf. Acts 10:3; 16:9, etc.) is a common Lukan narrative device. The vision of Christ intensifies the drama of the scene. It makes good redactional sense, since it not only explains the long duration of Paul's stay in Corinth (verse 11, eighteen months), but illustrates the significance of the Corinthian community in Luke's time. In addition, it provides a transition to the Gallio episode which follows, by announcing in anticipation that Paul will not undergo any suffering.

## THE TRADITION WORKED OVER BY LUKE

It was previously suggested that Luke combines all information about a given locality into one report; let us now observe how Luke did this in his report on Corinth. Acts 18:1–17 contains five groups of traditions:

1. Paul travels from Athens to Corinth (verse 1).
2. Paul meets Aquila and Priscilla—who as Jews had to leave because of the edict of Claudius—in Corinth and works with them (verses 2–3).
3. Paul preaches the gospel in Corinth (verses 5–8).
4. Paul stays in Corinth for eighteen months (verse 11).
5. The Gallio episode (verses 12–17).

## HISTORICAL ELEMENTS

(a) *Absolute dates*

From the Gallio inscription we know that Gallio held office in 51–52 C.E.[24] With the date of the first visit in Corinth set (cf. Acts 18:1), it is readily apparent that Paul's second or third visit could well have occurred during Gallio's tenure of office in 51–52 C.E.

The date of the expulsion of the Jews from Rome is usually set in

49 C.E. (see above, p. 22) on the basis of a combination of Acts, Suetonius, and Orosius.

The Roman biographer Suetonius (early second century C.E.)
writes, "Claudius expelled the Jews from Rome who were exceed-
ingly riotous because of the instigator Chrestus."[25]

The expulsion of the Jews by Claudius is also reported in Acts
18:2. But the date 49 C.E. rests on the information supplied by the
church father Orosius (from 417–418 C.E.), whose source derived it
by subtracting the eighteen months found in Acts 18:11 from the
dates of Gallio's term in office, which could be figured out by check-
ing the records in the archives. Hence it is certainly secondary.[26]

Now, the Roman historian Dio Cassius reports an imperial command regarding the Jews for the year 41 C.E. He writes:

> As for the Jews, who had again increased so greatly that by reason of
> their multitude it would have been hard without raising a tumult to
> bar them from the city, he did not drive them out, but ordered them,
> while continuing their traditional mode of life, not to hold meetings.[27]

The wording of the passage seems to indicate that Dio Cassius
might be using as a source either the above quoted text by Suetonius
or—this is more probable—a tradition that was available to Suetonius, too, while at the same time correcting this information: I am
referring to Dio Cassius's denial that Claudius expelled (all) the Jews.

The historical kernel of these reports is no doubt the following:
In 41 C.E., Claudius issued a decree regarding the Jews; it pertained
to the disturbances that had arisen in a synagogue and had involved
Chrestus. The decree entailed the expulsion of those Jews who had
been directly involved in the disturbances. One may, therefore, conclude that the tradition in Acts 18:2–3 could very well derive from
Paul's first visit to Corinth around 41 C.E. This date fits in well with
the chronology developed solely on the basis of the letters.

### (b) Individual pieces of tradition with a historical value

Two of Paul's letters reflect his close association with Aquila and
Priscilla. First, 1 Cor. 16:19 notes their presence with Paul in Ephesus,

and extends their greetings to the Corinthian congregation. Thus it seems certain that they were personally acquainted with the members of that church, and likely that they had met Paul during his founding visit to that city. Later, in Rom. 16:3 it is Paul who sends greetings to them. A quite reasonable explanation of the couple's presence in Rome at this time is that after having been expelled in the year 41 C.E. they returned to Rome at the end of Claudius's reign. All this renders it plausible that Paul met them in Corinth in 41.

Also, since 1 Cor. 1:14 mentions Crispus, the third element of tradition indicated above (i.e., Acts 18:5-8), with its reference to Crispus in verse 8, also derives from the first visit to Corinth.

Further confirmation of this view is found in the report of the arrival of Silas and Timothy from Macedonia (verse 5), for this corresponds exactly with 1 Thess. 3:6 (the reference to Timothy's arrival from Thessalonica in Corinth), and 2 Cor. 1:19 (the indication that Paul, Silvanus, and Timothy were active during the founding mission in Corinth; cf. 2 Cor. 11:9).

The above considerations allow us to reconstruct the following rough chronology:

## Chronological Chart[28]

30: The crucifixion of Jesus

32: Conversion of Paul in or near Damascus; one year stay in Arabia; return to Damascus (for two years)

35: Paul's first visit to Jerusalem (Gal. 1:18)

35: Journey to Syria and Cilicia (Gal. 1:21); mission there and in South Galatia together with Barnabas (Acts 13-14). Conversion and circumcision of Timothy (Acts 16:1-3)

37: Independent mission in Europe: Philippi (1 Thess. 2:2; Acts 16:12-40), Thessalonica (Phil. 4: 16; Acts 17:1-9); defeat at Athens (Acts 17:16-34; 1 Thess. 3:1)

41: *The decree of Claudius regarding the Jews*

41: Paul in Corinth: 1 Thessalonica. He stayed in Corinth for eighteen months (Acts 18:11)

*circa* 44: Founding of the Galatian congregations due to sickness (Gal. 4:13)

47: Incident at Antioch (Gal. 2:11–14; Acts 15:1–2)

47: Paul's second visit to Jerusalem: the Jerusalem conference (Gal. 2:1–11/Acts 15:6–29), followed by the journey to the Pauline congregations for the organization of the collection

48: Paul for the second time in Galatia

49–53: Paul in Ephesus (1 Cor. 15:32; 16:8; Acts 19)

49: Sending of Timothy to Macedonia and Corinth (1 Cor. 4:17); the previous letter to the Corinthians (1 Cor. 5:9) with instructions about the collection (or else the instructions were sent by messenger)

50–51: Timothy in Macedonia

*51–52: Gallio proconsul of Achaia*

51 (spring): Letter of the Corinthians with questions regarding the collection (or else the questions were delivered orally)

51 (around Easter): 1 Corinthians

51 (between Easter and summer): Timothy in Corinth

51 (summer): After bad news about Corinth by Timothy on his return to Paul in Ephesus, short visit of Paul to Corinth (cf. 2 Cor. 1:23; 2:1); Paul before Gallio (Acts 18:12–17); precipitate return to Ephesus; "letter of tears" (2 Cor. 2:3–9; 7:8–12); sending of Titus to Corinth (2 Cor. 8:5)

51–52 (winter): Paul in danger for his life (imprisonment in Ephesus, 2 Cor. 1:8); composition of Philemon; Philippians

52 (spring): Paul's journey with Timothy from Ephesus to Troas (2 Cor. 2: 12); further journey to Macedonia

52 (summer): Arrival of Titus in Macedonia from Corinth (2 Cor. 7:6–7); bad news from Galatia (Gal. 1:6–9); composition of 2 Cor. 1–9; 10–13 and Galatians; sending of Titus with parts of 2 Corinthians to Corinth in order to complete the collection

52–53 (winter): Paul in Macedonia; completion of the collection there

53 (spring/summer): Journey of Paul with Macedonian escorts to Corinth; completion of the collection there

53–54 (winter): Paul in Corinth; composition of Romans

54 (spring): Journey to Jerusalem in order to deliver the collection

55–57: Imprisonment in Caesarea (Acts 24:27)

57: Journey as a prisoner to Rome (Acts 27)

## NOTES

1. For the following, see my *Paul: Apostle to the Gentiles* (Philadelphia: Fortress Press, 1984). While recent monographs on the chronology of Paul by Jerome Murphy-O'Connor, *A Critical Life of Paul* (Oxford/New York: Oxford University Press, 1996), and Niels Hyldahl, *The History of Early Christianity* (Frankfurt: Peter Lang, 1997), pp. 134–52, are based on the same method and have in fact received an impetus to move in that direction by my own work (see my *Paul: Apostle to the Gentiles*, pp. 289–94), a new massive book has recently been published which tries to set the clock back. I have in mind Rainer Riesner, *Paul's Early Period: Chronology, Mission, Strategy* (Grand Rapids, Mich.: Wm. B. Eerdmans Publishing Co., 1998). Riesner treats Acts and Paul's letters as sources of the same rank and therefore, in spite of all his erudition, has little to contribute.

2. E.g., Luke writes that Paul the Christian traveled to Jerusalem five times: Acts 9, 11, 15, 18:22, 21. From Paul's letters we know that he went there only three times: Gal 1:18, 2:1 and the (planned) visit reflected in Rom 15:25.

3. We hear with the possible exception of Acts 13:38f. very little from Luke about Paul's doctrine that justification is by faith alone.

4. Ferdinand Christian Baur, *Paul, the Apostle of Jesus Christ*, (London/Edinburgh: Williams & Norgate, 1875–76), vol. 1, pp. 4ff. (The German original was published in its first edition 1845.)

5. John Knox, *Chapters in a Life of Paul*, revised by the author and edited with introduction by Douglas R. A. Hare (Macon: Mercer University Press, 1987).

6. See my *Opposition to Paul in Early Christianity* (Minneapolis: Fortress Press, 1988), pp. 97–103.

7. Martin Hengel and Anna Maria Schwemer, *Paul between Damascus and Antioch: The Unknown Years* (Louisville: Westminster John Knox Press, 1997), p. 110.

8. Other purposes in connection with the journey to Arabia are discussed by Hengel and Schwemer, *Paul between Damascus and Antioch*, p. 109.

9. For a critique of my suggestion, see Bradley H. McLean, "Galatians 2.7–8 and the Recognition of Paul's Apostolic Status at the Jerusalem Conference: A Critique of Gerd Luedemann's Solution," *New Testament Studies* 37 (1991): 67–76. For support see Andreas Schmidt, "Das Missionsdekret in Galater 2.7–8 als Vereinbarung vom ersten Besuch Pauli in Jerusalem," *New Testament Studies* 38 (1992): 149–152; Hyldahl, *History of Early Christianity*, pp. 202–203.

10. Robert Jewett, *A Chronology of Paul's Life* (Philadelphia: Fortress Press, 1982), pp. 30–33.

11. Paul's statement that the purpose of his mission to the Gentiles is to arouse the envy of his fellow Jews and thereby to save some of them (Rom. 11:14) attests to his strong sense of commitment to an exclusively Gentile mission.

12. Meaning that they made no demands that Paul alter his message or the religious praxis required of his converts.

13. Some would not even rule out the possibility that Paul eventually gave in to their demand, without being *forced* to do so.

14. Cf. Günther Bornkamm, *Paul* (New York: Harper & Row, 1971), pp. 37–42, 97–101.

15. Josephus *Jewish Antiquities* 14.110.

16. See Isa. 2:2–4; 60:3, 11–22, etc.

17. See my *Opposition to Paul in Jewish Christianity*, pp. 58–62. The remarks on the collection there go back to a dialogue with the late Morton Smith.

18. Cf. below, pp. 100–107.

19. Let me hasten to add that if my suggestion of a chronological reversal of conference and incident at Antioch should be incorrect, the above chronology does not automatically collapse. See the remarks in my *Paul: Apostle to the Gentiles*, p. 291.

20. Literally, "in the beginning of the gospel."

21. Acts contains traditions about both locations: see Acts 13–14,16 on the founding of the communities in the southern part of Galatia and Acts 16:6 as a reflection of Paul's work in the northern part. At any rate, the location has no bearing on the chronology.

22. For a detailed analysis of Acts 16:1–5 see my *Early Christianity*, pp. 173–77.

23. See my *Early Christianity*, p. 14.

24. See my *Paul: Apostle to the Gentiles*, pp. 163f.

25. Suetonius *Life of the Caesars*. Claudius 25.

26. See my essay "Das Judenedikt des Claudius (Apg 18,2)," in *Der Treue Gottes trauen: Beiträge zum Werk des Lukas*, ed. Claus Bussmann and Walter Radl. Festschrift für Gerhard Schneider (Freiburg/Basel/Wien: Herder 1991), pp. 289–98.

27. Dio Cassius *Roman History* 60.6.6.

28. I presuppose two years as a probable interval between Jesus' death and Paul's conversion.

# 3

# PAUL'S LETTER
# TO PHILEMON

There is a wide consensus among students of Paul that his

theology was polemical because it was wrought in controversy. His letters struggle for the authentic meaning of the gospel. They never argue with persons or positions outside the Christian community, but with Christians within it. . . . The more seriously the authentic meaning of the gospel was threatened, the more intense was Paul's response. Sometimes he wrote warmly (1 Thessalonians 1–3); at times magnanimously (as in Phil. 1:12–18); sometimes he was sarcastic (1 Cor. 4:8) or crude (Gal. 5:12). Paul's letters manifest his total engagement with the subject matter, his passionate commitment to the truth of the gospel.[1]

But this general statement fails to consider one of Paul's letters, Philemon, a document which is seldom accorded sufficient notice. This is so because it seems to be irrelevant for the study of Paul. This neglect notwithstanding, anyone interested in Paul's religion must regard Philemon as a pearl among his letters. Indeed, one would do well to accept the insight of the great German scholar Adolf Deissmann (1866–1937) who some seventy years ago wrote:

He who would most easily learn to know the intimate character of Paul's letters must not begin with the Epistle to the Romans. . . . It is better to start with the Epistle to Philemon. This is the shortest, as it is also the most letter-like of Paul's letters, written upon a single sheet of papyrus, just like numbers of Greek letters of the same date now known to us from Egypt. In it there is nothing of the doctrinaire and literary. If one regards this precious leaf as a tract on the attitude of Christianity to slavery, he misses his way not only in historical criticism but also in human taste. It is turning people into ideas and making a book out of a confidential letter: Paul is depersonalized into Christianity and the slave Onesimus has become "slavery".[2]

While Deissmann is correct in emphasizing the uniqueness of Philemon, his distinction between literary and unliterary, epistle and letter seems overdone. For one thing, no papyrus letter yet discovered can properly be compared to Philemon.[3] One of the nearest approaches, a letter from Caor of Hermupolis to the officer Flavius Abinnaeus,[4] will suffice to demonstrate the typical brevity, bluntness, and defective syntax of these missives:

> To my master and beloved brother Abinnaeus the prefect, Caor, Papas (priest) of Hermopulis, greetings. I send many greetings to your children.
>     I want you to know, lord, concerning the soldier Paul, i.e., his flight. Pardon him this time, for right now I have no time to come to you (in order to settle this). And, not desisting (but carrying out your orders) he will come back to you.
>     Farewell, I pray, many years, my lord (and) brother.

In spite of being three centuries newer, this correspondence is clearly ill-conceived and crudely executed. Philemon, on the other hand, will show under close analysis its considerable literary merit. For the moment, it is enough to note that in dealing with an extremely delicate matter, Paul displays great tact and eloquence. We should also do well to consider the opinion of a contemporary of Deissmann. Johannes Weiss (1866–1914), his successor in the Heidelberg chair of New Testament Studies, offered a quite different viewpoint on Philemon:

> One cannot deny that this letter-writer writes not only because it is necessary to do so, but also because he loves to produce polished literary pieces, and he certainly possesses the ability to do so.[5]

Taking all these factors into consideration, it is difficult to sustain Deissmann's judgment that Philemon is little more than an elegant papyrus autograph. Nonetheless, his suggested strategy of using this epistle as a window to Paul's thought and personality has much to recommend it.[6] Let me therefore offer a few additional reasons to carry this out:

1. Along with Galatians it is the only of Paul's letters that is certainly free from any addition by an editor.
2. It contains no explicit ethical teaching or theological reflection.
3. Many of the usual topics of Pauline theology are missing: human sin, Holy Spirit, reference to the "Christ-event," baptism, justification by faith, etc.
4. It is the only letter which Paul has not dictated, but written himself (cf. verse 19).
5. It is the briefest of Paul's letters. If despite its brevity this letter allows some general conclusion about Paul, the chances of successfully using it to shed new light on the man and his work are enhanced.
6. This letter shows no concerns for other communities. Thus for example neither rhetorical shading nor the twisting of a specific case is to be expected. We must always be aware that Paul's attempt to "become all things to all men" (1 Cor. 9:22) allowed him to be quite flexible in both language and the reporting of facts. Hence in this letter we meet Paul in a spontaneous act of communication, candid and uncontrived, and thus come quite close to what he really felt, thought, and wanted.

Some thoughts about the date of and place from which Philemon was written are appropriate here: Today a consensus is emerging among scholars that Philemon was written while Paul was in prison in Ephesus (see above, p. 62). In 2 Cor. 1:8 Paul refers to an imprisonment in Asia, and Ephesus as the place of writing becomes all the more probable when one takes into account that this city was the metropolis of the province of Asia, in which Colossae, the home of Onesimus's master, was situated (see Col. 4:9).[7] This means that

Philemon was written after 1 Corinthians and before 2 Corinthians (i.e., before all of its fragments).

## PLINY TO SABINIANUS—A SIMILAR CASE?

Before analyzing Philemon, I would also like to draw the reader's attention to a letter of Pliny the Younger (61–112 C.E.) to Sabinianus that deals with a case similar to that facing Paul. A freedman who had run away from Sabinianus turned to Pliny for help. Here is Pliny's letter to Sabinianus:

> To Sabinianus. Greetings!
> (1) Your freedman, whom you had mentioned as having displeased you, has come to me; he threw himself at my feet and clung to me as if I were you. He cried much, begged constantly, even with much silence. In short, he convinced me of his genuine penitence. And I am persuaded he has reformed, because he recognizes that he has been delinquent.
> (2) You are *angry*, I know, and I know too that your *anger* was deserved, but mercy wins most praise when there was a just cause for *anger*. You loved the man once, and I hope you will love him again, but it is sufficent for the moment if you allow yourself to be appeased. You can always be *angry* again when he deserves it, and will have more excuse if you were once appeased. Make some concession to his youth, his tears, and your own kind heart, and do not torment him or yourself any longer—*anger* can only be a torment to your gentle self.
> (3) I fear I may seem rather to compel than to request, if I add my prayers to his—but this is what I shall do, and all the more freely and fully because I have given the man a very severe scolding and warned him firmly that I will never make such a request again. Although it was proper to say this to him, who should become more fearful (of offending), I do not say so to you; for maybe I shall make another request and obtain it, as long as it is nothing unsuitable for me to ask and you to grant. Farewell.[8]

*Outline*

1. A freedman of Sabinianus has turned for help to Pliny in connection with a wrong done to Sabinianus. Pliny is convinced that his remorse is genuine.
2. While emphasizing that Sabinianus's anger is justified, Pliny asks him to forgive his freedman and adduces various reasons to comply with the request (youth of the freedman, his tears, Sabinianus's own well-being).
3. After a further plea to forgive the freedman, Pliny notes that he has scolded the freedman and asserts his prerogative of making further claims on their friendship.

A second letter that Pliny wrote in this matter reveals that the entreaty he had made on behalf of the freedman was successful. He compliments and thanks Sabinianus for granting his request, and at the end of the letter advises him to be more naturally disposed to clemency in the future:

> Pliny to Sabinianus. Greetings!
> You have done the right thing in taking back into your home and favor the freedman who was once dear to you, with my letter to mediate between you both. This will help you greatly, it certainly helps me, first because I see you are willing to be pliant enough to be governed in your anger, and then because you have paid me the tribute of *bowing to my authority, or, granting my request.* So accept my compliments as well as my thanks, but, at the same time, a word of advice for the future: be ready to forgive the faults of your household even if there is no one there to intercede for them. Farewell.[9]

Pliny here takes up the case of an emancipated slave who chose to remain under the authority of his former owner. While the parallel to Paul's letter on behalf of Onesimus is evident, we see important differences. For one thing, Paul seems unwilling to address the moral issue directly; he finesses the difficulty by insinuating his authority and by claiming the sanction of Christian love. He is cautious and subtle: he does not deny, but he minimizes the fault of Onesimus. He has recourse throughout to abstract concepts (e.g., verses 5–6), to emotional pleadings (verses 10 and 13), and theological propositions (verses 15–16). And although one may see an implicit call for forgiveness in verse 17 ("Welcome him as you would welcome me"), Paul never directly calls on Philemon to forgive Onesimus.

Pliny, on the other hand, makes repeated and compelling mention of the runaway freedman's repentance, and explicitly pleads with Sabinianus to forgive his unfaithful servant. His man-to-man approach is considerably more straightforward: Since your anger was deserved, he argues, your mercy will be the more praiseworthy, and if the situation should recur your future anger would be the more justified. He favorably notes Sabinianus's self-control and acceptance of authority. Where Paul is convoluted and "rabbinic" (dare one say devious?), Pliny is analytic and cooly rational. And at the end of his first letter, Pliny displays, I would say, a refreshing and effective undercurrent of humor: "Hey, maybe I'll need another favor someday!" Similarly, the second letter ends in a self-assured and no-nonsense manner: "You did well; now my advice for the future is this: Wise up!" His orientation is human, not supernatural.

Indeed Pliny is polite, but he is direct, sometimes to the point of bluntness. He says what has to be said and little more. Paul is less disciplined: overall his ideas are well marshaled, but on occasion the emotionalism of his appeal renders it all but irrelevant. Surely the use of flattery to buy good will at the outset (verses 5–7) does not rise to the level of reasoned persuasion. Perhaps we can reasonably discern an element of insecurity in Paul's manner of dealing with an affluent member of one of his congregations.

The fact that we find missing in Paul's letter much of what we would naturally expect suggests the possibility of another motive, a hidden agenda. Is it not possible that far from a tender appeal on behalf of a runaway slave in whom Paul had taken a fatherly interest, what we really have here is Paul's attempt to obtain the young man as his own servant? His feelings show too clearly to imagine it is a totally disinterested appeal. And Paul wants the servant, once he has made his peace with his owner, to be returned to Paul.

Further, his use of numerous words having distinctly legal or commercial overtones (see my comment on verse 17 below, p. 81), however obliquely they may be employed, suggests that their selection might reflect the concerns of the writer. Legal ownership may be on his mind.

Last, it is interesting to observe that Pliny in his second letter (see the words put in italics) like Paul (Philem. 18–19) vacillates between authority to give orders and the appeal to do what one could have ordered.

## THE STATUS OF ONESIMUS—A FUGITIVE SLAVE?

While earlier commentators proceeded on the assumption that Onesimus was a fugitive, it is increasingly accepted today that he had solicited Paul as a mediator who might restore him to his master's good graces.[10] And no longer are we terribly concerned whether Paul sought his client's manumission, for it is clear that the "libertus," or freedman, remained his master's dependent. Further, it seems significant that although Paul knows him to be a slave and assumes him to have wronged his master—at the very least by willfully removing himself from his master's control—Paul never refers to Onesimus as a runaway. Paul attempts to solve the problem of mediating between master and slave by the gambit of converting the slave to the master's Christianity, and then sending him back in order to gain a servant for himself.

Again, Paul's intercession "to obtain for Onesimus an assured return to his master's house,"[11] seems not to have been the real purpose of the letter. Paul wants to secure the slave Onesimus as his own servant. In order to reach that goal he first had to settle Onesimus's dispute with his master Philemon, all the more since all of them now belonged to Christ. Indeed it may well be that the real meaning of the letter is to be found not in what it says, but in what it omits and thereby suggests. Paul's failure to speak directly to the sticky moral issue, the lack of any mention of repentance on the part of Onesimus, and the absence of a direct call for Philemon to forgive, are best explained by the understanding that both men are "in

Christ." It is highly doubtful that Paul could have brokered such a reconciliation between two Gentiles.

*Commentary on Philemon*

*Verses 1–3: Introductory Greeting (Prescript)*

> (1) Paul, a prisoner for Christ Jesus, and Timothy, our brother, to Philemon, our beloved and fellow worker (2) and Apphia, our sister, and Archippus, our fellow soldier, and to the church at your house: (3) Grace and peace to you [sing.] from God our Father and the Lord Jesus Christ.

These verses follow the so-called oriental form of the prescript which consists of two parts. In contrast, the Greek form of the letter prescript contains only one part. It can be found in Acts 15:23 ("The apostles and the elders, [your] brothers, send greetings to the brothers who are of the Gentiles in Antioch and Syria and Cilicia") and James 1:1 ("James, servant of God and of the Lord Jesus Christ, sends greetings to the twelve tribes in the dispersion"). The first part of the oriental form gives the name(s) of the sender(s) (cf. verse 1a) and afterward the person(s) the letter is sent to (cf. verses 1b–2). The second part is a blessing (verse 3) which corresponds to Jewish benedictions (see Apoc. Bar. 78:2) and may echo the priestly blessing of Num. 6:24–26. The oriental form is used in all the extant letters of Paul and also Rev. 1:4–5. The distinction between the two types of prescripts helps to determine the relationship of early Christian documents to one another.[12]

*Verse 1a*: Paul calls himself "a prisoner of Christ" which is both a historical reference to his present situation (see also verses 9, 10, 13) and a designation of honor. Though Timothy ("our brother") is mentioned as the cosender, Paul is the sole author of the letter. This follows from the emphatic "I" used throughout the letter (see verses 4, 5, 7, 8, and esp. verse 9).

Note that in all the other Pauline letters save one there are cosenders (Galatians gives no names, but 1:2 identifies "all the brothers"). Romans, the exception, is a lengthy theological tractate to a community whose members did not know Paul or his coworkers individually, and mentioning them would not have made any sense.

In all the other letters it did, for the communities knew his coworkers in question.

*Verses 1b–2:* The letter is being sent to Philemon who later is addressed as "you" (verses 4, 5, 6, 7, 9, 10, 11, 12, 13, etc.). Yet in verse 2 Paul greets two other individuals as well as the whole congregation that meets in Philemon's house. Apphia seems to be Philemon's wife or sister, and Archippus a fellow missionary of Paul. Since the letter is addressed to them, too (as the Greek plural form of "your" in verse 25 also indicates), Paul's appeal to Philemon is not an entirely private matter. It is not difficult to imagine that his purpose is to multiply his moral leverage: if two intimates who are leading members of the church have direct knowledge of Paul's exhortation, and the rest are at least generally aware of the issue, Philemon will find it all but impossible to ignore the plea of their founding apostle. However ingratiating and petitionary the body of the letter, the prescript must have made Philemon aware that Paul is a wily and formidable hierarch who means to have his way.

*Verse 3:* The salutation, "grace . . . and peace", corresponds to the second part of all other extant Pauline prescripts. It is identical word for word with Rom. 1:7. Its first part has an echo at the end of this letter in verse 25.

*Verses 4–7: Thanksgiving and Transition*

> (4) I give thanks to my God, as I always remember you [sing.] in my prayers, (5) because I hear of your [sing.] **love** and of the **faith** which you [sing.] have toward the Lord Jesus and for all the *saints*, (6) in order that your [sing.] partnership in the **faith** may become effective in the recognition of all the good that is ours until [the coming of] Christ. (7) For I have derived much joy and comfort from your [sing.] **love**, because the hearts of the *saints* have been refreshed through you, brother.

The thanksgivings in each of Paul's letters with the exception of Galatians (and possibly 2 Corinthians) have several common features that may be listed here:

*Remembrance:* Rom. 1:8b; 1 Cor. 1:4a; Phil. 1:3–4; 1 Thess. 1:2, 2:13, 3:9: cf. verse 4.

*Reference to the status of faith*: Rom. 1:8b; 1 Cor. 1:4b–7a; Phil. 1:5; 1 Thess. 1:3–5: cf. verses 5–6, 7 (implied).

*Reference to the special relationship between Paul and the recipients*: Rom. 1:9–13; Phil. 1:7; 1 Thess. 1:6–9, 2:1–12, 3:1–8: cf. verse 7a.

*Prayer on behalf of the recipients*: Rom. 1:11; Phil. 1:9–11; 1 Thess. 3:10–13: cf. verse 4b.

*Eschatological outlook*: Rom. 1:17–18;[13] 1 Cor. 1:7–9; 2 Cor. 1:10–11; Phil. 1:6, 10; 1 Thess. 1:9–10, 2:12, 3:13: cf. verse 6.

*Verse 4*: This contains the recurrent expression that Paul keeps the addressee in his prayers.

*Verses 5–7*: Note the chiastic structure of the words in boldface. The statement about faith is sandwiched in between words about the love that Philemon has displayed to all the saints. (Note also the chiastic structure of verse 5: the love for all the saints sets in brackets the faith towards the Lord Jesus Christ.) Verse 7 picks up the thread of verse 5. "Saints" is an old name for the Christians and is often used in Paul: Rom. 1:7; 16:15; 1 Cor. 1:2; 2 Cor. 1:1; 13:12. In two places it may even reflect a self-designation of the Jerusalem community: Rom. 15:27 and 1 Cor. 16:15. "Saints" is repeated in verse 7, which is itself a transition to the body of the letter.

In verse 6 it is Paul's prayer that Philemon's faith toward Christ (cf. verse 5) will be productive of a deeper recognition of all the good that comes to the saints through incorporation into Christ until his Second Coming. For the temporal meaning of "until Christ" see Gal. 3:24; 2 Cor. 1:21–22 and the parallel eschatological outlook in the thanksgivings of other letters of Paul (see above). If one does not see the eschatological outlook reflected here, one would have to introduce rather torturous interpretations such as: "in view of Christ," or, "for the glory of Christ," or even, "to the fullness of Christian fellowship, i.e., Christ." But the Greek says not "in (in Greek, *en*) Christ" but "until (in Greek, *eis*) Christ."

Apparently what Paul has in mind is that from faith acting out of love (cf. Gal. 5:6), and the fellowship it creates, there comes a new understanding of the higher life to which the Christian is called. While "the good" is unfortunately vague here (as also in 1 Thess. 5:15 and Rom. 15:2), in this case the context better allows us to see it as referring to a new recognition of selfhood, a new reality in Christ.

The difficult expression "partnership in the faith" seems to designate the faith the Christians hold in common. I would like to stress that "partnership in faith" results in equality (cf. Gal. 2:9; 3:26–28) and includes partnership in the Spirit (cf. 2 Cor. 13:13; Phil. 2:1–2; Rom. 15:27). Such an idea of equality has parallels in the Greco-Roman tradition, as in the proverb that friendship is equality (*isotes philotes*) and the conviction expressed by many writers that friendship is not possible between a slave and a master.[14] Thus Christian partnership is possible only in Christ, not at the level of society (see below, p. 79).

In any case, "partnership" in verse 6 anticipates the request in verse 17 (see below, p. 81). In the same way and even more clearly, the reference to the fact that "the hearts of the saints have been refreshed through you" in verse 7 prepares the way for the later appeal in verse 20: "Refresh my heart in Christ" which already was prepared for in verse 12 (see below, p. 77). This has a parallel in 1 Corinthians where the thanksgiving alludes to the subject of the letter. Note how the thanksgiving in 1 Cor. 1:4–9 is related to 1 Corinthians as a whole in that some of its major themes (verse 5a: "enrichment": cf. 1 Cor. 3:18; verse 5b: "knowledge": cf. 1 Cor. 8:1–4; verse 7: "spiritual gifts": cf. 1 Cor. 12) are mentioned.

### Verses 8–20: Intercession for Onesimus and Indirect Claim on Onesimus by Paul (Body of the Letter)

(8) Therefore, though I have full authority in Christ to command you to do what is fitting, (9) for love's sake I prefer to appeal to you—I, Paul, an elderly man and now a prisoner also of Jesus Christ—(10) I appeal to you for my child, Onesimus, **whom** I have begotten in (my) *imprisonment*. (11) Formerly he was useless to you, but now he is indeed useful to you and to me, (12) **whom** I am sending back to you, him, my very own heart, (13) **whom** I would have been glad to keep with me, in order that he might serve me on your behalf during my *imprisonment* for the gospel. (14) But without

your consent I would not do anything in order that the good you do might not be forced but come of your own free will. (15) Perhaps this is why he was separated from you for a while, that you might have him back forever, (16) no longer as a slave but more than a slave, as a beloved brother, especially to me but how much more to you, both in the flesh and in the Lord.

(17) So if you consider me your partner, receive him as you would receive me. (18) If he has wronged you, or owes you anything, charge that to my account.—(19) I, Paul, write this with my own hand, I will repay it—to say nothing of your owing me even yourself. (20) Yes, brother, may I be joyful about you in the Lord. Refresh my heart in Christ.

*Verse 8:* "Therefore" links the body of the letter to the preceding thanksgiving. Verse 8 serves as a heading for what follows. As apostle, Paul does have the authority to give orders. This prerogative is insinuated again and again throughout the letter (cf. verses 13, 19). However, Paul wants it to be replaced by a more reciprocal relationship.

*Verses 9–10:* Just as Pliny's plea for the fugitive freedman calls upon Sabinianus's love ("You loved the man once, and I hope you will love him again" [2]), so Paul here solicits Philemon's love, and reinforces the appeal by invoking his advanced age and his own imprisonment. Regarding Paul's reference to his age (verse 9), it is necessary to point out that in all Greek manuscripts the word is *presbytes*, "an elderly man," which in that society would have indicated someone over fifty, but not yet sixty. It should be noted, though, that some commentators have chosen to follow Richard Bentley's inventive proposal to add an epsilon, so as to read *presbeutes*,[15] a noun cognate with the verb *presbeuein* found in 2 Cor. 5:20, and thus to confer on Paul the title "ambassador of Christ." Bentley supports this emendation by arguing that since Acts 7:58 identifies Saul/Paul as a young man (*neanias*) at the time of Stephen's death, Paul could not some twenty-five years later be calling himself an old man. The resulting contrast in Bentley's rendering, "As once an ambassador, but now a prisoner too," is rhetorically effective, but founders on the fact that *presbeutes* is not to be found in any other known Pauline text. Several other commentators—and surprisingly both RSV and NEB—

presume incorrectly that *presbytes* can mean an ambassador or envoy. Similarly, Norman Petersen informs us that it can mean both "old man" and "ambassador," while *presbeutes* is properly rendered by the latter.[16] Unfortunately for his thesis, lexicons do not indicate ambiguity in either word. Last but not least, Fitzmyer correctly observes that Paul's self-identification (implying authority) and his mention of seniority both add weight to his plea with the younger Philemon.[17]

Thus in addition to his special authority[18] Paul applies emotional leverage in an effort to move Philemon to a posture of forgiveness. It is interesting to note that here he uses the image of fatherhood to describe his relation to Onesimus (cf. 1 Cor. 4:14–17 for a similar claim relative to the Corinthians and to Timothy; cf. also 1 Thess. 2:11), but that in other cases he employs maternal metaphors to describe his relation to converts: cf. Gal. 4:19 ("suffering birth-pangs"); 1 Thess. 2:7 ("a nurse taking care of her children").

*Verse 11*: The acceptance of the gospel by Onesimus makes him useful to both Paul and Philemon. Note the wordplay in Greek: Onesimus recalls the Greek *oninemi*—to be useful, to have joy from (see verse 20).

*Verses 12–14*: These verses explain why Paul is sending Onesimus back even though he would have liked to keep him. (In all likelihood Onesimus is the letter carrier.) Verse 12 expresses that Paul is thinking of Onesimus as part of himself. The Greek for "my very own heart" is *ta splanchna mou* which literally means: "my very own innards." This expression was already used in verse 7 and will again be employed in verse 20 in order to show Paul's personal involvement in the whole matter. In verse 13 and verse 14 two different motives are standing side by side: Verse 13 expresses the wish that Onesimus might serve Paul on Philemon's behalf, whereas verse 14 states that Onesimus should serve Paul only with the *free will* of Philemon. (Cf. Pliny's letter to Sabinianus: "I fear I may seem rather to compel than to request" [3].) See above on the relationship of verse 8 to verse 9 and below on the relationship of verse 18 to verse 19.

"Imprisonment" (verse 13) echoes "imprisonment" in verse 10. "Gospel" means both the evangelization (cf. Gal. 2:7; Phil. 4:3, etc.) and the gospel that Paul preaches (1 Thess. 3:2; Gal. 1:7, etc.).

Indeed, it is a sort of summary of the "new reality" based in Jesus Christ. "Good" of verse 14 echoes "good" of verse 6: Paul seeks to receive from Philemon the good which stems from the new reality or the faith active in love.

*Verses 15–16:* The Greek word in verse 15 for "have back" occurs only one other time in Paul, in Phil. 4:18 ("I have all things"). The verb was used in writing receipts and clearly has something of that sense in the passage from Philippians in which Paul acknowledges receipt of a gift. In Philemon the word apparently intends an absolute transfer of ownership. It is, however, a new and different sort of ownership. While Philemon will take back Onesimus forever, it will not be as a slave. In verse 16 the term "slave" is used for the first time in the letter and here twice, although the issue of the relation of the slave Onesimus to his owner Philemon must have been on Paul's mind all the time. Paul also suggests a possible reason for Onesimus's separation from Philemon: without it he would not have come to know Paul, and consequently would not have become a Christian. Having become a Christian, however, means that he is united with Philemon both as a slave in the flesh and forever as a brother in the Lord. "Forever" includes an eschatological aspect, i.e., a prospect of eternal life (see Rom. 2:7; 5:21; 2 Cor. 4:19; 5:1) which has been bestowed on all Christians.

Note that Paul does not discuss the possibility of Philemon's giving Onesimus his freedom. He showed little interest in changing the institution of slavery and expected Christians to remain in the state into which they were born or into which their life circumstances brought them. An illustration of this is contained in a passage from the Corinthian correspondence, 1 Cor. 7:17–24:

> (17) *Only let each one walk according to the lot the Lord has apportioned him, as God has called him.* This is the charge I give in all the churches. (18) Was any one called in the state of circumcision? Let him not undo his circumcision. Has any one been called uncircumcised? Let him not be circumcised. (19) Circumcision is nothing, uncircumcision is nothing, but keeping the commandments of God. (20) *Every one should <u>remain</u> in the calling in which he was called.* (21) Were you a slave when you were called? Never

mind. But if you can become free, make use of your present condition instead. (22) For he who was called in the Lord as a slave is a freedman of the Lord. Likewise he who was free when called is a slave of Christ. (23) You were bought at a price; do not become slaves of men. (24) *Let each man, brothers, <u>remain</u> with God in that state in which he was called.*

The above translation of 1 Cor. 7:21 has always been debated, for some scholars have translated it quite differently. Following the lead of the RSV they render it, "avail yourself of the opportunity" (cf. NEB, "take it"). But the context definitely favors the above translation, for verses 17a, 20, and 24—set in italics—are almost identical in language and encourage the person to remain where he or she was when called. Much to the chagrin of many modern exegetes, Paul displays a consistently conservative attitude toward issues of socioeconomic status, including slavery. The chief reason for this is his imminent expectation of the end. Paul thought that this world was about to come to an end. Why then bother about the preliminary things? He relativizes slavery and freedom because what counts is freedom in Christ.

The inner freedom that Paul advocates has some similarity with the Stoic notion of freedom as defined in Epictetus's tractate, *Discourses* 4.1.128–131:

(128) The unhampered man, who finds things ready to hand as he wants them, is free. But the man, who can be hampered or subjected to compulsion, or hindered, or thrown into something against his will, is a slave. (129) And who is unhampered? The man who fixes his aim on nothing that is *not his own*. And what are the things that are *not our own*? All that are not under our control, either to have, or not to have, or to have of a certain quality, or under certain conditions. (130) Therefore, the body *is not our own*, its members are not our own, property is *not our own*. If, then, you conceive a strong passion for some of these things, as though it were your immediate possession, you will be punished as he should be who fixes his aim upon what is *not his own*. (131) This is the road which leads to freedom, this is the only surcease of slavery.[19]

But how can one discover what is one's own? To this Epictetus gives an impressive answer at the beginning of his Encheiridion 1.1–2:

> (1) Some things are under our control, while others are not under our control. Under our control are conception, choice, desire, aversion, and, in a word, everything that is our doing; not under our control are body, our property, reputation, office, and in a word, everything that is not our own. (2) Furthermore, the things under our control are by nature free, unhindered, and unimpeded; while the things not under our control are weak, servile, subject to hindrance, and not our own.[20]

Thus, while the Stoics' inner distancing is grounded in the nature of the self and in the ability to discover what is and what is not one's own, Paul's is related to both the "reality" in Christ and the imminent expectation of the return of Christ.

Paul describes the experience of "reality in Christ" in an inspired confession, in Rom. 8:31b–35, 37–39:

> (31b) If God is on our side, who can be against us? (32) He did not spare his own Son, but on behalf of us delivered him up; how then can he fail to bestow on us all things, with him? (33) Who can bring a charge against God's elect? It is God who justifies. (34) Who can condemn us? It is Christ Jesus who dies, indeed was raised, who is at the right hand of God, who is actually interceding on our behalf. (35) Who can separate us from the love of Christ? Shall tribulation, or anguish, or persecution, or famine, or nakedness, or danger, or the sword? . . . (37) No, in all these things we are more than conquerors through him who loved us. (38) For I am confident that neither death nor life, neither angels nor their princes, neither things present nor things to come, nor spiritual powers, (39) whether above or below the level of the earth, nor any other created thing, shall be able to separate us from the love of God which is in Christ Jesus our Lord.

Paul's expectation of Jesus' imminent return is expressed with equal fervor and assurance in 1 Cor. 7:29b–31:

(29b) The time is short; henceforth let those who have wives be as though they had none, (30) and those who weep as though they did not weep, and those who rejoice as though they did not rejoice, and those who buy as though they did not possess, (31) and those who use the world as though they had no full use of it; for the form of this world is passing away.

*Verse 17*: This verse encourages Philemon to receive Onesimus like Paul himself, a request that renders Onesimus no longer vulnerable to Philemon's anger or retribution. Implied here is the concept of "partnership," a term already explicit in verse 6. This term taken from the world of business means essentially the same as it does today. In this context, it functions as a reminder to the owner that he and Paul are, as it were, shareholders in an enterprise of the highest consequence, and therefore must share what they hold in common.

*Verses 18–19*: These verses again develop an argument at two levels: Paul will take care of whatever debts Onesimus owes to Philemon. At the same time, talking from the other level of authority, Paul suggests in verse 19 that since in a spiritual sense Philemon owes Paul his life, he should accede to Paul's request, and even seems to intimate that the offer to repay any losses (verse 19a) really means to charge them against his standing debt to Paul—that is, to cancel them. Perhaps we may discern a bit of dry humor on the Apostle's part: "Charge it to my account . . . oh, and remember you owe me everything."

*Verse 20*: Paul calls upon Philemon to live up to his highest ideals. In effect, the immediately preceding notice of Philemon's indebtedness to Paul prompts this request for recompense, which in turn leads into an imperative form of the prayer of thanksgiving in verse 7. To this latter he appends "in Christ" as a parallel to "in the Lord" in the first half of the verse.

### Verses 21–25: Greetings and Travel Plans (Conclusion)

(21) Confident of your obedience, I write to you, knowing that you will do more than I ask. (22) One other thing: prepare a guestroom for me, for I hope through your prayers to be restored to you. (23)

Epaphras, my *fellow* prisoner in Christ Jesus sends greetings to you (24) and so do Mark, Aristarchus, Demas, and Luke, my *fellow* workers. (25) May the grace of the Lord Jesus Christ be with your [pl.] spirit.

*Verse 21*: Paul is confident that Philemon will do all he can and even more. Indeed, he will be obedient. (This remark reminds Philemon of what was said in verse 8.) Does Paul think about obedience to himself (cf. 2 Cor. 7:15; 10:5–6), or to God (see Rom. 5:19; 6:16b; 15:18; 16:19), or to Christ (see 2 Cor. 10:5)? The context suggests that the apostle aims at Philemon's obedience to himself. The comment above on verse 20 suggests that Paul has good reason to believe that Philemon will comply, and thus will do the same for him that he had previously done for the saints (verse 7).

*Verse 22*: The expectation of a future visit may reflect form critical redaction, for it can be found in other Pauline letters (cf. Rom. 1:10–11; 15:23; 1 Cor. 16:2; 1 Thess. 3:11). At the same time, by announcing his visit, Paul lends strong emphasis to his demand.

*Verse 23*: This list of names, which appears also in Col. 4:10–14, begins with the name of Epaphras, who is called "my fellow prisoner in Christ." In Colossians he was described as the founder of the community in Colossae (Col. 1:7–8; 4:12–13), here he shares Paul's imprisonment.

*Verse 24*: Mark, Aristarchus, Demas, and Luke are introduced as fellow workers of Paul (cf. Col. 4:14). By greeting Philemon, the "fellow worker" of verse 1, these other fellow workers of Paul express their common interest in the same work and seem to put additional pressure on Philemon to fulfill Paul's request.

*Verse 25:* The blessing echoes verse 3 as it concludes the letter.

## TEN THESES: PHILEMON AND OTHER THEOLOGICAL TOPICS IN PAUL

1. Paul did have a close relationship to affluent people like Philemon, who in Colossae gathered the church in his house. Otherwise Paul would not have dared to send this letter. Cf. the

similar cases of the married couple Aquila and Priscilla (Rom. 16:4; 1 Cor. 16:19) and Stephanas (1 Cor. 16:15), all of whom had believers gather in their houses and all of whom had been converted by Paul himself.

2. Paul claimed authority over and demanded obedience even from rich people, however delicate the matter was. On the whole he seems to have been quite successful.

3. Paul displayed great rhetorical skill in presenting his argument and his request even though he lacks the forthrightness that Pliny in his two letters displays. (This deficiency led to occasional confusion in Paul's communication with his Corinthian community.) Still, Paul felt bound to preach the gospel, even at the expense of being imprisoned for the gospel (verse 13). Indeed, he used every opportunity, including imprisonment, to preach Jesus Christ.

4. The basis for his preaching and the arguments in his letter was the new "reality" in Christ (see verse 23 and elsewhere) in which both Philemon and—from now on—Onesimus participated, not a general idea of clemency that Pliny refers to in his letter.

5. Those belonging to this "reality" he called "saints" (verses 5–7). In other words, all the designations of honor ("the sanctified," "the Elect," "the Believers," etc.) apply to them and can be substituted from the other extant Pauline letters.

6. They are saved through faith which they demonstrate by practicing love (see verse 6). The problem of justification by faith without the law was not an issue for Gentile Christians.

7. This "reality," since it was not dependent on one's social status, had no consequences at the level of society. In this specific case, though, it meant that a slave had to be treated as a fellow human or better: a partner in Christ.

8. This "reality" will achieve its consummation at the return of Christ from heaven (cf. verses 6 and 25). Christians are "in Christ" and will be united "with Christ."

9. Not only was Paul bold, but he possessed an intuitive grasp of human nature and individual character that enabled him to challenge and bring forth the best in others.

10. Paul's self-assurance and sangfroid may on occasion have risen to the level of self-deception. In the case of Philemon, these qualities seem to have carried the day; in other cases (like the debacle in Athens) they seem to have failed.

*In summary*, it is evident that practically all the paradigmatic items of Pauline thought and practice are contained in Philemon though it admittedly contains little theological reflection. It must be admitted, however, that with Paul sharp distinctions between religion and theology, piety and thought, may not be appropriate.

## BEING IN CHRIST: THE NEW REALITY?

Before concluding this chapter, one question must be answered: What constitutes that which we referred to as "(new) reality"? In a final section we shall address this issue.

In the letter to Philemon Paul twice uses the expression "in Christ" (in Greek, *en Christo*): verses 8 and 20. The meaning and implications of this phrase can be understood only by examining the contexts of this and such parallel expressions as "in the Lord" (in Greek, *en kyrio*), in the flesh (in Greek, *en sarki*), etc., which appear numerous times in the apostle's six other authentic letters (the expression "in Christ" alone occurs 162 times). Consider the following brief review:

(1) The notion of spiritual oneness or even mystical unity is clearly intended in passages like 2 Cor. 5:17:"If anyone is in Christ, he is a new creature." Phil. 4:13 ("I can do all things in him who

strengthens me") may be taken similarly, though an instrumental function (see no. 5 below) may be as reasonably imagined. Such passages may have to be interpreted in the light of Gal. 2:19b–20a: "I have been crucified with Christ; it is no longer I who live, but Christ who lives in me."

(2) In another group of passages, "in" has nothing to do with spiritual communion or Christ residing within, but simply indicates that the real and necessary prerequisite for salvation is present "in Christ": cf. Rom. 3:24 (redemption in Jesus Christ); Rom. 8:39 (see the text cited above: the love of God in Jesus Christ); 2 Cor. 5:19 (God was reconciling the world to himself in Jesus Christ).

(3) In yet another set of passages, "in" functions to represent individuals or include them in a category: e.g., 1 Cor. 15:22 (as in Adam all die, so in Christ shall all be made alive); 1 Cor. 7:14 (the unbelieving man is sanctified in the wife).

(4) In numerous cases, used with such words as hope, trust, and boast, "in" has its normal meaning ("though I have confidence in the flesh," Phil. 3:4) or is easily replaced with "of" ("Let him boast in the Lord," 1 Cor. 1:31) or "about"("So let us boast in men," 1 Cor. 3:21).

(5) In a number of passages, "in" has a clearly instrumental function, meaning "through," "by means of," or "in the name of." Note for example 1 Thess. 4:1–2 in which "in" (in Greek: *en kyrio Iesou*) and "through" (in Greek, *dia tou kyriou Iesou*) are essentially interchangeable.

From the above it must be evident that when Paul writes "in Christ" a good many interpretations are possible. Since he was evidently the first within the Christian tradition to use this expression, the variety of its possible renderings suggests that he must have used it frequently and over a long period of time. By contextual variation over several decades, thus, it became sufficiently ambiguous that we cannot be sure of its original meaning. By the time of his apostleship, Paul himself seems not to have had a single clear notion governing his use of "in" in combination with various nouns he frequently used. Perhaps the "new reality" in his life that he denominates "Christ" added a new dimension to his understanding of this slippery preposition. I am inclined to suppose that the phrase had its origin in baptism; Christians were in Christ (Rom. 16:7; 2 Cor. 12:2).

The degree to which baptism and other ritual practices of the early church involved mysticism (whether by invocation or evocation) we will never know. But our survey of Paul's use of the phrase "in Christ" makes it all but certain that Philemon, like the other authentic letters of Paul, reflects a Pauline ontology of grace, an implied claim on his part which must receive due attention in subsequent analyses.

## NOTES

1. Leander E. Keck, *Paul and his Letters*, 2d ed., rev. ed. (Philadelphia: Fortress Press, 1988), p. 79.

2. Adolf Deissmann, *Paul: A Study in Social and Religious History* (New York: Harper & Brothers, Torchbooks, 1957), pp. 18–19.

3. See the collection by John L. White, *Light from Ancient Letters* (Philadelphia: Fortress Press, 1986).

4. The letter dates from around 346 c.e., and was sent from a village priest who calls himself "Papas" to a Christian officer. In his book *Earliest Christianity: A History of the Period A.D. 30–150* (English translation edited with a new introduction and bibliography by Frederick C. Grant, 2 vols. [1937], New York/Evanston: Harper & Row, Torchbooks, 1959; reprint, Gloucester, Mass.: Peter Smith, 1970), Johannes Weiss gives a translation of the letter (p. 405, n. 13) that I have revised on the basis of the original of which there is a photograph in Adolf Deissmann, *Licht vom Osten*, 4th ed. (Tübingen: J. C. B. Mohr [Paul Siebeck], 1923), pp. 184–85. Unfortunately, the letter has not been included in White's collection of papyrus letters.

5. Weiss, *Earliest Christianity*, vol. 2, p. 406.

6. Let me emphasize that my analysis of Philemon derives from the historical critical method. While I find interesting such creative approaches as Norman Petersen's study of the narrative aspects of the letter (*Rediscovering Paul: Philemon and the Sociology of Paul's Narrative World* [Philadelphia: Fortress Press, 1985]), I note little in his study which cannot be discovered by traditional methodologies.

7. John Knox, *Philemon among the Letters of Paul: A New View of Its Place and Importance*, 2d ed. (New York and Nashville: Abingdon Press, 1959).

8. Pliny *Epistulae* 9.21. Translation with some modifications from: Pliny, *Letters and Panegyricus* in two volumes, II. Letters, Books VIII–X and Panagyricus with an English translation by Betty Radice, Loeb Classical

Library (Cambridge: Harvard University Press and London: William Heinemann, 1969), pp. 119, 121.

9. Pliny *Epistulae* 9.24 (translation from Pliny, *Letters*, p. 127).

10. See the survey by Joseph A. Fitzmyer, *The Letter to Philemon: A New Translation with Introduction and Commentary* (Anchor Bible, vol. 34 C, New York: Doubleday, 2000), pp.17–23.

11. Fitzmyer, *The Letter to Philemon*, p. 24.

12. For example the use of the oriental prescript in the Pauline letters and Revelation allows us to infer that the author of the latter knew the Pauline letters.

13. The very verb Paul uses in Rom 1:17–18 ("to reveal") confirms that he is thinking of a preliminary manifestation of that divine righteousness which, in Jewish thought, could be vindicated only at the last judgment.

14. Cf. Plato *Laws* 6.757a.

15. *Bentleei Critica Sacra*, ed. A. A. Ellis (Cambridge: Deighton, Bell & Co., 1862), p. 73, quoted and paraphrased from Fitzmyer, *The Letter to Philemon*, p. 105.

16. Petersen, *Rediscovering Paul*, p. 33 n. 4.

17. Fitzmyer, *The Letter to Philemon*, p. 103.

18. I write "special authority" rather than "apostolic authority" because the term "apostle" does not occur in Philemon. However, both expressions amount to the same thing for, being an apostle of Jesus Christ was part of Paul's identity. (See below, pp. 166–92.)

19. Translation on the basis of Epictetus, *The Discourses* as reported by Arrian, with an English translation by W. A. Oldfather, in two vols., Loeb Classical Library (Cambridge, Mass.: Harvard University Press, 1928), vol. 2, p. 289.

20. Translation ibid., p. 483.

# 4

# PAUL THE JEW

## PAUL—NOT REALLY A JEW?

At the beginning of this chapter it is appropriate to refute a thesis being propagated by some scholars, namely that Paul was not really a Jew. This opinion has been readily applauded by those who do not think highly of Paul anyway, and by Jewish critics of Paul who regard him as a primary source of anti-Semitism. Last but not least, those who presuppose that the church has generally suppressed the truth are also a responsive audience to the thesis of Paul's non-Jewish roots. What is the textual evidence for this?[1]

The church father Epiphanius of Salamis in the fourth century wrote a major work against all the heresies that had existed up to that time.[2] Although not very polite in his attacks, he remains an invaluable source, containing much otherwise lost material. Among others, he wrote about a group called Ebionites (from the Hebrew, meaning "the poor") who regarded themselves as the descendants of the Jerusalem community and its leader, James. In chapter 30 Epiphanius summarizes a source from an Ebionite community entitled "Ascensions of James" (I have placed in italics what is due to Epiphanius's polemic and therefore has to be subtracted from the older material). Haer. 30.16.6-9 reads:

> (6) They tell also of other Acts of the Apostles, *in which much that is godless is to be found, which they use to arm themselves against the truth.*
> (7) *They also fabricate* certain ascensions and speeches, namely, in

the Anabathmoi Jakobou ( = Ascensions of James), *as though* he (James) had spoken against the temple and sacrifice, or against fire and sacrificial altar, and much else *full of empty prattle they (attribute to him). (8) In the same way they say libelous things about Paul with lying, evil, and misleading words of their false apostles, saying that he was, to be sure,* a native of Tarsus, *which he himself acknowledges and does not deny, but they claim that he is from a Greek family. As the occasion for this claim, they use the passage in which Paul correctly says:* "I am from Tarsus, a citizen of no insignificant city."[3] *(9) They thus claim that* he was a Greek, a child of a Greek mother and a Greek father. After he had gone up to Jerusalem and remained there a long time, he wanted to marry the daughter of the (high?) priest. He therefore became a proselyte and had himself circumcised. But when he did not get the girl, he became angry and wrote against the circumcision, as well as against the Sabbath and the law.

The passage has a parallel in a tradition preserved in the Recognitions of Pseudo-Clement which in their Greek original stem from the third century. One of the basic features of that tradition is a hostile attitude toward Paul.[4] The contents of book 1 of the Recognitions are speeches of James against the altar and sacrifices which resembles James's polemic against these items in the passage just quoted. At one point a hostile man shows up who, defending the law against James's criticism, instigates the crowds against him. Struck to the ground, James barely survives the attack.

It is beyond doubt and almost universally accepted that the author of this text has used the canonical Acts of the Apostles, for the tale of the hostile man is based upon the tale of Saul in Acts 7–8. In other words, the author of this story employs the activity of the pre-Christian Saul to attack Paul the apostle. That is not very fair. But what does fairness mean in a situation of conflict?

There is an important agreement between the *Ascensions of James* and the story in the Recognitions. Both seem to use the canonical Acts of the Apostles, and they do so for a polemical purpose: in the Recognitions, to attack Paul in any way possible, and in the *Ascensions* to make Paul a Greek. These observations arouse suspicion as to the historical value of the report of Paul's Greek origins, all the more so since the tale of the failed love is totally gossip. It smacks of the same vulgar polemic as the tale in the Recognitions, being utterly remote from genuinely historical concerns. Apart from that, the Jewish origin of Paul is well attested (see below, pp. 91–93).

## HOW ANTI-PAULINE POLEMIC DEVELOPED

If the historical value of the story is nil, how can we explain its formation? One has to realize that for many members of the Jerusalem congregation, Paul was an apostate from the law almost from the beginning and certainly from the Jerusalem conference on. As was demonstrated earlier (see above, pp. 39–44), Paul had to fight a fierce battle at the conference and only after a protracted struggle obtained a sort of compromise. Even then the fight was not settled, but went on. We must not be so credulous as to take at face value propaganda like that in Acts 15 where Luke smoothes the waves with holy oil; for Paul indicates that the proceedings were all too human. To him the earliest period does not appear in the mist of sacred history; he allows himself to speak quite ironically of men like James and Peter. It should also be noted that the dispute was not settled and brought to an end with the apostolic decision, as it appears in Acts, but continued for a long time afterward.

We catch a glimpse of it when in Acts Luke has James report an oral tradition as to what was being said about Paul among the Jewish Christians and which according to Luke is of course not true, in Acts 21:21:

> Paul teaches all Jews who are among the Gentiles to forsake Moses,
> telling them not to circumcise their children or observe the customs.

The Greek term that is used here to describe Paul's activity is *apostasia tou nomou*, and indeed that is the way many Jerusalem Christians looked at Paul. For them he was nothing but an apostate. This charge runs like a scarlet thread through the stories told by Jewish Christian groups that claimed to be the successors of the original Jerusalem church.

## A SUMMARY REPORT ABOUT
## THE ANTI-PAULINE EBIONITES

One example may suffice. A summary report of the Jewish Christians appears in the antiheretical work of bishop Irenaeus of Lyons which has as its title "Unmasking and Refutation of the Gnosis Falsely so Called". It was written around 180 c.e. but certainly derives from earlier accounts. The bishop writes in Haer. 1.26.2:

> Those who are called Ebionites agree (with us) that the world was made by God; but their opinion with respect to the Lord is similar to those of Cerinthus and Carpocrates (namely, that Jesus was a mere man). They use the Gospel according to Matthew only, and repudiate the apostle Paul, maintaining that he was an *apostate from the law*. As to the prophetic writings, they endeavor to expound them in a somewhat singular manner; they practise circumcision, persevere in the observance of those customs which are enjoined by the law, and are so Judaic in their style of life that they even adore Jerusalem as if it were the house of God.

Such an anti-Pauline attitude seems to have been a common feature of these groups despite their differences in theology. Note that in the *Ascension of James* and in the tale from the Recognitions (see above, p. 89) James had a critical attitude toward the temple, even while Paul was observing the law. In other words, although their theologies developed, the hostility to Paul remained intact. Considering the trajectory of opposition to Paul in Jewish Christianity, it is impossible to accept the historical trustworthiness of the tale about Paul's Gentile origin. In view of the shaky historical standing of the story about Paul the Greek, nobody should use it even to suggest that Paul was not really a Jew.

## PAUL—PROUD OF HIS JEWISH HERITAGE

By his own account he was not only a real Jew but also a committed Jew who must have been very proud of his heritage. It shines through in a number of his later statements. We may very well see a reflection of Paul before his conversion to Christ in the legal expert he depicts in Rom. 2:17–23:

> (17 . . . You call yourself a Jew and rely upon the law and <u>make your boast</u> of God (18) and know his will and—instructed by the law—are able to judge what is significant and good (19) and . . . you are sure that you are a guide to the blind, a light to those who are in the darkness, (20) a corrector of fools, a teacher of babes, provided with the embodiment of knowledge and truth in the law—(21) you teach others ... you preach against stealing. . . . (22) You say that one must not commit adultery. You abhor idols. . . . (23) You <u>make your boast</u> in the law. . . .

The apostle writes about his origin in Phil. 3:5–6:

> (5) [I was] circumcised on the eighth day, of the people of Israel, of the tribe of Benjamin, a Hebrew born of Hebrews; as to the law a Pharisee, (6) as to zeal, a persecutor of the church, as to righteousness under the law, blameless.

This summary statement is written against intruders into his own Philippian community who had boasted of their Jewish origin. Against this Paul emphasizes that he has as much or even more to offer. Although the statements are made in an apologetic context, this does not mean that they are false. Here as elsewhere (cf. the oath in Gal. 1:20) Paul had to be accurate. Besides, many of the statements in Phil. 3 are corroborated by other passages in his letters. For the tribe of Benjamin see Rom. 11:1; for the persecution of the church cf. Gal. 1:13 and 1 Cor. 15:9. Only Paul's association with the Pharisees cannot be confirmed by another passage from his letters. However, Acts (23:6; 26:5) confirms it.

By his own account Paul was circumcised on the eighth day (Phil. 3:5). Every Jew had an obligation to circumcise his own son (according to Gen. 17:12 on the eighth day). Usually this was followed by the giving of a name as the narratives about John the Baptist and Jesus in Luke 1:59 and 2:21 illustrate. Paul received the Hebrew name "Saul" after his famous royal ancestor of the tribe Benjamin, to which he himself belonged. (On the name "Paul" see below, p. 134.)

Paul also calls himself *Hebrew of Hebrews* (Phil. 3:5). This is occasionally taken as proof that he spoke Aramaic. But "Hebrew" can also denote the ethnicity of Jews as opposed to that of Gentiles. At all events, that Paul's mother tongue was Greek is strongly suggested by the fact that scriptural citations in his letters are in most cases from the Septuagint, the Greek translation of the Hebrew Bible.

Moreover, in Phil. 3:5 Paul calls himself a *"Pharisee according to the law."*[5] The word Pharisee probably arose as a term given to the group by others meaning "the separated ones." As often in the history of religions, an originally alien designation was adopted by those to whom it was applied as a description, here all the more appropriately, since the Aramaic root of the word denoted the Pharisees as holy ones. Their goal was the sanctification of everyday life by adopting the strict regimen of the temple priesthood. The goal of sanctification by segregation meant that regulations of the Torah, which applied to priests and related to the temple cult, became requirements for individual Jews. One might recall Lev. 19:2: "You shall be holy. For I the Lord your God am holy." However, this holiness in everyday life, an ancient analogue to the priesthood of all believers, was possible outside the temple only by reinterpretation. Achieving the Pharisaic ideal therefore required the collaboration of scribes, who were the guardians and interpreters of the Law. The Pharisees thus developed the theology and practice of Judaism, while methodologically keeping the letter of the Hebrew Bible. For example, unlike the Sadducees, they put forward a doctrine of resurrection, which appears only at the periphery of the Hebrew Bible (Mark 12:18: "The Sadducees . . . say that there is no resurrection").[6]

The Pharisees organized themselves in communities. There was probably a probationary period, a set of regulations and a disciplinary law. Therefore one of their most important features was communal fellowship, as the contemporary Pharisee Josephus reports: "The Pharisees are friendly to one another, and are for the exercise of concord, and a regard for the public."[7] This fellowship was expressed in shared meals, especially every Friday evening at the beginning of the Sabbath. Any male Jew could become a member. And though scribal erudition was commonly prerequisite for leadership roles, the learning of the "typical" Pharisee should not be underestimated.[8]

Regulations about purity played a major role in the precepts of the Pharisees even if some modern scholars put the fulfillment of purity regulations only in third place.[9] These regulations primarily represented separation from other Jews and Gentiles. The New Testament Gospels also mention Pharisaic emphasis on good works (Matt. 6:2), prayer (Matt. 6:5), and fasting (Luke 18:12: twice a week).

The separation of written and oral law was also important for the Pharisees; Paul alludes to this in Gal. 1:14 when he speaks of the traditions of the elders. According to Josephus there were more than six thousand Pharisees at the time of Paul.[10] They were to be found mainly in the homeland of Judaea. In Jerusalem, Paul joined a Pharisaic community and received special training in scripture.

Paul's activity as a tentmaker or leatherworker (Acts 18:3; cf. 1 Thess. 2:9; 1 Cor. 4:12; 9:6–18, etc.) either derives from the rabbinical custom of learning a trade or stems from a familial context, likely from his father. If the latter is true, "Paul's family may have acted in accordance with specifically Jewish prescriptions, but we need to realize that the plausibility structure for their action extended far beyond the Jewish community."[11]

## PAUL'S METHODS OF INTERPRETING SCRIPTURE

Paul's Jewishness is also apparent from his knowledge and employment of the protocols of interpretation then current. Indeed, his customary hermeneutic methodology indicates that in addition to purported legal studies under Gamaliel (Acts 22:3) he must have attended Jewish schools in Tarsus and/or Jerusalem. The rules for scriptural exegesis he learned there and the strict canons of rabbinical argument so guided the apostle's thinking process that to understand them is to gain considerable insight into his Christian epistles. For this reason it will be useful to define and give an example of each of the two most commonly used interpretive methods. The first is inferring or deriving the greater from the lesser (*a minori ad maius*). It is employed in drawing the contrast between Adam and Christ (Rom. 5:15; 17). The second is analogy, that is, demonstrating the relation of two passages by adducing similar wording or phraseology. In Rom. 4:3–8, for example, Paul, by quoting Gen. 15:6, interprets the imputing of faith as righteousness. Naturally, Paul had mastered these and other argumentative strategies before his conversion: before he became a Christian he was already a theologian.

A more systematic analysis of interpretive principles is beyond our present scope; unfortunately, we have little detailed knowledge of whether the seven rules of interpretation, the first two of which I have just illustrated, really go back to Hillel.[12] Besides, these rules or some of them most likely have a Hellenistic provenance and were thus often variously employed by teachers and exegetes not bound by the rabbinic tradition.[13] Therefore it will prove more useful to adopt an ad hoc approach, and seek to understand the way Paul uses Scripture by examining specific passages.

One thing we should note at the outset is that Paul is not greatly concerned with the original significations of words in the text, nor with their contextual settings. He cares only for what will advance his line of argument. In other words, he has the solution in mind before he searches the scriptural texts for his evidence. A clear example of this occurs in Rom. 10:8, where to demonstrate that justification comes by faith he cites Deut. 30:14a: "The word is near you and in your mouth." But in Deuteronomy the clause refers not to faith, but to God's demand that the Law be fulfilled. In fact, verse 14b concludes with the statement, "you can do it," an assurance totally antithetical to Paul's doctrinal denial of free will. In another case his emphatic insistence on the singular nature of the common noun in "the seed of Abraham" (Gal. 3:16) flies in the face of both Hebrew and Greek usage, in which it is a collective noun which clearly refers to the Hebrew people as a whole. In that same passage, he employs it again, but this time collectively (Gal. 3:29; and cf. Rom. 4:13; 9:7), thus showing himself arbitrary as well as deceptive.

Furthermore, Paul proceeds on the basis of a tacit claim that God arranged for the insertion into Holy Scripture of hidden meanings that only the apostle is privileged to reveal. We should not be surprised at this, for he asserts that the intended beneficiaries are those whose feet now straddle the borderline between the old and the new ages of creation (Rom. 10:4; 1 Cor. 10:11). It means also that a number of passages containing the title "Lord" are subject to ambiguity, for even when in the original setting it means "The Lord of Hosts," i.e., God, Paul does not hesitate to assign it to Christ. For example, he not only misquotes a passage from Jeremiah, "He who boasts, let him boast of the Lord" (1 Cor. 1:31; but cf. Jer. 9:23–24), but he replaces God with Christ. Indeed, Paul can with apparently total conviction apply the word to either: in Rom. 11:34 he assigns Isa. 40:13: "Who has known the mind of the Lord?" to God; whereas in 1 Cor. 2:16 the same quote is used, but Christ is signified.

Another reinterpretation arises from Paul's personal history, and especially from his successful Gentile mission: the faith of Abraham comes to take on a whole new meaning. Paul has arrived at the conviction that when, many centuries earlier, the author of Genesis reported that Abraham's faith was taken as a sign of his righteousness (Gen. 15:6), God had thereby revealed the essential principle on which his plan of salvation was based, although his Chosen People had never understood or accepted it (Rom. 10:3). Here, of course, Paul is using the analogy method which, as we noted above, allowed him to use Gen. 15:6 in Rom. 4:3–8. And thus it becomes clear how Abraham's faith in the God who offered him a new life is the appropriate prototype of the Christian's faith in Christ's resurrection (Rom. 4:19–21; 24). All at once we see the full significance of the teaching that in Abraham all Gentiles shall be blessed (Gen. 17:15; 12:3). And finally we see the crucial importance of the often overlooked notice that Abraham's faith preceded his circumcision: it was thus that he could be held up as the spiritual father of the uncircumcised (Rom. 4:10–11). Indeed, the pronouncement of Abraham's faith (Gen. 15) precedes that of his circumcision (Gen. 17).

It is crucial for Paul's scheme of salvation that God's covenant with Abraham antedated by more than four centuries his revelation of the Law to Moses (Gal. 3:17). That means that the earlier covenant cannot be abrogated by the later one. For Paul, the revelation to Abraham signifies the true relation between God and mankind; the Law, which was "added to it" (Gal. 3:19) or "slipped in between" (Rom. 5:20) is more than merely an unreliable indication of God's intention, it is an encitement to sin and death (cf. Rom. 5:20; 7:5, 7b–11a).

Predictably enough, Paul sees many indications of the Law's dubious value. Jewish tradition informs him that the Law itself had not come directly from God, but was handed on by angels (Gal. 3:19). And Paul tells us that when Moses shielded his face from God's glory (Ex. 34:33; 35), his real purpose was to prevent the Israelites from seeing how that glory (presumably reflected in his face) was fading away (2 Cor. 3:13).

Also of rabbinic origin is a kind of midrash in which Paul supplements the scriptural record with his own redactive explanations, and then by implication assigns scriptural status to his glosses. Consider an example: He begins by taking out of context an excerpt from Deut. 30:12: "Who will ascend into heaven . . . ?" and further distorts it by an anachronistic explanation, "That is, to bring Christ down" (Rom. 10:6). Next, he changes Deut. 30:13 from "Who will go over the sea?" to "Who will descend into the abyss?" and then appends another imaginative paraphrase: "That is, to bring Christ up from the dead." In a similar manner he so misconstrues Ps. 143:2 as to make it deny justification by works, and then bases Rom. 3:20 and Gal. 2:16 upon it. To the text of Gen. 2:7, "The first man Adam was made a living soul," he adds a useful invention of his own: "the last Adam, a life-giving spirit" (1 Cor. 15:45). Then he goes on to base his demonstration of human immortality on the clause he has added!

Clearly, Paul is employing what we may term scribal license: to wit, that which can be extracted by exegesis is as valid as the scripture from which it is drawn. But this was not something new for Paul. Long before his encounter with Christ he had learned the Scriptures, the traditions of the Elders (Gal. 1:14), and patterns of thought and interpretation. Turning Christian did not change his way of thinking; rather he conceived that as a Christian he was one with the divine Spirit from which the Scriptures emanated. How could his interpretation fail to be in harmony with the divine mind? If the legendary Daniel could be inspired to interpret dreams and visions, surely he, Paul, specially designated and elevated by God's own Son, could glean from the mysteries of Scripture (1 Cor. 2:13) the wisdom inspired by the Spirit (1 Cor. 2:6) and the knowledge which is above all others (1 Cor. 13:2).

## PAUL'S ZEAL AND THE CONSEQUENCES RESULTING FROM IT

Given Paul's scribal training, it is surprising that unlike most of the Jewish teachers known to us he was evidently not married.[14] Only one scholar, the mystic Simon Ben Azzai (early second century C.E.), is supposed to have remained unmarried. When asked why, he gave the following reason: "What should I do? My soul hangs on the torah; let the world be maintained by others."[15] One may suppose it was the same for Paul: his soul, in fact, hung on the Torah. This led him, indeed drove him to persecute Christians (cf. Phil. 3:6; 1 Cor. 15:9; Gal. 1:23). More than most of his contemporaries he was moved by his zeal to become involved in matters he considered to involve transgressions of the law. Here his gaze fell upon the followers of Jesus, who claimed that a crucified man was the Messiah. For one trained in the law that was impossible, simply because "cursed is the one who hangs on the tree" (Gal. 3:13/Deut. 21:23).

And there was a second factor: possibly in Jerusalem and surely a little later in Damascus, Paul had come to know Christians—both Jews and Gentiles—who thought of themselves as being brothers and sisters in Christ. Probably at baptismal celebrations (see Gal. 3:27: "For as many of you as were *baptized* into Christ have put on Christ") they cried out in joy, "Here is neither Jew nor Greek; here is neither slave nor free; here is neither male nor female; for you are all one in Christ" (Gal. 3:28).

That could not be permitted, because it put the purity of the Jews at risk: fellowship between Jews and Gentiles was a pollution that extinguished Jewish identity.[16] For reasons to be explained later (see below, pp. 187–91), Paul joined these groups. At this point of the investigation we must point out that despite his departure from Judaism Paul continued to use Jewish concepts when preaching the Good News to the Gentiles. Therefore the following sections belong here.

Paul taught his Gentile converts two basic things: Jewish monotheism and Jewish ethics.

## PAUL'S TEACHING TO THE GENTILES: JEWISH MONOTHEISM

The major point of Paul's instructions during his founding visit to a community was the proclamation of the one living and true God, which included a complete exclusiveness and intolerance toward all other religions. The I-am proclamation of God in Isa. 45:5 ("I am the Lord, and there is no other, besides me there is no God") looms large and permeates most of the Jewish literature in postexilic times. It is against this background that Paul's explanation to the Corinthians (1 Cor. 8:5–6a) has to be understood:

> (5) For indeed, if there be so-called gods, whether in heaven or on earth—as indeed there are many "gods" and many "lords"—(6a) yet for us there is one God, the Father, from whom all being comes.

Here was a novel notion indeed: devotion to the Lord entailed rejecting all the old, familiar deities as mere idols. No doubt the Corinthians, like other Gentiles, found this doctrine difficult to grasp, for one did not offend Father Zeus by honoring Serapis. Nor did an offering to "the Savior" Asclepius for curing an illness preclude offerings to another god or, for that matter, the whole pantheon. In 1 Thess. 1:9 (cf. 4:5b) Paul reminds the Thessalonians of how they "turned to God from idols, to serve a living and true God." This is fundamental to Israel's religion and can be illustrated by many parallels.[17]

*Letter of Aristeas 132, 134:*

> (132) [Eleazar] began first of all by demonstrating that God is one, that his power is shown in everything, every place being filled with his sovereignty. . . . (134) He proceeded to show that all the rest of mankind . . . believe that there are many gods.[18]

*Sibyline Oracles, Fragment 3:*

> There are gods which by deceit are leaders of mindless men, from
> whose mouths pour deadly poisons. But he (God) is life and imper-
> ishable eternal light, and he pours out a delight sweeter than
> honey for men. . . . Bend the neck to him alone.[19]

The serving of one God is already central in the Hebrew Bible:
see in addition to the just cited text from Isa. 45 the first commandment Exod. 20:2. (It is connected with the turning away from idols:
cf. Exod. 20:3–4.) In other words, Hellenistic Jews derived from the
Hebrew Bible their monotheism along with the turning away from
idols. Since most of them did not know Hebrew they were dependent
on the Greek version of the Hebrew Bible, the Septuagint.

## PAUL'S TEACHING OF THE GENTILES: JEWISH ETHICS

In his earliest extant letter, 1 Thessalonians, Paul partly reiterates
what he had told his converts during the founding visit and thereby
allows us to catch a glimpse of his ethical instructions. Let me hasten
to add that this teaching is rooted in Paul's conviction that God wants
human beings to behave in a certain way. "Thy will be done, on earth
as in heaven" (Matt. 6:10b) is the Jewish maxim which is also the
basis of Gentile Christian ethics. Paul writes in 1 Thess. 4:2–12:

> (2) For you know what instructions we gave you through the Lord
> Jesus Christ, (3) For this is the *will of GOD*, your **sanctification**: that
> you abstain from fornication; (4) that each of you know how to take
> a wife for himself in **sanctification** and honor, (5) not in the pas-
> sion of lust like the Gentiles who do not know GOD; (6) that no
> man defraud or take advantage of his brother in business, because
> the Lord is an avenger in all these things, as we told you before
> with all emphasis. (7) For GOD has not called us for uncleanness,
> but for **sanctification**. (8) Therefore whoever disregards this, dis-
> regards not man but GOD, who gives his Holy Spirit to you.
>     (9) But concerning love of the brothers you have no need to
> have anyone write to you, for you yourselves have been taught by

GOD to <u>love one another</u> (10) and indeed you do <u>love all the</u> <u>brothers</u> throughout Macedonia. But we exhort you, brothers, to do so more and more, (11) to aspire to live quietly, to mind your own affairs, and to work with your own hands, as we charged you; (12) so that you may command the respect of outsiders, and be dependent on nobody.

The passage in 1 Thessalonians is Jewish through and through. The Gentile Thessalonians (see 1:9) are told not to behave like Gentiles (see 4:5). In other words, Paul gives them instructions almost as if they were Jewish. At the same time, we see that the service of God is fundamental to the teaching of the ethical standards preserved in 1 Thess. 4:2–12 and for the prediction that "the Lord is an avenger in all these things" (1 Thess. 4:6b = Ps. 94:1). However, circumcision was not part of the teaching. It was deliberately omitted.

The ethical standard that Paul transmitted to the Thessalonians (and all the other communities he founded during his early missionary preaching) consists in the *sanctification* of the Christians (verses 3, 4, 7) which specifies: "that you abstain from fornication" (verse 3), "that each of you take a wife for himself in sanctification and in honor" (verse 4),[20] "that no man defraud or take advantage of his brother in business" (verse 6), "to love one another" (verse 9), "to aspire to live quietly, to mind your own affairs, and to work with your own hands" (verse 11).

Beyond the material contained in 1 Thessalonians, lists of virtues and vices must have been part of Paul's instruction. This can be said with confidence because in another letter, Galatians, Paul emphasizes that he proclaimed similar doctrines during the founding visit, and we may conclude that he instructed his converts everywhere along the same lines. In Gal. 5:19–23 the apostle writes the following (the italics stress that this is repeated instruction):

(19) Now the works of the flesh are plain: fornication, impurity, licentiousness, (20) idolatry, sorcery, enmity, strife, jealousy, anger, selfishness, dissension, party spirit, (21) envy, drunkenness, carousing, and the like. I tell you, *as I told you before*, that those who do such things shall not inherit <u>the kingdom of God</u>. (22) But the fruit

of the Spirit is love, joy, peace, patience, kindness, goodness, faith-
fulness, (23) gentleness, self-control; against such there is no law.

In 1 Cor. 6:9–10 Paul presents a similar doctrine, and clearly it is
one the Corinthians have heard before. The term "kingdom of God"
(underlined both in the above text from Galatians and in the text
from 1 Corinthians below) is repeated, indicating that Paul is
drawing upon pre-Pauline material, for the term "kingdom of God"
is not central in his theological language (see below, p. 194). The
text of 1 Cor. 6:9–10 reads thus:

> (9) Do you not know that the unrighteous will not inherit the
> kingdom of God? Do not be deceived; neither people who practice
> fornication, nor idolators, nor adulterers, nor homosexuals, (10)
> nor thieves, nor the greedy, nor drunkards, nor revilers, nor robbers
> will inherit the kingdom of God. (11) And such were some of you.
> But you were washed, you were sanctified, you were justified in the
> name of the Lord Jesus Christ and in the Spirit of God.

## JEWISH AND GENTILE ETHICS—THEIR RELATIONSHIP

Of course Jewish and Gentile ideas of proper behavior corresponded
to a considerable degree. No one approved of murder, fraud, theft, or
lying. Indeed, Paul's catalogues of virtues and sins often agreed
pretty closely with pagan parallels.[21]

But there were two areas of fundamental disagreement: idolatry
and certain sexual practices. Jewish attacks on Gentile morality
nearly always emphasized these two issues (see e.g., Wisd. of Sol.
13–14). Certainly they predominate in Paul's lists of vices: in 1 Cor.
5:11 fornication heads the list and idolatry ranks third; in 1 Cor.
6:9–10 sexual immorality and idolatry are first and second, followed
by specific sexual evils (adultery and homosexuality). The list in Gal.
5:19–21 (see above, p. 101) begins with fornication, impurity, licentiousness, and idolatry. The influence of the synagogue is evident.

Note the connection between idolatry and fornication in Wisd. of
Sol. 14:12: "For the idea of making idols was the beginning of forni-

cation, and the invention of them was the corruption of life." Paul must be seen in this ethical Jewish tradition.

## THE ORIGIN OF JEWISH ETHICS

As to the origins of such teachings about ethics, one has to realize that they stem from the Hebrew Bible and its exegesis by Greek-speaking Jews. Let me demonstrate this by citing two verses from 1 Thessalonians, followed by their parallels in the Septuagint, which had become part of Hellenistic Judaism:

On abstention from sexual immorality (1 Thess. 4:3) cf. Exod. 20:16–17; Lev. 19:13.

On loving one's brother (1 Thess. 4:9) cf. Lev. 19:18.

To be sure, the passages from the Septuagint are in some cases only slightly reminiscent of the Pauline exhortations.[22] However, in order to recognize their importance to Paul, their appropriation by Hellenistic Judaism has to be taken into account. For Paul and other Hellenistic Jews, knowledge of the will of God (cf. 1 Thess. 4:3) could have had its origin only in the revelations and events recorded in Scripture.

It must be noted in passing that scholars like Wayne A. Meeks opine that Paul borrowed directly from Hellenistic moralists. For him, 1 Thessalonians exemplifies Paul's method of adopting the Greco-Roman style and content of moral instruction, and adapting them to the situations existing within a specific community.[23] But that disregards the role of the synagogue, which played a formative role in Paul's identity. It seems an unlikely assumption that Cynic teachers had a greater influence on Paul than did the Jewish diaspora Synagogue of Tarsus. In a like manner, Nock derives from stylistic similarities between the epistles and the diatribe,[24] a contemporary pagan genre, the proposal that Paul adopted both the form and content of Cynic philosophers he had heard engaged in public debate.[25] But the casual acquaintance with one contemporary rhetorical parallel no more demonstrates Paul's reliance on their example than does Meeks's citation of a literary model. Eminently more striking is the fact that there is not a paragraph in Paul's writing which does not include subconscious recollections of the Greek Old Testament. He "shows only the slightest acquaintance with pagan Greek literature, but he knew his Old Testament very well."[26]

It should further be noted that in the case of both Paul and other Hellenistic Jews we would be missing the point if we were to presume that their appropriation of biblical law involved distinguishing between moral and ritual precepts of the law. It is not true that Paul has kept only the moral law, for neither the service of the one and living God nor the turning away from idols can be regarded as moral law.

Another point deserves consideration. It seems clear that the Hebrew Bible's concept of purity underlies much of what Paul says about the community. For Paul, sanctification involves not only following certain commandments, but also separation from all things that would defile, e.g., the impure Gentiles (cf. 1 Thess. 4:4; 1 Cor. 5:1; Gal. 2:15). The reason for this lies in the holiness of the community which is "the temple of God" (cf. 1 Cor. 3:16; 6:19), and thus corresponds to the holiness of God (cf. Lev. 19:2).

## A FAMOUS EXAMPLE OF JEWISH ETHICS: 1 COR. 13

In order to complete our journey through the ethical standards of Jewish origin that Paul transmitted to his newly founded churches, we must now turn to the famous hymn about love, 1 Cor. 13. I have heard Christian theologians say that a Jew could not possibly have written that hymn and that Paul must have taken it from Gentile Christians, discovered it in a non-Jewish literary source, or have drawn on purely Christian inspiration.

*1 Cor. 13*

> (1) *If I* speak with the tongues of men and of angels, but have no **love**, I am a noisy gong or a shrill cymbal. (2) And *if I* have the gift of prophecy, and know all mysteries and all knowledge, and *if I* have all faith, so as to remove mountains, but have no **love**, I am nothing. (3) *If I* give away all that I possess, and if I deliver my body to be burned, but have no **love**, that does me no good whatever.

(4) Love is patient; love is kind; love is not jealous or boastful; (5) it is not arrogant or rude. Love does not insist on its own way; it is not irritable or resentful; (6) it does not rejoice at unrighteousness, but rejoices in the truth. (7) It bears all things, believes all things, hopes all things, endures all things.

(8) Love never ends; *as for* prophecies, they will be done away with; *as for* tongues, they will cease; *as for* knowledge, it will be done away with. (9) For we know in part, and prophesy in part; (10) but when the wholeness comes, the partial will be done away with. (11) When I was a child, I used to speak like a child, I used to think like a child, I used to reason like a child; but now I have become a man I am done with this that belongs to childhood. (12) For now we see in a mirror obscurely, but then face to face. Now I know in part; then I shall know, even as also I have been known.

(13) So faith, hope, love endure, these three; but the greatest of these is love.

Although it would surely be an exaggeration to suggest that by itself 1 Cor. 13 suffices to secure Paul's undying fame, still in chapters 12–14 Paul the pastor appears at the height of his powers. Not only does he have his priorities right, but his style of presentation is direct and persuasive. Elsewhere his handling of the law is marred by confusion and casuistry (see below, pp. 215–17); here his exaltation of love over mere protestations and displays of faith is honest and on the mark. It should nevertheless be noted that however powerful a blending of Jewish ideas and Greek rhetoric we have here, two quintessentially Jewish elements are missing. Paul's triad of virtues omits "truth" and "justice." We do not remember the Old Testament prophets primarily as champions of love; we speak of them as the "ethical" prophets. Whether we like it or not, the history of mankind attests that truth and justice are necessary preconditions for the flowering of faith, hope, and love. Yet even with this proviso, and amazing as it may seem to a Christian theologian or believer, this passage is certainly of Jewish origin and stems almost entirely from Paul's Jewish acculturation.

## THE JEWISH ORIGIN OF 1 COR. 13

*First* of all, one must observe that it is altogether lacking in teachings about Christ.

*Second*, the traditional character of the hymn is confirmed in that it can be removed from 1 Cor. 12–14 without causing any contextual disruption. For example, 1 Cor. 14:1 ("Pursue love as your aim, but strive for spiritual gifts, and especially that you may prophesy") links up with 1 Cor. 12:31 ("But strive for the greater gifts; and I am going on to show you a yet better way").

*Third*, "faith" in verse 2 has a meaning quite different from that of salvific faith in Jesus Christ. It designates an unshakable trust, a perseverance that moves mountains, a concept that likely goes back to the historical Jesus. It is preserved in both Mark 11:23 and Q (Matt. 17:20b/Luke 17:6) as well as Thomas (48; 106).

*Fourth*, the triad "faith, hope, love" which forms an emphatic conclusion to the hymn already occurs at the level of tradition in 1 Thess. 1:3 and 5:8 and elsewhere in the Pauline letters.[27]

*Fifth*, passages like Wisd. of Sol. 3:9; 7:25 or 4 Macc. 17:2–4 shed further light on the traditional character of the triad in 1 Cor. 13.

## A JEWISH PARALLEL OF 1 COR. 13

The following hymn about truth from 1 Esd. 4:34–40 (first century B.C.E.) gives us ideas of how integral to the Jewish tradition were hymns about truth or the closely related concepts of justice, wisdom, or love. Note that there are many parallels in the Hebrew Bible for what is said about truth in this hymn. (I have listed these parallels in brackets according to the Greek translation, the Septuagint, whose division of the text sometimes varies from that of the Hebrew Bible.)[28] The hymn is inserted into the narrative framework of the competition of the young men before King Darius. One of them delivers the following paean in 1 Esd. 4:34–40:

> (34) "Men, are not women strong? Great is the earth, high is heaven and swift is the sun in his course, for he moves around his

circuit of the heavens and returns again to his place in a single day. (35) Is he not great who does these things (Ps. 76:14)? But great is the **truth**, and stronger than all things. (36) The whole earth calls on the **truth** and the heavens bless her (Ps. 88:6); all works shake and tremble at it (Nah. 1:5), and with it there is no unrighteous thing (Dan. 3:27–28).

(37) Wine is <u>unjust</u>, the king is <u>unjust</u>, women are <u>unjust</u>, all the children of men are <u>unjust</u>; and such are all their <u>unjust</u> works, and there is no **truth** in them; in their unrighteousness they shall perish (Ez. 3:18c; Prov. 11:18; 13:23b).

(38) As for the **truth**, it endures, and is always strong; it lives and conquers for evermore (Ps. 116:2; 145:6) (39) With her there is no accepting of persons or rewards (cf. Deut. 10:17). But she does the things that are just, and refrains from all unjust and wicked things; and all (men) take delight in her works. (40) Neither in her judgment is any unrighteousness; and to her belongs the strength, the kingdom, the authority, and the majesty of ages. Blessed be the God of **truth** (Ps. 30:6b)."

(41) And with that he held his peace. And all the people then shouted, and said, "Great is **truth**, and mighty above all things."

Note the following parallels between this text and 1 Corinthians:

Verses 34–36/1 Cor. 13:1–3: Introduction; true values.
Verse 37/1 Cor. 13:4–7: Denial of other values.
Verses 38–40/1 Cor. 13:13: The endurance of value.

In sum, we may conclude that the hymn in 1 Cor. 13 can be derived from Hellenistic Jewish motifs and traditions. What many Christians regard as a jewel of Christian ethics has solid Jewish roots and was directly transported from Judaism to Christianity. Indeed, the whole of Pauline ethics derives from Judaism. As far as ethics is concerned Paul remained firmly rooted in the tradition of his Jewish mother religion.

## JERUSALEM REMAINS THE CENTER OF THE WORLD

It comes therefore as no surprise that Paul—even as a Christian—continued to regard Jerusalem as the center of the world. Though we do not know precisely what role the temple cult played for Paul before his conversion, Jerusalem remained a most important place. This can be said with great confidence for the pre-Christian Paul, because for Paul the Christian Jerusalem remained the point of origin of his missionary activity. See Rom. 15:19b: "From Jerusalem and as far as around Illyricum I have completed the gospel of Christ." The ideological importance of Jerusalem was such that even as a Christian Paul had to go to the Jerusalem community in order to receive their approval for his preaching, because otherwise his work would be in jeopardy (see Gal. 2:2b: "lest somehow I should be running or had run in vain"). The preeminent place of that community in early Christianity *including* Paul is beyond dispute, in considerable measure because it was located at the center of Israel then and now: Jerusalem. (For the tension between this ideology and Paul's Christianity—two ideologies which he seldom managed to synthesize—see below, pp. 156–63.)

### The Enduring Election of Israel

Furthermore, the election of Israel was a firm ingredient of Paul's religious conviction.[29] That was and is a basic tenet of every Jew's worldview.[30] How deeply rooted it was in Paul's soul one can infer from his manner of dealing with it during his activity as a Christian missionary. While at first he seemed to have deprived Israel of all privileges unless it turned to Christ, at the end of his career things had changed, and he steadfastly defended the election of Israel whether repenting or unrepenting. All this is being formulated accompanied by emotional turmoil.

*Rom. 9:1–5:*

> (1) I am speaking the truth in Christ, I am not lying; my conscience bears me witness in the Holy Spirit (2) when I say that I feel in my heart great grief and ceaseless pain. (3) For I could wish myself

accursed and cut off from Christ for the sake of my brothers, my natural kinsfolk. (4) They are Israelites, and to them belong the sonship, the glory, the covenants, the giving of the law, the worship (in the temple), and the promises; (5) to them belong the patriarchs, and from them, in natural descent, is the Christ. God who is over all be blessed forever. Amen.

It does not really matter that we find Paul flip-flopping in order to combine the election of (unbelieving) Israel and the election of the church. In the end he combines them by claiming in Rom. 11:28:

As regards the gospel, they [the unbelieving Israelites] are enemies, for your [the Gentile Christians'] sake; but as regards election they are beloved for the fathers' sake.

Whether these statements are logically sound does not concern us here (see more on this below, pp. 161–63). More important is the observation that after being a Christian for more than twenty years, Paul could still maintain—or again maintain—the enduring election of Israel. How much more must he have believed in Israel's election before he had ever heard anything of the Christian movement?

## NOTES

1. For the following, see my *Opposition to Paul in Early Christianity* (Minneapolis: Fortress Press, 1989), pp. 169–96.

2. Cf. Frank Williams, *Panarion of Epiphanius of Salamis*, bk. 1 (secs. 1–46) (Leiden/New York/Köln: E. J. Brill, 1987). Williams's translation of chap. 30 (pp. 132ff.) differs slightly.

3. See Acts 21:39.

4. See F. Stanley Jones, *An Ancient Jewish Christian Source on the History of Christianity: Pseudo-Clementine Recognitions 1.27–71* (Atlanta: Scholars Press, 1995).

5. Present research into the Pharisees produces a chaotic picture. The problem relates to whether or not we have sources for the reconstruction of Pharisaism in the first century. The only Pharisee from the period before 30 c.e. about whom sources survive is the apostle Paul. The other source is

Josephus, who at the beginning of the second century claims to have been a Pharisee (Life 10–12) and whose work is the basic source for the history of Judaism in the first centuries B.C.E. and C.E. There is argument over the attribution to the Pharisees of individual sources such as the *Psalms of Solomon* and the *Assumption of Moses*. At the same time, the importance of the New Testament Gospels from the period after 70 C.E. should not be underestimated, although they contain a polemical picture of the Pharisees. The earlier research of Julius Wellhausen (1844–1918) is still important. In his monograph *Die Pharisäer und Sadducäer* (3d ed., Göttingen: Vandenhoeck & Ruprecht, 1967) he was the first to regard the *Psalms of Solomon* as Pharisaic and was probably right in assuming that the influence of the Pharisees on the people was considerable. However, his remarks are highly polemical. He uses Pharisaic teaching as the dark background for spelling out the light of the New Testament message. See his statements: The Pharisees "never took the human side in matters of God but always opposed it . . . the remarkably indirect approach in relation to God, the lack of freedom, that Paul attributes to the Pharisees, is a main characteristic of the dominant Pharisaic piety of his day" (p. 101). For a good assessment in English see Steve N. Mason, *Flavius Josephus on the Pharisees: A Composition-Critical Study* (Leiden: E. J. Brill, 1991).

6. See also Dan. 12:2–3: "And many of those who sleep in the dust of the earth shall awaken, some to everlasting life, and some to shame and everlasting contempt," and Ezek. 37:12: "These are the words of the Lord God: O my people, I will open your graves and bring you up from them, and restore you to the land of Israel."

7. Josephus *Jewish War* 2.166.

8. See Josephus *Life* 196f.

9. See E. P. Sanders, *Jewish Law from Jesus to the Mishnah* (Harrisburg, Pa.: Trinity Press International, 1990), p. 236. According to Sanders, study of the law and of the extrabiblical traditions, along with belief in life after death, were the two main marks of the Pharisees—not purity and tithes.

10. Josephus *Jewish Antiquities* 17.42.

11. Ronald F. Hock, *The Social Context of Paul's Ministry: Tentmaking and Apostleship* (Philadelphia: Fortress Press, 1980), p. 24.

12. See Hermann L. Strack, *Introduction to the Talmud and Midrash* (New York: Jewish Publication Society of America, 1931), pp. 93–98.

13. See Saul Lieberman, *Hellenism in Jewish Palestine*, rev. ed. (New York: Jewish Theological Seminary of America, 1962).

14. Renewed efforts by some scholars to defend the thesis that Paul

was married are unlikely to succeed in view of 1 Cor. 7. Yet in his *Paul: A Critical Life* (Oxford/New York: Oxford University Press, 1996), pp. 62–65, Jerome Murphy-O'Connor goes so far as to claim knowledge that Paul's wife and his children had died in an accident.

15. *Tosefta Jebamoth* 8.4. Cf. Paul Billerbeck, *Kommentar zum Neuen Testament aus Talmud und Midrasch*, vol. 1 (Munich: C. H. Beck'sche Verlagsbuchhandlung, 1926), p. 807.

16. It is ironic that Paul seems to have reintroduced purity laws into his own churches; on this see above, p. 104.

17. For details see John J. Collins, *Between Athens and Jerusalem: Jewish Identity in the Hellenistic Diaspora* (New York: Crossroad, 1983).

18. Translation following James H. Charlesworth, ed., *The Old Testament Pseudepigrapha*. Vol. 2, *Expansions of the "Old Testament" and Legends, Wisdom and Philosophical Literature, Prayers, Psalms, and Odes, Fragments of Lost Judeo-Hellenistic Works* (New York: Doubleday & Company, 1985), pp. 21–22 (R. J. H. Shutt).

19. Translation following James H. Charlesworth, ed., *The Old Testament Pseudepigrapha*. Vol. 1, *Apocalyptic Literature and Testaments* (New York: Doubleday & Company, 1983), p. 471 (John J. Collins).

20. JB offers the following translation: "(He wants) each one of you to know how to use the body that belongs to him in a way that is holy and honourable." NEB reads: "Each one of you must learn to gain mastery over his body, to hallow and honour it." One must note that "body" is not the correct translation of *skeuos*, which means *"vessel."* "Vessel" is a metaphor for the wife into which the husband puts his semen.

21. See the collection by Abraham Malherbe, *Moral Exhortation: A Greco-Roman Sourcebook* (Philadelphia: Westminster Press, 1986).

22. Note also that Pliny describes Christians as having similar ethical standards (*Epistulae* 10.96.7: "to bind themselves by oath . . . to abstain from theft, robbery, and adultery, to commit no breach of trust and not to deny a deposit when called upon to restore it").

23. Wayne A. Meeks, *The Origins of Christian Morality: The First Two Centuries* (New Haven and London: Yale University Press, 1993), p. 80.

24. See Stanley K. Stowers, *The Diatribe and Paul's Letter to the Romans* (Chico, Calif.: Scholars Press, 1981).

25. Arthur Darby Nock, *St. Paul* (New York and Evanston: Harper & Row, Torchbooks, 1963): Paul's "style with its homely, if occasionally artificial, illustrations and metaphors has one contemporary pagan counterpart, the diatribe. . . . The essential similarity lies in the fact that the dia-

tribe, like the Epistles, was intended to produce the effect of a spoken style; both have the same loose vigour. . . . Cynic philosophers talked at street corners to any and all would listen, and Paul must have heard them at times; and much of what they said was reasonably congenial, for the Cynics attacked popular vices, and popular superstitions" (pp. 234ff.).

26. Nock, *St. Paul*, p. 236.

27. In the passages from 1 Thessalonians the order of the triad is in each case "faith, love, hope," thereby making hope central because the community is waiting for Jesus to come back in the very near future.

28. See A. Hilhorst, "The Speech on Truth in 1 Esdras 4:34–41," in *The Scriptures and the Scrolls: Studies in Honour of A. S. van der Woude on the Occasion of his 65th Birthday*, ed. F. García Martínez, A. Hilhorst, and C. J. Labuschagne (Leiden: E. J. Brill, 1992), pp. 135–51. Hilhorst observes that "neither the Hebrew Bible nor the Septuagint have any example to offer of truth as the supreme power *tout court*" (p. 147). At the same time, he notes that the Hebrew Bible offers many instances of personifications (Isa. 59:14; Ps. 85:11–12, etc.).

29. See E. P. Sanders, *Paul and Palestinian Judaism: A Comparison of Patterns of Religion* (Philadelphia: Fortress Press, 1977), pp. 33–428; E. P. Sanders, "The Covenant as a Soteriological Category and the Nature of Salvation in Palestinian and Hellenistic Judaism," in *Jews, Greeks and Christians: Religious Cultures in Late Antiquity*. Essays in Honor of William David Davies, ed. Robert Hamerton-Kelly and Robin Scroggs (Leiden: E. J. Brill, 1976), pp. 11–44.

30. See Jacob Neusner, *Children of the Flesh, Children of the Promise: A Rabbi Talks with Paul* (Cleveland: Pilgrim Press, 1995).

# 5

# PAUL
# THE GRECO-ROMAN

**P**aul was born into the Mediterranean world and its dominant Hellenistic civilization, in which Greek and Roman cultures had so permeated one another that he belonged to both.[1]

In this chapter I shall first deal with Paul the Greek by analyzing Paul's speech to Greek philosophers on or before the Areopagus and its setting (Acts 17). Whether this is a trustworthy account or not does not matter for the moment. Indeed I think, and most scholars agree, that the report and Paul's speech are for the most part a fiction, and therefore cannot settle the issue of how typically Greek Paul was. But since in previous research and among the general public the account of Acts is regarded as an answer to the question, I shall use it as a vantage point for exploring the subject of "Paul the Greek." By addressing the question through an analysis of the text of Acts which was hitherto considered a classic document of Paul's dealing with Greek culture, other aspects of "Paul the Greek" will be clarified almost by themselves.

Second, I shall deal with "Paul the Roman" by focusing on the question whether Paul really was a Roman citizen as the Book of Acts claims. Depending on the answer to that question, other aspects of the Romanness of Paul will be illuminated almost automatically (see below, pp. 130–35 for details).

## PAUL THE GREEK: AN ANALYSIS OF ACTS 17:16–34

The speech to the Greek philosophers in Athens has been regarded by many as proof that a certain inner proximity connects the Gospel and Greek philosophy, Jerusalem and Athens, Paul's transcendental faith and human wisdom. Let us therefore examine that assumption and analyze the report of Acts by using standard exegetical procedure. After a translation, I shall give an outline both to present an overview of the content and to gain insight into its structure. The syntactic design of sentences and clauses will suggest their purpose, both of which considerations will be a key element in the subsequent analysis of Luke's intention. In that section I shall essay a brief and necessarily incomplete analysis of elements of Luke's language, including a discussion of the redactional meaning of the text and its apologetic aims. The presumably redactional elements are printed in italics. Next we shall investigate whether elements of tradition can be found. Starting points for this may already exist in the previous section on redaction—for example by indicating tensions which do not derive from redactional intent, or by un-Lukan expressions—but the probability of tradition must be demonstrated apart from these observations. The last section subjects the reconstructed traditions to historical verification. Here the Pauline letters play a decisive role.[2]

*Acts 17:16–34:*

(16) While Paul was waiting for them (Silas and Timothy) at Athens, *his spirit grew angry within him as he saw that the city was full of idols.* (17) *So he argued in the synagogue with the Jews and the devout persons, and in the market place every day with casual passers-by.* (18) Some also of the Epicurean and Stoic philosophers joined issue with him. And some said, "What is this babbler trying to say?" Others said, "He seems to be a proclaimer of <u>strange</u> divinities"—because he preached about Jesus and the Resurrection. (19) And they *took* him and brought him to the Areopagus, saying, "May we know what this new teaching is that you propound? (20) *For you are introducing ideas that sound <u>strange</u> to us; we wish to know therefore what they mean.*"

(21) *Now all the Athenians and the foreigners who lived there spent their time in nothing except telling or hearing something new.*

(22) So Paul, standing in the middle of the Areopagus, said: "Men of Athens, I perceive that in everything that concerns religion you are uncommonly scrupulous. (23) For as I passed along, admiring your sacred monuments, I found also an altar bearing the inscription, 'To an unknown god.' Now then, that which you worship but do not know—this is what I proclaim to you. (24) The God who made the world and everything in it, being Lord of heaven and earth, does not live in shrines made by man, (25) nor is he served by human hands, as though he needed anything, since he himself gives to all men life and breath and everything. (26) And he made from one every nation of men to live on all the face of the earth, having determined allotted periods and the boundaries of their habitation, (27) that they should seek God, in the hope that they might feel their way toward him and at last find him. Yet he is not far from each one of us, (28) for 'In him we live and move and have our being'; as even some of your poets have said, 'We, too, are descended from him.'

(29) Being then descendants from God, we ought not to think that the Deity is like gold, or silver, or stone, a representation by the art and imagination of man. (30) The times of ignorance God overlooked, but he commands all men everywhere to repent, (31) because he has fixed a day on which he will judge the world in righteousness by a man whom he has appointed, and of this he has given assurance to all men by raising him from the dead."

(32) Now when they heard of the resurrection of the dead, some scoffed; but others said, "We will hear you again on this." (33) So *Paul went out from among them.* (34) But some men *joined* him and became believers, among them Dionysius the Areopagite and a woman *called* Damaris *and others with them.*

*Outline*

Verses 16–20: Paul's arrival in Athens and encounter with the philosophers

16a: Travel note

16b: Paul's anger at the idols in the city

17–18: Paul in the synagogue and in the market place. Reaction of the Stoics and Epicureans

19–20: Paul on/before the Areopagus. Content of his teaching

Verse 21: Explanation about the Athenians for the reader

Verses 22–31: Paul's speech on/before the Areopagus
22–23: Introduction
24–25: I. God the creator needs no temple
26–27: II. The seasons and limits given by God's creative
       impulse, his allotment of eras and boundaries, and
       his intended human response and the determination
       of human beings
28–29: III. The affinity of human beings to God
30–31: The possibility of repentance and the judgment to come

Verses 32–34: Reaction of the audience: some reject Paul and
       some join him

## LUKE'S INTENTION

*Verses 16–20*: These verses are shaped by Luke throughout.

Verse 16, which speaks of Paul's anger about the idols in Athens, prepares for verse 23. It is a Lukan transitional verse. Verse 17 contains the Lukan scheme of making Paul go to the Jews first, but it is striking that in contrast to other passages we are told that Paul debated with Jews in the synagogue and with Gentiles in the marketplace almost *at the same time*. Verse 18 outlines a scene with local coloring (cf. similarly Acts 19:23–40). It is to be regarded as a literary creation. Here the contrast between the two schools merely serves to create a milieu. Luke seems to produce a parallel to Socrates. Socrates *argued* with the representatives of philosophical schools, who accused him of introducing new gods. Paul speaks in the market place to everyone—like Socrates. They think he is introducing new gods—like Socrates. As later in verse 32, in verse 18 Luke contrasts two groups in the audience both of which have reservations about Paul's preaching (cf. Acts 2:12; 28:24). When Luke identifies the subject of Paul's proclamation as "Jesus and the <u>Resurrection</u>," he probably alludes to a Gentile misunderstanding of Christian preaching: they take it to mean "Jesus and the <u>Anastasis</u>," a divine couple. But that is exactly what Luke intended. In verses 19–20 Luke mentions the best-known place of judgment in Athens in order to produce a worthy scene for Paul's speech. "Areopagus" could mean the hill of Ares, but this would be far too small for the scene. Therefore the other possible meaning for Areopagus is more likely: the Athenian council. This is also suggested by the expressions "in the middle" (verse 22; cf. verse 33), "took him" (verse 19) and "the Areopagite" (verse 34). Paul is taken along to give an account of the new teaching. But the subsequent "sermon" is not a speech in his defense, and verse 21 makes it quite clear that there is no accusation. Moreover verse 20 again shows the author at work when, taking up motives mentioned earlier (verse 18), he recalls the accusation against Socrates: Paul is accused of introducing strange things. This obviously picks up verse 18 in which Paul "seems to be a proclaimer of strange divinities." This echoes the accusation against Socrates that he was introducing "new demons."[3] Only the charge of leading youth astray is absent.

*Verse 21*: This verse is addressed directly to the reader (cf. Acts 8:26; 16:12; 23:8). The curiosity of the Athenians was proverbial in antiquity. Demosthenes had said to them three hundred years earlier, "Instead of guarding your liberties, you are forever gadding about and looking for news."[4] Including this theme lends a further touch of local color to the scene.

*Verses 22–31*: This set piece serves as the theological explanation of the note about "preaching" in verse 18. It contains the only discourse addressed to Gentiles in Acts (cf. 14:15–17). Its starting point in verse 22 is a commonplace often expressed in praise of Athens, namely its claim because of its many cultic images and festivals to be the most pious city in Greece. The reference to the inscription on the altar in verse 23 may also derive from Luke. It is patterned after a type of inscription known (despite the lack of of archaeological evidence) to have existed in Athens; but those referred to unknown gods (plural). Luke has served his monotheistic agenda by replacing the plural with the singular.

At the redactional level the speech shows its concern to allude to previous knowledge of the Christian God by means of the theme of an affinity between God and the works of creation. The first part of verse 28 is an echo of a poem of Epimenides the Cretan, the second part—a stock quotation in Stoic circles—stems from Aratus (b. 310 B.C.E.). Luke hardly imagines that the discourse he assigns to Paul was the model for sermons to Gentiles, since the Areopagus speech was not a sermon. Here, however, as is the case in all the discourses in Acts, there remains the question of how this discourse is related to various types of sermons in Luke's time.

It has sometimes been argued in previous scholarship that the Areopagus speech derives from a secondary revision of Acts, but the parallels between the speech and other passages in Luke-Acts tell against this. I shall list a number of them following the sequence of the speech, along with the singular features of the speech which are printed in italics:

God the creator (verse 24)—cf. Acts 4:24; 14:15.

God, the Lord (verse 24)—cf. Acts 10:36, "He is the Lord of all."

God does not dwell in temples (verse 24)—cf. Acts 7:48.

*God is not served by human worship because he does not need anything* (verse 25).

God is the giver of being and of all gifts (verse 25)—cf. similarly Acts 14:17.

Descent of all beings from the one (verse 26)—cf. how Luke makes Jesus descend from Adam in Luke 3:23–28.

God who guides the history of the nations (verse 26)—cf. similarly Acts 14:16.

The task imposed on human beings of finding God (verse 27)—cf. Acts 14:27.

God is near to every human being (verse 27)—cf. Acts 10:35.

*Pantheism* (verse 28).

*Divine race of humankind* (verses 28–29).

*Idols are not permitted (because they are nonsensical)* (verse 29).

The previous ignorance of all men, from whom God has looked away in disapproval (verse 30)—cf. Acts 3:17; 13:27; 14:16.

A new revelation of God has been given in the present to all men (verse 30)—cf. Luke 2:10 (the whole people).

The new preaching begins with repentance (verse 30)—cf. Acts 2:38; 3:19; 13:24; 20:21; 26:20.

The coming judgment (verse 31)—cf. Acts 24:25.

The man appointed (verse 31)—cf. Acts 10:42.

The resurrection of Christ (verse 31)—cf. Luke 24; often in Acts.

Of these 18 points only four are not attested in Luke-Acts, but they are the characteristic features of a speech which Paul (alias Luke) would deliver to Gentiles in this solemn didactic discourse, and they further develop Luke's own ideas.

*Verses 32–34:* For verses 32–33 cf. the comments above on verse 18; both groups in the audience have reservations about Paul's preaching (see Acts 2:12). For verse 33 see Luke 4:30; verse 34 has Lukan linguistic coloring.

## THE TRADITION AVAILABLE TO LUKE

*Verse 16a:* The arrival of Paul in Athens from Thessalonica as reported in verse 16a reflects tradition (cf. 1 Thess. 3:1).

*Verses 22–31:* We can discover three different motifs in the Areopagus speech: creation (verses 24–26a, 27–28), preservation (verse 26b), and redemption (verse 31). The same scheme of motifs occurs in missionary (or propaganda) literature of Hellenistic Judaism as well as in Jewish and early Christian writings.[5] The frequency of this structural pattern in tradition makes it advisable not to take the combination of the three themes in the Areopagus speech as Luke's theological conception. Rather, the pattern of the mission speech is probably not Luke's creation, but a model he knew from missionary practice. Therefore we are led to assume a traditional basis for the Areopagus speech on the basis for a history-of-religions comparison.

*Verses 32–34*: The name of Dionysius the Areopagite probably comes from a tradition which also enabled Luke to have Paul appear before the Areopagus. Luke's logic runs as follows: If Dionysius was converted as an Areopagite, then Paul must have appeared before the Areopagus.

That the name of Damaris was also part of the tradition is supported by the consideration that Damaris—not elsewhere instanced as a woman's name—does not fit in the context of a speech before the Areopagus. A pious Jewish woman or a woman in the community would, of course, not appear in public with men.

However, it must be reiterated at this point that these traditional elements are not necessarily related to a specific time, but only in general terms to Athens (see further on this above, p. 25).


## HISTORICAL ELEMENTS

*Verse 16a*: Paul's journey from Thessalonica to Athens during the founding mission of communities in Macedonia and Achaia is historical. Cf. 1 Thess. 2:2; 3:1, 6, and above, pp. 49, 61.

*Verses 22–31*: It should be stressed that Paul, too, in various remarks reflects the scheme of motifs of the Areopagus speech, a scheme rooted in tradition as well as evident in the formulation of 1 Thess. 1:9–10 and Rom. 1:18–2:10.

As was indicated previously (see above, p. 99), there is a summary of Paul's founding proclamation in 1 Thess. 1:9b–10:

> (9b) You turned to God from idols, to serve a living and true God,
> (10) and to wait expectantly for the appearance from heaven of his

Son Jesus, whom he raised from the dead, Jesus our deliverer from the wrath to come.

Note the list of motifs in Romans parallel with this summary of the apostle's missionary preaching:

Creation (Rom. 1:20, 25)

Knowledge of God (Rom. 1:19–20)

Worship of God (Rom. 1:23, 25)

Repentance (Rom. 2:4)

Judgment (Rom. 2:5–6, 8)

Salvation (Rom. 2:7, 10)

By way of qualification it must first be allowed that the theme of preservation does not appear explicitly either in 1 Thess. 1:9–10 or in Rom. 1:18–2:10. But it is presupposed as an extension of remarks of creation.

And of course there are noteworthy *differences* between Paul's epistolary message and the tradition of the Areopagus speech. The latter has two proofs for the knowledge of God by natural man: first, from the works of creation (Acts 17:24–25), second, from affinity to God (Acts 17:28–29). The first appears in Paul only as a lost possibility (cf. Rom. 1:20) while the latter seems to be incongruous with his view of the alienation of human beings from God.

*Rom. 1:21–22:*

(21) Although they (the Gentiles) know God they did not honor him as God or give thanks to him, but their thoughts became directed to worthless things and their confused minds were darkened. (22) Claiming to be wise, they became fools.

As was just pointed out, the two proofs for the knowledge of God would seem to be inconceivable in Paul, while the preservation theme might be understood as a corollary of the topic of creation. On the other hand, one has to ask whether one could not imagine Paul occasionally departing from his negative view of the human capability of knowing God in order to win Greeks to the gospel. In any case, one should avoid any absolutism here in deciding what he could or could not have said, and fully take into account Paul's flexibility in order to be "all things to all men" (cf. 1 Cor. 9:19–23).

Furthermore, the parallels between 1 Thess. 1:9–10 and the tradition behind Acts 17 remain valid. In addition, it is safe to assume that in Athens Paul tried to convert Gentiles as well as Jews. True, his missionary activity did not begin with a reference to the unknown god, for such an altar dedicated to the unknown god did not exist. Nevertheless it can be assumed that in the course of his mission at Athens Paul gave one speech (or more—see the explanations below) to the Gentiles, the essence of which may have been preserved in the Areopagus speech. Since this was a *type* of speech, a genetic relationship between the tradition behind Acts 17 and Paul's epistolary sermons cannot be established with certainty. However, such a link seems more and more probable to me, for Luke has Paul deliver a speech in Athens along the same lines that Paul is accustomed to follow. Since it is likely that Luke did not know Paul personally, the coincidence of parallels has to be fully taken into account.

Moreover, one should not adduce 1 Cor. 2:1–5, where Paul disclaims all "plausible words of wisdom" (verse 4), as proof that Paul can never have said anything like that in his speech in Athens. As noted above, Paul was quite flexible and often said contradictory things. On the other hand, the content of 1 Cor. 2:1–5 seems to reflect his experience in Athens (see below, p. 129).

There are various possible places for such a sermon: the synagogue (many Gentiles attended synagogue services), the market place, indeed also Paul's workshop. This is not to suggest that Paul delivered only one sermon when founding the community. Rather, we should think of several, each of which contained the themes we have enumerated.

## HOW EDUCATED GREEKS WOULD HAVE
## OBJECTED TO PAUL

In addition, we must assume that as Acts 17 indicates, Paul's audience included a number of educated persons. They must have protested against Paul's message of the resurrection of Jesus, which during the founding mission in Achaia included an apocalyptic drama of the kind that Paul had outlined in 1 Thess. 4:15–17. It is therefore worth listening to what an educated Gentile of the third century, the Neoplatonist philosopher Porphyry, had to say about such a hope. In his "Fifteen Books Against the Christians" Porphyry raises the following objection to Paul's view on Jesus' return on the clouds of heaven:

> Another of his astonishingly silly comments needs to be examined: I mean that wise saying of his, to the effect that, "We who are alive who are left shall not precede those who have fallen asleep until the Lord comes; for the Lord himself will descend from heaven with a cry of command, with the archangel's call; and the trumpet of God will sound; and the dead in Christ shall rise first; then we who are alive, who are left, shall be caught up together with them in the clouds to meet the Lord in the air; and so we shall always be with the Lord."[6]
>
> Indeed there is something here that reaches up to heaven: the magnitude of this lie. When told to dumb bears, to silly frogs and geese—they bellow or croak or quack with delight to hear of the bodies of men flying through the air like birds or being carried about on clouds. This belief is quackery of the first rank: that the weight of our mortal flesh should behave as though it were of the nature of winged birds and could navigate the winds as easily as ships cross the sea, using clouds for a chariot! Even if such a thing could happen, it would be a violation of nature and hence completely unfitting.[7]

True, Porphyry lived more than two hundred years after Paul. However, it seems clear that something like what Porphyry objected to in Paul's apocalyptic hope may very well have told against Paul when he attempted to preach the Good News in Athens.

But not only the specific idea of an aerial reunion between Christ and believers would have come under attack at Athens. Bodily res-

urrection was always a stumbling block for the educated world of
antiquity. Some five hundred years before Paul's purported speech to
the council, the tragedian Aeschylus had enunciated the Greek view
of the matter. In the course of dramatizing the mythic origin of the
Aereopagitican court under the aegis of the city's eponymous god-
dess Athena, he put these words on the lips of the divine Apollo:

> When the dust has soaked up a man's blood, once he is dead, there
> is no resurrection.[8]

It is worth noting that his word for resurrection, *anastasis*, is the
same as Paul's in Acts 17:18. And opposition to the idea of bodily
resurrection continued in Athens over the centuries.

In order to illustrate this, let me quote what two critics who lived
in the second century said about the Christian notion of bodily resurrection and judgment. The first critic is the Roman Fronto (d.
before 175 c.e.), the teacher of the emperor Marcus Aurelius, and the
second the Greek Platonist Celsus.

Part of Fronto's speech against the Christians has been preserved
in the work of the Christian apologist Minucius Felix, who composed
his work *Octavius* around 200 c.e. We have a unique opportunity of
listening to Fronto's objections:

> (7) Yet I should be glad to be informed whether or no you rise again
> with bodies; and if so, with what bodies—whether with the same
> or with renewed bodies? Without a body? Then, as far as I know,
> there will neither be mind, nor soul, nor life. With the same body?
> But this has already been previously destroyed. With another
> body? Then it is a new person who is born, not the former one
> restored; (8) and yet so long a time has passed away, innumerable
> ages have flowed by, and what single individual has returned from
> the dead either by the fate of Protesilaus[9] with permission to
> sojourn even for a few hours, or that we might believe it for an
> example? (9) All such figments (are) of an unhealthy belief, and
> vain sources of comfort.[10]

The work of the Platonist Celsus can be reconstructed on the
basis of the "refutation" by Origen who, for lack of time, fortunately

left many passages of his opponent's treatise "True Doctrine" intact. In one of them Celsus makes the following point:

> It is foolish of them [the Christians] also to suppose that, when God applies the [hell-]fire, all the rest of mankind will be thoroughly roasted and that they alone will survive, not merely those who are alive at the time but those also long dead who will rise up from the earth possessing the same bodies as before. This is simply the hope of worms. For what sort of human soul would have any further desire for a body that has rotted? . . . For what sort of body, after being entirely corrupted, could return to its original nature and that same condition which it had before it was dissolved? As they have nothing to say in reply, they escape to a most outrageous refuge by saying that "anything is possible to God."[11] But, indeed, neither can God do what is shameful nor does he desire what is contrary to nature. If you were to desire something abominable in your wickedness, not even God would be able to do this, and you ought not to believe at all that your desire will be fulfilled. For God is not the author of sinful desire or of disorderly confusion, but of what is naturally just and right. For the soul he might be able to provide an everlasting life; but as Heraclitus says, "corpses ought to be thrown away as worse than dung." As for the flesh, which is full of things that it is not even nice to mention, God would neither desire nor be able to make it everlasting contrary to reason. For he himself is the reason of everything that exists; therefore he is not able to do anything contrary to reason or to his own character.[12]

## CONTINUATION OF THE ANALYSIS OF ACTS 17:16–34

*Verse 34:* Damaris and Dionysius the Areopagite are probably historical, but they should not be connected with the mission during which Paul founded the community. Rather, the house of Stephanas (from Corinth), with whom Paul had not yet come into contact during his stay at Athens, was designated as "the first fruits of Achaea" (1 Cor. 16:15), of which Athens was a part. Moreover, we may consider well founded the historical assumption that Paul did not have much missionary success in Athens, for an Athenian com-

munity plays no recognizable role in his missionary plans, his journeys, or the collection for the Jerusalem church. There is no attestation of a Christian community in Athens until around 179 c.e.[13]

One further point deserves notice here: Athens is the only place
in which Paul preached without prompting a *persecution*. Some
explain this as being due to apologetics: the educated Gentiles of
Athens dispute but do not turn violent. Furthermore, the absence of
the theme of persecution is explained by the fact that in this chapter
Paul turns exclusively to the Gentiles. Yet it has to be pointed out
that Jews do appear in verse 17a. Be that as it may, the historical
record shows that except in this case, Gentiles did start persecutions
against the Pauline communities (cf. 1 Thess. 2:14) and caused Paul
trouble in Ephesus (1 Cor. 15:32; 2 Cor. 1:8; Acts 19).

Therefore I would suggest that the absence of a persecution
theme in Acts 17 is an argument *in favor of* solid historical information in the narrative.


## PAUL'S PAINFUL DEFEAT IN ATHENS

Such an assessment of the account in Acts 17 has consequences for
the subject "Paul the Greek," for it demonstrates that Paul suffered a
painful defeat in the home of Greek philosophy. Not only was he
unable to found a community there, but Greek philosophers seem to
have gotten the better of him by invoking reason and human wisdom,
and thereby left him with a painful memory. It seems clear that Paul
did not find in Athens the same reception he had been accorded elsewhere. Athens was, after all, a different place. In Paul's day it was, to
use the modern phrase, a university city. It attracted both the serious
would-be philosophers and the would-be distinguished Roman who
sought the cachet of culture and the recognition of his peers. Arthur
Darby Nock once rightly observed: "It is easier to convert the Prodigal
Son than his brother or his uncle who is a professor."[14]

Nearly as problematic as the doctrine of resurrection would have
been the idea of a final day of judgment. Paul's audience was quite
accustomed to the notion of a post-mortem assessment of an indi-

vidual's life, and even amenable to the concept of some sort of reward or punishment on the basis of one's deeds. But to imagine that Jesus' resurrection made him eligible to judge the lives of others was simply silly; to propose a general resurrection at which he presided and judged was ludicrous, and a sure way to be rejected out of hand.

## SOME GENERAL REMARKS ABOUT
## PAUL'S RELATIONSHIP TO THE GREEK ENLIGHTENMENT

The Jewish Christian theologian Paul had become a Gentile to the Gentiles, a Jew to the Jews. Where then was his commitment? Throughout his activity there was not only a dash of arrogance but also a trace of flexibility which must have been perplexing to honest spirits and maddening to others. One is hardly surprised to find Porphyry attacking him thus:

> How is it that Paul says, "Being free, I have made myself the slave of all so that I might win them all";[15] how, even though he called circumcision "mutilation,"[16] he nevertheless circumcised a certain man named Timothy, as the Acts of the Apostles[17] instructs us. Ah! The asinine nature of all this. Such scenes are used in the theater in order to get a laugh. Jugglers give exhibitions like this! For how can a free man be everyone's slave? . . .
>
> These are not the teachings of a healthy mind. . . . The words indeed suggest someone who is mentally feeble and deficient in reasoning powers. And if he lives among the lawless yet accepts the religion of the Jews with an open heart, taking a piece from each, he is confused by each. He participates in their worst shortcomings and makes himself everyone's companion.[18]

But as Paul's life work attests, this openness on all sides was a good way to succeed. Only once did it run into a brick wall, and that was when he went up against the Athenian intelligentsia. However much he claims to value the right use of reason, his religion, grounded as it was in mystical experience, was not up to the intellectual challenge of Greece. The fact that he founded no community in Athens speaks volumes in this matter.

Paul did not come to a knowledge of the truth through a mind trained in logic which examines strictly the content and viability of all concepts and views, which heedlessly fights against the phantasms of the imagination and acknowledges no authority over itself, whether that of a god or of a human being. Of a very different nature is the oriental mysticism which Hellenistic Christianity and its leading figure Paul represent. Its orientation is supernatural; it calls for unquestionable subjection to authority and surrender to divine guidance; its ultimate appeal is not to the intellect, but to the emotions; and its final goal is to be seized by the Spirit. For this reason, spiritual enthusiasts ("pneumatics") are elevated high above people of a more everyday mind ("psychics"), because to them alone is disclosed the vision of the mysterious truth which can never be grasped by reason.

But the deepest reason for the victory of the Christianity of Paul and his pupils lay in the spirit of the time. The world had become weary of thought. In a more convenient way, large numbers of people attempted to secure their immortality through initiation into mysteries, of which baptism and the Lord's supper were only two of many. The defeat of the human spirit, and a public which had become willing to believe anything while the public had become completely believing—this description fits Paul and his time.

In Paul and his religion we see reflected the orientalization of the Western world and the reaction against the Greek enlightenment. The free spirit of ancient Greece was being strangled by authoritarianism; the republican virtues of the Roman state were drowning in commercialism. And as faith replaced knowledge as the highest goal of the human spirit, the proud and responsible individual was called upon to bow in submission to an otherworldly deity who demeaned the affairs of this world as unimportant preliminaries to another existence. This future reality, alas, was not subject to inspection or certification. And it was precisely this reality which the Athenian philosophers repudiated.

## THE RESULT OF THE FAILURE IN ATHENS

A defeat of this sort would predictably leave its mark on Paul's soul. When he founded the community in Corinth a few weeks later, he said some very negative things about the Greeks' search for wisdom which, in its extreme form, he had just encountered in Athens. An accurate reflection of Paul's first visit in Corinth may be found in the epitome of his founding mission, namely 1 Cor. 2:1–5:

> (1) When I came to you, brothers, I did not come proclaiming to you the testimony about God with preeminent eloquence or *wisdom*. (2) For I decided to know nothing among you except Jesus Christ, and him crucified. (3) And I was with you in weakness and in much fear and trembling; (4) and my speech and my message were not in persuasive words of *wisdom*, but in manifestation of Spirit and power, (5) that your faith might depend not on men's *wisdom* but on God's power.

For Paul it is clear why human wisdom is doomed to failure. He writes in 1 Cor. 1:17–25:

> (17) Christ did not send me to baptize, but to preach the gospel, and not with eloquent *wisdom* lest the cross of Christ be emptied. (18) For the word of the cross is **folly** to those who are perishing, but to us who are being saved it is God's power. (19) For it is written, "I will destroy the *wisdom* of the *wise*, and the cleverness of the clever I will set aside." (20) Where is the *wise* man? Where is the scribe? Where is the debater of this age? Has not God made the world's *wisdom* **folly**? (21) For since, in God's *wisdom* the world did not know God through *wisdom*, God chose through the **folly** of what we preach to save those who believe. (22) For Jews demand signs and Greeks seek *wisdom*, (23) but we preach Christ crucified, a stumbling block to Jews and **folly** to Gentiles; (24) but to those who are called, both Jews and Greeks, Christ, God's power and God's *wisdom*. (25) For God's **folly** is *wiser* than men, and God's weakness is stronger than men.

The upshot of this is very clear: Paul demonizes wisdom insofar as it does not agree with his own faith. As we know from another passage in 1 Corinthians, the apostle does know another wisdom that is hidden and, indeed, can be equated with Christ himself (cf. verse 24 above and 1 Cor. 2:6–8). But that wisdom is closely connected with mystery and revelation and not with reason. Thus in the end Paul suffered what Gilbert Murray a century ago called a failure of nerve.[19] Like so many of his contemporaries he became an apostate to the Greek heritage in which he and other Hellenistic Jews had been nurtured. Certainly the advocacy of the risen and the returning Christ in Thessalonica (cf. 1 Thess. 1:9–10) shows that religious enthusiasm had taken precedence over reason, at least once Paul had become a Christian. Then came the experience of Athens. Having lost this argument, he may very well have felt himself driven to the conclusion that God was calling him to serve by preaching this divine folly. We can see the effect of this in 1 Corinthians. From now on Paul sold Christianity as a mystery religion that satisfied his and his converts' needs for hidden wisdom and divine folly. That made him immune against any objection and allowed him to continue his missionary zeal among the Greeks. The incipient dialogue between Christianity and Greek philosophy was over for a long time.


## PAUL THE ROMAN

### Did Paul Have Roman Citizenship?

Paul's Roman citizenship is not mentioned in the Pauline letters, but only in Acts, and there twice. After translating and analyzing the two texts I shall deal thematically with Paul's alleged Roman citizenship.

### Acts 16:16–39:

[Verses 16–18 relate Paul's healing of a slave-girl through exorcism.]

> (19) [The girl's owners] seized Paul and Silas and dragged them into the marketplace before the rulers; (20) and when they had brought them to the magistrates they said, "These men are causing a disturbance in our city; they are Jews; (21) they advocate customs which

are illegal for us Romans to adopt or to follow." (22) The crowd joined in the attack against them; and the magistrates tore the garments off them and gave orders to beat them with rods. (23) And after inflicting many blows on them, they threw them into prison, charging the jailer to keep them safely. (24) Having received this charge, he put them into the inner prison and fastened their feet in the stock.

[Verses 25–34 relate the miraculous release of the two of them and the conversion of the jailer.]

(35) But when daylight came, the magistrates sent the police, saying, "Release those men." (36) And the jailer reported the message to Paul, saying, "The magistrates have sent to release you; now therefore come out and go in peace." (37) But Paul said to them; "They have beaten us publicly without a trial, men who are Roman citizens, and have thrown us into prison; and now they want to get rid of us secretly? No! Let them come themselves and escort us out." (38) The police reported these words to the magistrates, who were alarmed to hear that they were Roman citizens; (39) so they came and apologized to them. And they escorted them out and begged them to leave the city.

## LUKE'S INTENTION

The charges mentioned in verses 20–21 have nothing to do with Paul's exorcism that was narrated before in verses 16–18. Luke presents them in such a way that they can be rejected. Verses 35–39 resume the main action. Verse 37 gives Luke's understanding of verse 20. Silas and Paul are Romans: insofar as being a Jew is associated with magic—a traditional association which is also instanced in Acts (cf. 13:6; 19:13, 16)—Silas and Paul are not Jews. The order for them to be released from prison and the way in which they are escorted out of the city (verses 35–39) vindicate Silas and Paul in the eyes of the Roman readers.

For the question of whether Luke based his story on a tradition of Paul's Roman citizenship, see the second text from Acts.

*Acts 22:24–29:*

> (24) The commander ordered him [Paul] to be brought into the barracks, and gave instructions to examine him by <u>flogging</u>, to find out what reason there was for such an outcry against him. (25) But when they had tied him up for the lash, Paul said to the centurion, who was standing there, "Is it lawful for you to <u>flog</u> a man who is a Roman citizen, and moreover has not been found guilty?" (26) When the centurion heard this, he went and reported it to the commander and said to him, "What are you about to do? For this man is a Roman citizen." (27) So the commander came and said to him, "Tell me, are you a Roman citizen?" And he said, "Yes." (28) The commander answered, "I bought this citizenship for a large sum." Paul said, "But I was born a Roman citizen." (29) So those who were about to examine him withdrew from him hastily; and the commander also was alarmed, for he realized that Paul was a Roman citizen and that he had him put in irons.

## LUKE'S INTEREST IN PAUL BEING A ROMAN CITIZEN

This section depicts Paul's appeal to his Roman citizenship. The information that he is a Roman citizen fits well with the apologetic bias of Luke-Acts. The first real Gentile convert to Christianity is a Roman centurion (Acts 10). Further, the way that Roman officials treat Christians who have been denounced by Jews is exemplary (cf. the portrayals of Gallio in Acts 18:12–17, Felix in 24:24–26, and Festus in 26:24–29). These apologetic tendencies shed light on other less-known passages that also deserve to be classified as apologetic: John the Baptist's sermon on the responsibilities of people of various ranks (Luke 3:10–14), a Lukan compendium,[20] ends with a prescription for soldiers. Though the soldiers are not at all concerned about the baptism of John, the ethical advice in Luke 3:14, "Do violence or injustice to no one, and be content with your wages," indicates that they should be loyal to the state.

# THE TRADITION ABOUT PAUL'S ROMAN CITIZENSHIP

Still, the author's intention and the testimony of the tradition are not necessarily incompatible. The parallel relationship between this scene and the previous one (Acts 16:16–39) is instructive. In both passages the appeal to Roman citizenship is delayed (cf. 22:25 with 16:37), and accordingly Paul is first open to acts of violence by the Roman authorities (cf. 22:24 with 16:22–23). On each occasion the cruelty of the Roman authorities is contrasted with their fear when they discover that Paul is a Roman citizen (cf. 22:29 with 16:38). The probable narrative intent of all this is to stress Paul's Roman citizenship and to make the apostle appear all the more clearly to be safe under the protection of the Roman state against Jewish acts of violence.

# REBUTTAL OF VARIOUS ARGUMENTS
# AGAINST PAUL'S ROMAN CITIZENSHIP

1. At no point does Paul mention his Roman citizenship. *Against that,* it must be admitted, he had no particular occasion to—not even in the catalogue of vicissitudes in 2 Cor. 11:23–27. (Still his failure to claim Roman citizenship in 2 Cor. 11:25 does not permit one to conclude that he did not attach any importance to it.)

2. Paul was flogged three times (2 Cor. 11:25). *Against that,* while indeed the flogging of a Roman citizen as a punishment was forbidden, this rule was often violated. Further, it is not certain whether Paul would have appealed a flogging sentence on the basis of his Roman citizenship. In addition, there remains the problem of how he could have proved his citizenship.

3. The contradiction between Paul's manual labor (suggesting that he came from the lower middle class) and his Roman citizenship (indicating that he belonged to the upper class) tells against the latter, as the former is indisputable. *Against that,* in the early Empire bestowal of citizenship was in no way restricted to prominent citizens. Moreover, since his rabbinical training probably motivated Paul's manual labor, it is hardly to be used as conclusive evidence of

his social status. To be sure, the rabbinical texts about the study of
the Torah and manual labor come only from the middle of the
second century c.e., but this does not exclude an earlier provenance.
There are no rabbinical texts before the middle of the second century
in general, though quite a few go back to earlier material.

## CONSIDERATIONS IN FAVOR OF
## PAUL'S ROMAN CITIZENSHIP

1. The apostle bears a Roman name, Paul, which *against* the information of Acts 13:9 he had together with the Semitic name Saul since
his childhood. (There are many examples from Roman Judaism that
Jews had dual names.) Paul is a *cognomen* or *praenomen*. The name is
rare in the East and suggests high birth. Its adoption can be
explained in two ways: For one thing, it could reflect an attempted
assimilation, a way of facilitating social contacts or even dealings
with the Roman authorities. Paul may have been chosen as a pho-
netic equivalent of Saul. Or perhaps it indicates that the apostle was
a Roman citizen. Roman citizens had the right and duty to bear a
Roman name. Jews who became Roman citizens commonly took
Roman names. Here it seems worth taking into consideration the
possibility that Paul had citizenship as the descendant of a
freedman, for the legal freeing of a slave by a Roman citizen secured
him citizenship without further ado, without the need for any state
consent. However, the freedman and his children did not get unlim-
ited citizenship immediately. Therefore in fact they could be
regarded as second-class citizens.

    2. If the apostle's imprisonment in Jerusalem is a fact, his trans-
portation to Rome can best be explained by an appeal to the Roman
emperor by the Roman citizen Paul (Acts 25:10–11). One should not
argue the other way around that Luke concluded from Paul's transportation to Rome that Paul had appealed to the emperor, since that
would beg the question of why he was transported to Rome in the
first place.

    3. The fact that while a prisoner Paul could write to Philemon

and carry on his work (see Philem. 24) is strong evidence that he was not kept in harsh confinement but in liberal detention. This may well have been due to his citizenship, for as a rule Roman citizens were not allowed to be kept in harsh confinement.

4. Paul traveled frequently, widely, and freely through Roman colonial territories (Pisidian Antioch [Acts 13:14], Philippi, Corinth) and regularly uses the names of the Roman provinces when writing about his travel plans and his missionary activity: Syria-Cilicia (Gal. 1:21); Asia (2 Cor. 1:8); Macedonia (Phil. 4:15; 2 Cor. 7:7; 8:1); Achaia (2 Cor. 9:2); Galatia (1 Cor. 16:1; Gal. 1:2). One explanation of his plan to go to Spain (Rom. 15:28) would be that he could be sure of finding Roman colonies there. For along with Gaul, Spain was at the center of a deliberate policy of Romanization. And Roman citizenship was both his passport and his shield on these wide-ranging missionary journeys.

## RESULT

In all probability Paul was a Roman citizen. Whether at the same time he was also a citizen of Tarsus (Acts 21:39) is not so easy to decide. At all events, being a citizen of Tarsus did not rule out being a Roman citizen, for the rule that Roman citizenship was incompatible with citizenship of another city had already been relaxed at the end of the Republic and in the early Principate.

## CONCLUSION

A tree grows best in its native soil, and a fish has to swim in those waters where it finds itself. Yet even the salmon, whose journeys are as far-ranging as Paul's, eventually comes home to spawn. And it was long before Paul had to go swimming in *mare nostrum* to survive a shipwreck that he had taken the Roman name we have been taught to perceive as a symbol of his new-found faith and exploited his Roman passport to spread that faith; nevertheless, his mind remained Rabbinic to the end.

And even though he strove mightily to uproot and transplant himself, he found, to paraphrase Gibran, that the mighty cedar does not thrive in the shadow of the groves of academe. The taproot once sunk deep in the soil of Palestine did not draw the same nourishment from the Attic earth.

Put another way, Greece and Rome were garments in which the apostle wrapped himself against a cold world, but the God of Israel was the source of his inner fire. Paul the Greco-Roman never lost his Jewish soul.


## NOTES

1. See the useful collection of essays by Troels Engberg-Pedersen, ed., *Paul in His Hellenistic Context* (Minneapolis: Fortress Press, 1995).

2. For a detailed analysis of Acts 17:16–34 see my *Early Christianity according to the Traditions in Acts: A Commentary* (Minneapolis: Fortress Press, 1989), pp. 189–95.

3. Plato *Apology* 24c.

4. Demosthenes *Philippics* 1.43.

5. See my *Early Christianity*, pp. 192–93.

6. 1 Thess. 4:15b–17.

7. R. Joseph Hoffmann, ed., *Porphyry's Against the Christians: The Literary Remains* (Amherst, N.Y.: Prometheus Books, 1994), p. 68. (I have slightly changed Hoffmann's translation.)

8. Aeschylus *Eumenides* 647f.

9. Greek mythological hero who after his premature death in the Trojan War was allowed by the gods to return to his bride Laodameia for three hours from the underworld.

10. Minucius Felix *Octavius* 11.7–9.

11. Cf. Mark 10:27; Luke 1:37.

12. *Contra Celsum* 5.14. (My translation follows Henry Chadwick, ed., *Origen: Contra Celsum* [Cambridge: University Press, 1965], pp. 274f.)

13. That record comes from the church father Eusebius (fourth century), who writes in his *Ecclesiastical History* 4.23.2–3 about a letter of bishop Dionysios of Corinth to the community of Athens. (It should be noted, though, that the letter's assertion that Dionysius the Areopagite had been the first bishop of Athens belongs in the realm of legend.)

14. Arthur Darby Nock, *St. Paul* (New York and Evanston: Harper & Row, Torchbooks, 1963), p. 128.

15. 1 Cor. 9:19.

16. Phil. 3:2f.

17. Apg 16:3.

18. Hoffmann, *Porphyry's Against the Christians*, pp. 58ff.

19. Gilbert Murray, *Four Stages of Greek Religion* (London: Watts & Company, 1935), p. xiii.

20. For exegetical details see my *Jesus After Two Thousand Years: What He Really Said and Did* (Amherst, N.Y.: Prometheus Books, 2001), pp. 276–78.

# 6

# PAUL
# THE CHRISTIAN

## THE ORIGIN OF THE NAME "CHRISTIAN"

At first sight it may seem anachronistic to deal with Paul as a Christian, for he never uses this name for himself and his fellow believers but rather prefers other names: "the Saints," "the Sanctified," "the Chosen," "the Called," "the Believers," "Israel of God," the "People of God," the "Body of Christ," etc. On the other hand we have solid evidence that Paul and his adherents—previously the members of his mother church, the Hellenists at Antioch—received the name "Christians" almost from the beginning in places outside Jerusalem where non-Jews were in the majority. This follows from a statement in Acts (11:26d). Since Acts 11:19–26 is generally accepted as based on reliable information (see below, pp. 281–82), one may reasonably assume the same for the notice about the origin of the label *Christianoi*, i.e., "Christians," in Acts 11:26d.

The ending *-anoi* is a Latinism and denotes the supporters of a person (Pompeians, Herodians, etc.). In the second century names of sects were formed in an analogous way (Valentinians, Simonians, etc.). For this reason it is uncertain whether the name Christians denotes *political* followers of Christ, but tradition is surely correct in reporting that the name "Christian," like the above parallels, was a term used by outsiders. In other words, the name does not derive from the program of the group concerned, but is a term probably assigned by political authorities seeking to classify it, or by rival groups intent on defining boundaries.

Soon, however, Christians adopted the name, probably because it aptly reflected their primary concern. Only two generations later Bishop Ignatius of Antioch, the very place where this designation first arose, in a letter to the Magnesians not only spoke of "Christianity" (in Greek, *Christianismos*) as a matter of course, but triumphantly proclaimed: "For Christianity did not base its faith on Judaism, but Judaism on Christianity" (10:3).[1]

Since Paul became part of the Hellenist movement in the early Church and in addition worked for a while as a missionary for the community of Antioch where the name "Christians" was first given to the members of this movement, we are justified in speaking of him as a Christian. Furthermore, to name the movement that Paul helped to shape "Christian" was equally appropriate for those outside the movement and those inside, for in both cases it distinguished the church from Jewish and Gentile groups. 1 Cor. 10:32 is an interesting example of the view from within: "Give no offence to Jews or to Greeks or to the church of God." (See on this below, p. 154.) The church of God is where Christ is present. Hence those belonging to the church of God can justly be called Christians.

## PAUL'S SPIRITUAL ROOTS IN THE HELLENISTIC COMMUNITIES

Before turning to Paul himself in order to define him as a Christian, it will be worthwhile to summarize what we know about Paul's spiritual roots in the Hellenistic communities of Damascus and Antioch. (Since we have no extant sources dealing with Damascus, I must perforce take Antioch as a prototype of a Hellenistic community.) Such a step is all the more important because Paul learned the basic tenets of belief from such a community and developed his own interpretation of that Christian faith in constant dialogue with these tenets.

Paul's theology is rooted *not* in the proclamation of the Jerusalem community, but in the traditions of the Hellenistic church, whose reformulations of the earliest kerygma were Paul's primary source material. Only when we have come to recognize that Hellenistic

Christians—both Jewish and Gentile—had adapted as well as adopted the Good News that originated in Palestinian Judaism can we understand the thrust of Paul's message.

Further, it must be emphasized that Hellenistic Christianity was not all of one piece, and that its widely divergent forms did not all impinge on Paul's thinking. It was shaped by such diverse influences as the synagogue, the miracle and mystery religions, and Gnosticism in various strands, not all of which found a place in Paul's thinking, yet which lived on and evolved, some noticeably affected by Paulinism, some quite independent of the apostle's influence.[2]

A brief yet compendious account of Hellenistic Christianity not only before and during Paul's time, but in the immediate post-Pauline period as well, would therefore be of inestimable value to the student of Christianity in general and Paul specifically. But since scarcely any direct witnesses exist, what sources can permit us to essay such a delineation? We have several. *First*, a good deal of useful information can be derived from the source Luke used in Acts 6–8 and 11:19–30. (See below, pp. 259–61: Appendix 3). *Second*, we may draw a number of inferences from the Pauline letters. We have, of course, material that Paul identifies as part of the received tradition (e.g., 1 Cor. 11:23–25 and 1 Cor. 15:3–7), though to be sure we cannot be certain how old such traditions are. But in addition we can assume that terminology and concepts which Paul treats as axiomatic, as well as ideas which he feels no need to defend, must be part of the accepted tradition. Items subsumed under this heading include Christological titles, eschatological pronouncements, references to and ways of interpreting the Old Testament, and reports of sacramental formulas. *Finally*, we may draw reasonable inferences from post-Pauline texts which preserve Hellenistic Christian traditions.[3] This last point, however, will receive the least consideration in my reconstruction.

It is not difficult to imagine that a liberal attitude toward the Law characterized Hellenistic Jews who had returned to Jerusalem and established their own synagogues. Nor is it surprising that when they subsequently became members of the Christian fellowship, such less-than-orthodox believers should be critical of the temple apparatus and the strictures of the Law. The paradigm case, of course, is Stephen;[4] and the specific points of conflict are attested in

Acts 6:11, 13–14. Apparently it was this confrontation within the Jerusalem church that we see reflected in the election of the seven men (Acts 6:1–7) who, as their Greek names suggest, were not "deacons" at all, but representatives of the Hellenistic party. The story of Stephen and the career of Philip make it clear that they were not table stewards, but proclaimers of the Word. And the resulting uproar of their Jewish neighbors was not directed at the Jewish-Christian church as a whole, but at the Hellenistic reformers. Stephen's heresy was silenced by his stoning, his supporters were driven out of town, and both Jews and Jewish Christians fancied that the issue had been resolved.

But it soon broke out again, and in large measure because of the successful proselytizing of those they had ejected (Acts 8:4–40; 11:19–21), and whom they had thus provided with both a cause and a mission field. Indeed it was thus that there first arose Gentile Christian congregations for whom full adoption of the Law, and circumcision in particular, were no longer demanded for admission to the fellowship nor seen as necessary for salvation.[5]

## "CHRIST" AS A PROPER NAME

About this same time the word "Christ" began to be understood less as a title and increasingly as a proper name. It should be noted that "Christ" appears as a name already in the pre-Pauline tradition (1 Cor. 15:3) and throughout Paul's letters. This was even more evident in the churches Paul founded, and for two reasons. For one thing, the general populace came to label the disciples "Christians," intending thereby a less than sympathetic designation of the new sect. The nickname tagged them, in effect, as Christian partisans, just as later sects were named for the heretics whose teaching they followed: Basilidians, Valentinians, Arians, etc. Thus Christ was taken to be the leader of a party movement. Initially the appellation must have puzzled the Greeks: What could it mean to call someone "Anointed" or "Oily-head"? Indeed it is highly possible they were called Christians, mistaking their leader's name for "Chrestos," a common given name in Greek.

The other reason is the crucial one, of course: the disciples adopted as their name the name they gave their Lord. And the adopting took the form of a confession that they were his both in body and in spirit. Noteworthy are such statements as "we are of Christ" (1 Cor. 3:23; Rom. 8:9) and "servants of Christ" (1 Cor. 7:22; Rom. 1:1). The latter might better be rendered literally, "slaves of Christ," for the essence of the confession is not simply that his followers place themselves in his service, but that they become his property (1 Cor. 6:19b–20). Clearly indicative of this concept is the title "Kyrios" (Lord), and its repeated use in combination with the title Messiah (Christ) indicates that nothing less than a paradigm shift has occurred in the early church. Two closely related elements contributed to this.

## "CHRIST" AMONG GENTILES—
## A REALITY PRIMARILY IN THE PRESENT

As the church's geographical horizon widened, the once divisive issue of ethnicity waned, and with it the emphasis on eschatology abated somewhat. To be sure, the Risen Lord remained a potentially eschatological figure and, especially for Jewish Christians, the Second Coming was a central expectation: but most Gentile Christians felt themselves supported and their faith sustained by a religion focused largely in the present. And before too long, most Christians were Gentiles. The Lord they worshiped had supplanted all the pagan "gods and lords" Paul contemptuously refers to in 1 Cor. 8:5; and Christ alone bears "the name that is above every other name," raised as he was to glory by God the Father (Phil. 2:9–11). Already seated on his celestial throne, this royal Christ offered his worshippers a rich fulfillment in their present lives, and would require no further crown of glory on the Last Day to certify his Sonship. Thus the cosmic and catastrophic resolution of the problem of good and evil envisioned by the eschatologists gradually but inexorably gave way to an increasing emphasis on individual salvation.[6]

We must now turn to a careful consideration of two major rites which, as they developed within Hellenistic Christianity, exerted powerful formative influences upon it. I shall analyze both, in each case beginning with a key text and then seeking to clarify the related issue.

## BAPTISM

In Gal. 3:26–28 Paul makes the following statement:

> (26) You are all sons of God *through faith* in Christ Jesus. (27) For as many of you as were **baptized** into Christ have put on Christ. (28) There is neither Jew nor Greek, there is neither slave nor free, there is no male and female, for you are all one in Christ.

In the context of arguing that Christians are Abraham's descendants and therefore free from the law, Paul quotes a traditional formula which, as verse 27 shows, has its origin in the ritual of baptism. Here the apostle reminds the readers of their own baptism. Since for him faith is the main element in Christianity, he has added "through faith" to the formula. This renders the Greek syntax quite awkward, for you cannot speak of a "faith in (en)" but only of a "faith into (eis)." Be that as it may, by adding "through faith" Paul interprets a traditional baptismal formula in order to make it fit the context.

From the standpoint of form criticism the formula is recognizable as a blessing. It was spoken to every initiate immediately before being baptized. By participating in that ritual, Christians were inaugurated into the "new reality" of Christ where previous differences of ethnicity, religion, sex, and social condition were once and for all replaced or transcended.

The pair "male and female" deserves special attention. It is different from the other pairs, "Jew and Greek" and "slave and free," since in this case human sexuality is in effect cancelled; not only the social differences between man and woman are repudiated, but also the *biological* distinctions. In short, Gal. 3:28 seems to proclaim the abolition of the biological sex distinctions as a result of salvation in Christ. Such a claim may well be based on the idea of the androgynous nature of Christ himself, which in turn derives from Gen. 1:27 and other savior myths of Hellenistic religions.[7]

We can observe the result of such a theology of baptism among Corinthian women who after listening to baptismal formulae like Gal. 3:28 seem to have demanded full equality with men. In 1 Corinthians Paul had to respond to such claims. However, Paul did not translate the new reality in Christ into general practice as the case of the slave Onesimus has already shown (see above, pp. 78–79) and as 1 Cor. 11:2–16 vividly attests.

In order to illustrate this, let us turn our attention to 1 Cor. 11:2–16:

> (2) I commend you because you remember me in everything and maintain the traditions even as I have delivered them to you.
>
> (3) But I want you to understand that Christ is the <u>head</u> of every man, the man is the <u>head</u> of the woman, and God is the <u>head</u> of Christ.
>
> (4) Any man who prays or prophesies with his <u>head</u> covered disgraces his <u>head</u>, (5) but any woman who prays or prophesies with her <u>head</u> unveiled disgraces her <u>head</u>—it is the same as if her <u>head</u> were shaven. (6) For if a woman is not veiled, then she should cut off her hair; but if it is disgraceful for a woman to be shorn or shaven, let her wear a veil.
>
> (7) For a man ought not to cover his <u>head</u>, since he is the image and glory of God; but the woman is the glory of man. (8) For man was not made from woman, but woman from man. (9) Neither was man created for the sake of woman, but woman for the sake of man. (10) That is why a woman ought to have a means of exercising power [veil] on her <u>head</u>, because of the angels.
>
> (11) Nevertheless, in the Lord the woman is not independent of the man nor man of the woman; (12) for as the woman was made from the man, so also man is through the woman. And all things are from God.
>
> (13) Judge for yourselves; is it proper for a woman to pray to God with her <u>head</u> unveiled? (14) Does not nature itself teach you that for a man to wear long hair is degrading to him, (15) but if a woman has long hair, it is her pride? For her hair is given to her for a covering.
>
> (16) If any one is disposed to be contentious, we recognize no other practice, nor do the churches of God.

*Outline*

> Verse 2: Expression of benevolence in order to catch the
> Corinthians' attention
> Verse 3: General rule
> Verses 4–6: Critique of the Corinthian custom
> Verses 7–10: *First objection* on the basis of Gen. 2:21–22
> Verses 11–12: Parenthesis to avoid a possible misunderstanding
> Verses 13–15: *Second objection*: Nature is against changing the custom
> Verse 16: *Third objection:* If any doubt is left, the tradition of the
> churches is against changing the custom

## ANALYSIS

This passage shows the apostle engaged in an ongoing yet formalized thought process. After a *captatio benevolentiae* (verse 2) Paul in advance formulates a general thesis about the superiority of the man to the woman, this itself based on the overall hierarchy of God to Christ, Christ to the man, and the man to the woman (verse 3). The starting point for the discussion with the Corinthians, which may have been triggered by a question from Corinth, is that in worship the man has nothing on his head (verse 4), but the woman covers her head. If she does not cover it, "she disgraces her head—it is the same as if her head were shaven" (verse 5). Paul goes on to defend this custom against the criticism of Corinthian women. He advances three arguments for maintaining it:

*First*, it is an ordinance of creation (verses 7–10); see especially verse 7: "For a man ought not to cover his head, since he is the image and glory of God; but the woman is the glory of man."

After inserting a parenthesis in verses 11–12 that links with the general rule of verse 3, Paul *second* offers another objection in verses 13–15 by claiming that nature reaffirms the custom that he himself propagates. *Third*, a powerful statement with a reference to the custom of the churches of God (verse 16b) brings the debate to an abrupt end. This argument seems to show that Paul does not really trust in any of the reasons previously given.

One cannot help but recognize Paul's perplexity when dealing with what may have been an application of the content of Gal. 3:28 on the part of some Corinthian women. It is almost treacherous that when in 1 Corinthians Paul repeats the baptismal tradition of Gal. 3:28, he *omits* the pair "male-female." Now it simply runs: "For by one Spirit we were all baptized into one body—Jews or Greeks, slaves or free—and all were made to drink of the same Spirit" (1 Cor. 12:13).

These are certainly embarrassing expedients, but they do not, as some would have it, show Paul to be an enemy of women. Rather, in general he preferred not to translate the "reality" in Christ into political reality. At the same time this should warn anybody from the outset against using Paul as a champion of political reform in our time.

Despite these problems, it is nonetheless important to explore the meaning of baptism in primitive Christianity and in Paul in order better to understand the Christian movement. And while it is surely noteworthy that according to Paul, Christ sent him not to baptize but to preach the gospel (1 Cor. 1:17), it is nonetheless crucial to our understanding of Paul the Christian that we do two things. First we must summarize what is reasonably certain about baptism both before and during Paul's time, and after that we shall examine Paul's interpretation of the ritual.

*First,* we should recall that the baptism rituals of the early church cannot be said to reflect Jesus' practice, since there exist no authentic attestations that he ever baptized anyone.[8] Nonetheless, Christians began very early to baptize those who joined the faith and the fellowship. That it derived from the practice of John the Baptist is likely though uncertain, and in any case the significance assigned to it remains an open question.

*Second,* baptism functioned as an initiatory rite by which new members entered the Christian community.

*Third,* it probably entailed immersion (see below, p. 276, on Acts 8), involved an act of confession, and accepted the inductee "in the name of Jesus" (1 Cor. 1:13; Acts 8:16; 19:5; cf. Did. 9:5) or "into Christ" (Gal. 3:27).

*Fourth,* the question of infant baptism had not yet arisen in Paul's time. Those who freely confessed Jesus as Lord were baptized—

sometimes, according to Acts 16:15, along with their families and households; though as the case of Onesimus shows, household members were not always included: only after his conversion by Paul was Philemon's retainer baptized.

*Fifth*, it appears that from the earliest days of the movement, Christians understood baptism to be both symbolic and sacramental. The common view of the first century c.e. was that the efficacy of any rite depended primarily on the power to which it attested rather than on the ritual performance itself; it was by the power of this invoked "otherness" that the imitative or representational action was able to bring about results.

*Sixth*, for early Christians the all-important gift of the Holy Spirit was inextricably linked with baptism, for every baptized person was understood to have received the Holy Spirit.

Undoubtedly the baptism offered by Paul and his colleagues was informed by these common assumptions, but in their nuanced version the ritual also called upon the new Christian to be a participant in Christ's death. Even this, however, may have had a pre-Pauline origin, for in his letter to the Roman Christians, to whom he had never preached, he *assumes* this understanding on their part. In asking, "Do you not know that all of us who have been baptized into Jesus Christ were baptized into his death?" (Rom. 6:3) he takes for granted that for both the Gentile and Jewish Christians he addresses, the person receiving baptism is understood to be incorporated into both Christ's Lordship and his ignominious death.

Observe, however, that Paul does not relate baptism to Christ's resurrection. In Rom. 6:8 he writes: "But if we have died with Christ we believe that we shall also live with him." Still, it is clear that while sharing in his resurrection is reserved for the future, its ethical implications involve present realities: "We were buried . . . with him . . . so that as Christ was raised from the the dead . . . we too might walk in the newness of life" (Rom. 6:4). Recalling the Hellenistic baptismal formula in Gal. 3:26–28 which proclaimed the abolition of ethnic, social, and sexual distinctions by Christ's new reality (see above, p. 143), it seems reasonable to propose that in Rom. 6:4 Paul may be correcting a Hellenistic tradition which saw in Christ's resurrection a pledge of the present resurrection of Christians. This surmise is strengthened by the fact that in Rom. 6:8 he seems intent on correcting that tradition by emphasizing the death rather than stressing the resurrection, as Hellenistic Christianity was wont to do.

And yet his correspondence with the Corinthian church shows that in his interpretation of baptism he may sometimes have inclined toward the Hellenistic model. The Corinthians were apparently all too willing to suppose that their faith allowed them to share in Christ's resurrection and thus protected them from temptation and sin. Paul seeks to disabuse them of this error by comparing baptized Christians to the children of Israel freed from Egyptian bondage. He intensifies the metaphor by claiming that in passing through the sea, Israel had been "baptized into Moses," and then reminds his Corinthian flock that most of the Israelites were later destroyed: despite "baptism" their sins barred them from Canaan (1 Cor. 10:1–13).

## THE LORD'S SUPPER

Two features of worship services in the Hellenistic communities are all but certain: they were held on Sundays (Acts 20:7; Rev. 1:10; Did. 14:1), and their focal point was the Lord's Supper, which originally was an integral part of the church's common meal. This was one reason for the severity of the crisis at Antioch: When Jewish Christians withdrew from the common table, they left the communion table as well (Gal. 2:11–13). The ritual independence of the Lord's Supper is signaled by Paul's instruction to the Corinthians (1 Cor. 11:17–34, especially verse 34). As to Paul's understanding of the communion ritual that he originally taught the Corinthians, it appears in the tradition he passed on (1 Cor. 11:23–25) and in 1 Cor. 10:16–17, where in the course of condemning idol worship he reminds them of the real significance of this sacred meal.

*1 Cor. 11:23–26:*

> (23) For I received from the Lord what I also delivered to you, that the Lord Jesus on the night when he was handed over took bread, (24) and when he had given thanks, he broke it, and said, "This is

my body which is for you. <u>Do this in remembrance of me</u>." (25) In the same way also the cup, after supper, saying, "This cup is the new covenant in my blood. <u>Do this</u>, as often as you drink it, <u>in remembrance of me</u>." (26) For as often as you eat this bread and drink the cup, you proclaim the Lord's death until he comes.

Because it is at least fifteen years earlier than Mark, 1 Cor. 11 contains the oldest written form of the tradition. This, however, does not necessarily make Mark's version secondary.

*Mark 14:22–25:*

> (22) And while they were eating he took the bread, *gave thanks* and broke *it and gave* [it] *to them* and said, "Take, <u>this is my</u> body." (23) And he took a cup, *gave thanks and gave* [it] *to them*; and they all drank of it. (24) And he said to them, "<u>This is my</u> blood of the covenant which is poured out for many. (25) Amen, I say to you, I will no more drink of the fruit of the vine until that day when I drink it new in the kingdom of God."

Both accounts attest that "Christ died for our sins" (1 Cor. 15:3), but Paul stresses the point: not only does he preface his account of the last meal (1 Cor. 11:23–25) with "On the night when he was handed over," but he makes explicit what Mark only implies:

Mark: This is my body.

Paul: This is my body which is for you.

Mark: This is my blood of the covenant which is poured out for many.

Paul: This is the new covenant in my blood.

In the Pauline formulation the bread is specifically incorporated into the atonement theme, and the covenant motive makes all but explicit the proclamation of a new reality: "Look, the days are coming, says the Lord, when I will make a new covenant with the house of Israel and Judah" (Jer. 31:31).

Paul reiterates the injunction (underlined in the above text) that this rite be performed on a regular basis, an element absent from Mark. A liturgical origin is thus attested, and something more than remembering is indicated: this is a commemoration, an act in which the significance of a vital event of the past becomes a present reality.

In 1 Cor. 10:16–17 Paul writes the following about the Lord's Supper:

> (16) The cup of blessing over which we say the blessing, is it not a <u>participation</u> of the blood of Christ? The bread which we break, is it not a <u>participation</u> of the body of Christ? (17) Because there is one bread, we, many as we are, form one body, for we all partake of the one bread.

By twice using the word "participation" to characterize the Supper, Paul reminds the Corinthians that the cup and the bread (the reversal of order is of no significance) involve *koinonia*—communion with or participation in the blood of Christ. Paul's insistence that they could not eat the Lord's Supper and then join in a similar rite at some pagan shrine (1 Cor. 10:20–21) attests to a shared understanding that partaking of a sacred meal involves sharing in the reality that it commemorates.

## MALPRACTICE OF THE LORD'S SUPPER IN CORINTH

Yet from this very understanding of sacramental function arose a dangerously divisive malpractice. It must be understood that meetings were sponsored by wealthy members whose homes were large enough to accomodate the whole community. And since Sunday had no legal standing, nor was there a recognized end of the working day, a fixed hour for meeting would be all but impossible to arrange. Thus gatherings doubtless lasted for hours. Naturally enough, perhaps, the first to arrive began their meal, and by the time all were present, the best food and wine was gone, and some had already had more than enough to eat—and to drink (1 Cor. 11:21). And though the poor might be humiliated by their reception or by how little they contributed or received (verse 22), most Corinthians seem to have seen no overriding reason to alter arrangements. After all, did not religious eating and drinking mean communion with Christ, and in particular sharing the Risen Lord's power and spirit? What real difference did it make who might or might not be in attendance?

It was a thorny complex of socioeconomic, ritual, and theological issues with which Paul was obliged to deal; and true to character he did not hesitate to point out their error: "When you meet together, it is not the Lord's Supper that you eat" (1 Cor. 11:20). But why wasn't it?

*First,* because at the Lord's table the worshipper is participating not in the Lord's power and glory, but in his death. To drive home the concept he repeats in 11:23–25 the point he made in 10:16–17, and by way of further emphasis adds verse 26: "For as often as you eat this bread and drink this cup, you proclaim the Lord's death until he comes." *Second,* he charges that those who eat and drink in an unworthy manner profane the Lord's body and blood (verse 29). His concluding argument, that sickness and death have resulted from improper participation (verse 30), claims that abusing so powerful a sacrament calls down a curse rather than the expected blessing.


## PAUL AND THE HELLENISTS— OBJECTS OF PERSECUTION BY OTHER JEWS

We have pointed out above (pp. 139–41) that Paul was instructed in the Christian faith by the Hellenists. They were the object of his persecution and they later praised God for having bought about the sudden change in Paul: "He who once persecuted us is now proclaiming the faith he once tried to destroy. And they praised God for me" (Gal. 1:23–24). It seems possible to detect one more passage that is related to the Hellenists and that serves Paul to define his own faith.

In the earliest of his extant letters Paul directs a sharp polemic against the Jews.

*1 Thess. 2:14–16:*

> (14) *For you, brothers, became imitators of the churches of God in Christ Jesus which are in Judaea; for you suffered the same thing from your countrymen as they did from the Jews,*

(15) who killed the Lord Jesus and the prophets,
**and** drove us out
**and** displease God
**and** oppose all men
(16) *hindering us from speaking to the Gentiles that they may be saved*—so
as always to fill up the measure of their sins. But God's wrath has
come upon them at last.

Scholars have long recognized that at this point Paul is drawing
on tradition from pre-Pauline communities. The statement in verse
15 that the Jews displease God and are hostile to all men can be
found in previous polemics of pagan authors against the Jews. Thus
for example the Roman historian Tacitus writes that the Jews of his
time have become increasingly powerful and

> rigidly insist upon loyalty and faith, . . . whereas they adopt a
> spiteful and hostile attitude to all non-Jews. . . . Those who go over
> to their religion observe the same customs, and the first thing to be
> inculcated upon them is the precept to despise the gods, to deny
> their fatherland and their parents, and to regard their children and
> kinsfolk as worthless things.[9]

The accusation that the Jews killed the prophets corresponds to
the Old Testament-Jewish view of the violent end of the prophets, a
proposition which owes more to theological interpretation than to
history. Israel and Judaism had long ago formulated it against themselves. See Neh. 9:26:

> They were disobedient and rebelled against you and cast your law
> behind their back and killed your prophets, who had warned them in
> order to turn them back to you, and they committed great blasphemies.

The similar accusation that the Jews killed Jesus appears in the
gospel passion narratives written between ten and forty years after
Paul but likely reflecting pre-Pauline traditions. According to these
accounts the Jewish authorities initiate proceedings against Jesus,
condemn him to death, and hand him over to the Romans.

Paul's accusation that the Jews "drove us out" might derive from a tradition of the Hellenists who, after the killing of their leader Stephen, were in fact driven out of Jerusalem. Remember that Paul received instruction in the Christian faith by members of these groups.

The statement in verse 16 that God's wrath has come upon them at last may refer to a prophetic judgment which considers a future act already happening in the present.[10]

Paul has taken up a tradition which goes back to an earlier formulation—which in turn may derive from an early distortion of one of Jesus' parables.[11] In view of his problems with Jews and Jewish Christians, Paul would naturally have been inclined to adopt such a tradition; and for good measures he adds the comment, "hindering us from speaking to the Gentiles that they may be saved" (verse 16). This thesis is based, *first,* on the observation that the accusations against the Jews are each connected by "and" while Paul adds his own interpretation without a connecting "and." *Second,* in the original Greek all the accusations employ participial constructions, a form which strongly suggests tradition. *Third,* the alleged interpretation displays features of Pauline language.[12]

Similar comments on traditions also appear elsewhere in the Pauline letters without the apostle specifically noting the fact. (Cf. Phil. 2:6–11, expanded in verse 8b by "to death on the cross"; Rom. 3:25–26, expanded in verse 25 "through faith"; and Gal. 3:26–28, expanded in verse 16 by "through faith.") Note that, as becomes clear from the "us" of verse 16, Paul can apply the "us" of verse 15 to himself. This is an ecclesiastical "we" that surfaces here. Paul holds the conviction that he, along with the Hellenists, belongs to Christ and that what happened to them must also have happened to him.

Thus the direction of the text 1 Thess. 2:15–16 is clear: the unbelieving Jews who have earlier driven out the Hellenists and are now hindering Paul from preaching salvation to the Gentiles have already fallen victim to God's wrathful judgment. Paul's view of the church made up of Jews and Gentiles, a concept inherited from the Hellenists, is the positive parallel to the negative verdict on unbelieving Judaism. The Gentile Christians from Thessalonica have become imitators of the Hellenist communities of Judaea and beyond. Their fellowship is one in suffering and in Christ. At the beginning of 1 Thessalonians Paul reminds the members of his Gentile Christian community of their election (1 Thess. 1:4), but this equally applies to the Hellenist churches in Judaea.

So we can say that with the calling of the Gentiles God's election has been transferred from Israel to the Christian church made up of Jews and Gentiles.


## THE CHURCH OF JEWS AND GENTILES— THE THIRD RACE?

What kind of church was this? How was it organized and governed? How did Jews and Gentiles manage to get along? How did they conceive of salvation?

Concerning the last question, salvation was to be achieved through Christ (cf. 1 Cor. 15:3-5; 1 Thess. 1:9-10); indeed, it is important to note that Paul required the same confession, "faith in Jesus Christ," of Jew and Gentile alike. Even such righteous Jews as Peter and Paul had to present other credentials to become one of God's people: They had to confess faith in Christ (Gal. 2:15-16). However unarguable a person's Jewishness, Paul considered no one, himself included (Phil. 3:4-6), as thus a true descendant of Abraham; that distinction required that one belong to Christ (Gal. 3:29). Therefore Jew and Gentile were equally qualified and eligible to join the people of God, and in joining, both became members of a third group, as separate from Judaism as it was from Hellenism (cf.1 Cor. 10:32 and the previous comments on this passage, p. 139). It was a group created by an admission requirement (faith), an initiation rite (baptism), and a discrete social body (the church).

Yet E. P. Sanders is correct when he observes that "Paul would have been horrified to read that in claiming that both Jew and Greek had to have faith in Christ, he had made the Christian movement a third race."[13] For Paul's intent was *not* to found a new religion. He no more considered Christianity separate from Judaism than did the Jews who assailed him—just as he had railed at the Hellenists. As Sanders aptly observes, "Punishment implies inclusion."[14] Be that as it may, it was clear that Paul did create a new and separate socio-religious reality.

Despite the divisive nature of his proclamation of "the true Israel," he would surely have abjured the idea that his teaching had all but defined the new human type known in the second century as "the third race."[15] Indeed, he would later argue that the true Israel would at last include all of Israel (see below, pp. 159–62). On the other hand, from the outset Paul clearly thought of the church as the true Israel; this is evident from his characterization of the church as "the Israel of God" (Gal. 6:16). RSV correctly translates the verse in the following way: "Peace and mercy be upon all who walk by this rule, upon the Israel of God." A different translation in NEB has important consequences: "Whoever they are who take this principle for their guide, peace and mercy upon them, and upon the whole Israel of God." Most scholars dismiss this rendering, since it can be taken to imply that those following this new creation of faith might not comprise the whole of God's Israel. Two strong arguments support this. *First*, the argument from Abraham we find in Gal. 3 and Rom. 4, and the lengthy analysis in Rom. 9 (see below, pp. 157–58), make it evident that for Paul it is not Jewishness, but faith in Christ that confers the inheritance.

*Second*, Gal. 6:16 is both a benediction and the culmination of a postscript (verses 11–16) which forms a sort of thematic summary of the epistle (note that 6:12–13 recalls 2:14, and 6:14 echoes 2:20). In a sense this verse is the emphatic conclusion of the letter. And the point it drives home is that neither circumcision nor uncircumcision matters. It is all but unthinkable that in this climactic verse Paul would bestow the same blessing on his opponents as on those who accept with him the unimportance of circumcision. That would cancel the very attack he levelled against them at the beginning of the postscript.

*Gal. 6:12–13:*

> (12) It is those people who wish to make a nice appearance in the flesh that force you to be circumcised—only that they may not be persecuted because of the cross of Christ. (13) For not even the circumcised themselves keep the law, but they want you to be circumcised, in order that they may boast in the flesh.

For Paul it was of the utmost importance that Jewish and Gentile Christians should live in peace in the same community. This is clear from his rage at Peter's withdrawal from the common table in Antioch (Gal. 2:11–14). Surely he could not accept any policy which might have a like result elsewhere. So how were these two groups to coexist? He called on Jewish Christians to repudiate the dietary laws; after all, they were members of a church now, not a synagogue. Nor, conversely, were Gentile converts to become Jewish. Yet Jews who joined the church were, though often unaware of it, forsaking their old religion. In any case, according to Paul neither Jew nor Gentile could escape destruction except by adopting faith.

Could Paul persist in this clear verdict? In the assertion of the destruction of the Jews in 1 Thess. 2:16 is he thinking only of those Jews who are preventing him from preaching to the Gentiles? Does he leave some room for the salvation of the remainder of Israel which, while unbelieving, is not hindering his preaching? Is the harsh statement in 1 Thess. 2 to be explained by the effusive, fiery character of 1 Thessalonians? What would Paul say if the Jews rejected the gospel not only as individuals, but en masse? We should remember that 1 Thessalonians is Paul's earliest extant letter, written when he could hardly foresee such a development.

## THE REMARKS ABOUT ISRAEL IN ROM. 9–11

At the beginning of Rom. 9 Paul powerfully expresses his dismay at the obduracy of his fellow Jews, on whose behalf he feels ceaseless pain (verse 2); indeed, he says in verse 3, for their sake he would willingly be accursed and cut off from Christ (see the translation of Rom. 9:1–5 above, pp. 108–109).

However, this wish is clearly rhetorical and incapable of fulfillment. It stands in stark contrast to Rom. 8:39, where the apostle had emphatically asserted that nothing could separate him from the love of Christ. Now Paul would give up everything, indeed even his own bond with Christ, if he could save his unbelieving brothers by doing so. But he knows that this is impossible. The real reason for this clearly melodramatic wish, which Paul omits here but indicates in Rom. 10:16, is that for the most part Jews have not accepted the gospel, despite the gifts (listed in verses 4–5) by which God has bound himself to them and which culminate in the promises to the fathers.

But what is the status of the promises to Israel, which are contained in the list Rom. 9:4–5? Does what God once promised still hold? Can one no longer rely on God?

In the following passage three issues are intertwined and overlap: first, the meaning of the history of Israel; second, the validity of the promise; and third, the loyalty and truthfulness of God. In other words, he asks, doesn't the overwhelming rejection of the gospel by the Jews endanger the validity of God's promises? That is the unifying motif of Paul's reflections in Rom. 9–11, which had begun in Rom. 3:1–8 but were then dropped. E. P. Sanders offers a perceptive comment on Paul's attempt to wrestle with these matters:

> These partially contradictory assertions ebb and flow in the chapters as Paul seeks solid ground. On the question of God's justice, he has little to say, and one is almost embarrassed on his behalf. He proposes that the pot may not criticize the potter, and that similarly humans may not object to God, who predestines some to salvation but rejects others. This and other attempts in Romans 9–11 to deal directly with the problem of theodicy are standard in Jewish literature, and they show none of Paul's customary virtuosity and ingenuity.[16]

For understandable reasons, it is impossible to give a detailed exposition of the three chapters. Instead, we shall investigate how Paul describes the relationship between the Jews and the Gentile Christians in these chapters when he is tackling the questions listed above. In my view the apostle gives three different answers.

The first answer is contained in Rom. 9:6–29 and begins with the statement: "But it is not as though the word of God had failed. For not all who are descended from Israel belong to Israel." In other words, the promise relates not to physical Israel but to spiritual Israel, as the subsequent example of Abraham demonstrates. God's promise *a priori* relates to those who are elected by God's free grace. Here God has mercy on whomsoever he wills to have mercy (verse

15). Verse 22 refers to the unbelieving Jews of his time; verse 23 and more especially verse 24 to Christians. As "vessels of wrath" (verse 22), human beings are already prepared for destruction. In the manifestation of wrath, this predestination is realized in final destruction (cf. 1 Thess. 2:16b). Here, in an eschatological perspective, God's patience is aimed not at salvation, but rather at damnation. The fact that we know from Rom. 11 that this is not Paul's last word on the problem of Israel and salvation history must not be a reason for toning down the sharpness of Paul's argumentation in an interpretation of verses 22–23, or doing away with it on dialectical grounds. So God has fulfilled his word of promise as it was intended from the beginning, in the church made up of Jews and Gentiles (verse 24).

The second answer can be found in Rom. 9:30–11:10: Israel has heard the preaching of the gospel (10:18) but wants to become righteous through works (10:3), whereas by contrast the Gentiles have attained righteousness by faith. Israel has "stumbled over the stumbling stone" (9:32b). Nevertheless, it would be wrong to conclude that God has rejected his people (11:1). Granted, the majority of them have become stubborn, but a remnant has remained (11:5). So Paul demonstrates the realization of the promises by a reference to those Jewish Christians who in fact exist.

The third answer is found in Rom. 11:11–36. For the sake of clarity, I shall analyze this section verse by verse.

*Verse 11*: Paul begins with the question whether Israel has stumbled greatly so as to fall completely (see 11:1, "Has God rejected his people?"). Paul rejects such a conclusion and points out the positive consequence of Israel's "false step": because the (majority of) Jews did not accept the gospel, salvation has come *also* to the Gentiles. The whole section is addressed as a warning to the latter, the predominantly Gentile Christian readers of the letter in Rome.

*Verse 12*: If the refusal of Israel and its rejection (verse 15) have already resulted in "riches" (i.e., salvation) and reconciliation for the world and the Gentiles, so even more will their reincorporation when the "full number is redeemed." Accordingly, their "full number" denotes Israel as a whole, i.e., the filling up of the present remnant (i.e., the Jewish Christians) with the stubborn majority in order to make up the full number of Israel. Thus "their trespass" must mean the diminution of this full number which has come about through the fall of the unbelieving Jews. But how can we conceive the redemption of the full number to be possible despite the fall of the majority? The statement in verses 25–26 resolves this problem: the recovery of the unbelievers will be none other than God's promised deliverance of Israel (Isa. 59:20–21), the return to "life from the dead" pledged in verse 15.

*Verses 13–14:* Thus Paul sees his role of apostle to the Gentiles as consisting in making some Jews jealous (see 10:19; 11:1) in order to save them. For the first time Paul assigns himself responsibility for the salvation of Israel—but only indirectly. Remember that the mission to the Jews was assigned to Peter and the other apostles (see above, p. 39). Since their mission has failed, Paul claims this too is now up to him, with God's help.

*Verse 15:* See the end of the analysis of verse 12.

*Verse 16:* With an image, Paul seeks to explain to the Gentile Christians their relationship to the Jews: "If the dough offered as first fruits is holy, so is the whole lump; and if the root is holy, so are the branches. This "holy root" is a reference to the patriarch Abraham chosen by God (or to the patriarchs generally, see verse 28).

*Verses 17–24:* The image of the olive tree now shows God's (paradoxical) action: through their unbelief the Jews are cut off from the olive tree, and God has instead "grafted in" the Gentiles, thus making them children of Israel. But the Gentiles who have now been called to salvation are not to be arrogant toward Israel; for surely God, who has rejected Israel and given the Gentiles a share in the promise to Abraham in its place, can as easily remove the Gentile grafts as he accepts all of Israel again (verses 23–24).

*Verses 25–36:* The idea of the reacceptance of unbelieving Israel, of it being grafted back into the olive tree, permeates the whole section from verse 11 on and is summarized here. The apostle begins the passage with the phrase, "I do not want you to be ignorant."[17] Paul communicates a mystery to the Roman Christians, again with the warning that they should not be wise among themselves—that is, smug and complacent.

The mystery *first* has as its content the surprising news that all Israel, i.e., the Jews as a people, will finally be saved. However, this was already emerging in verses 11–12, 15, 23–24, albeit only as a remote possibility. *Second*, the hardening of Israel will last until "the full number of Gentiles determined by God" has come in. The Apostle clinches his conclusion with prophecies from the Books of Isaiah (59:20) and Jeremiah (31:33–34—the prophecy of the New Covenant, which elsewhere in the New Testament is always applied to the Church as the New Israel, and not, as here, to the salvation of the Jews).[18]


## HOW WILL ISRAEL BE SAVED?

Paul does not say anything here about how Israel will be saved. In recent discussions a dispute has flared up over this. Some speak of a special path to salvation which does not include the acceptance of the gospel but rests on the principle of grace. Yet in verse 23 Paul insists that only the acceptance of the gospel can ensure belonging to the olive tree. "There is only one olive tree, and the condition of being a 'branch' is faith."[19] Furthermore, talk of arousing the jealousy of the Jews makes sense only if it is hoped that they will accept the gospel. Note especially Rom. 11:13–14:

> (13) Now I am speaking to you Gentiles. Precisely because I am an apostle to the Gentiles, I make much of my office (14) in order to make my fellow Jews jealous, and so to save some of them.

But since in these verses Paul is speaking only of the immediate present in which some Jews may accept the gospel, they hardly demonstrate that in verses 25–26 Paul presupposes the conversion of all Israel, especially since here the apostle is speaking of the historical Israel, and thus so to speak infers salvation in the future from the election in the past (cf. 11:28–32). Any hope for a final resolution of the question is at best elusive.

Still, I cannot get rid of the suspicion that Paul is giving Israel an advantage. According to the proof texts in verses 26–27, iniquity will be removed from Jacob, that is from the people of Israel as defined by physical descent. And while Paul earlier rejected physical descent as the basis for salvation (Rom. 9), now in view of the failure of the mission among the Jews he seems to accept it. Note Paul's conviction throughout his career that the gospel is for the Jews first and only afterward to the Gentiles (Rom. 1:16, etc.). (See more on the Jewish bias of Paul above, pp. 108–109.)

## WHEN WILL ISRAEL BE SAVED?

When will the salvation of all Israel that Paul envisages in Rom. 11:26 take place?

In verse 15 he likened the reacceptance of Israel to returning from death to life. Furthermore, he grounded his statement on the salvation of all Israel in scripture (verses 26–27: "The deliverer will come from Zion, he will banish ungodliness from Jacob";[20] "and this will be my covenant with them when I take away their sins"[21]). Now for Paul the coming of the deliverer probably means the Second Coming of Jesus, and the expression "life from the dead" similarly focuses on the end-event. Therefore it seems likely that Paul is transferring the salvation of all Israel to the end of history, where the resurrection of the dead takes place with the coming of Jesus on the clouds of heaven.

In the following (verses 28–36), Paul once again attempts a comprehensive exposition of the basis and purpose of God's action toward Israel: Because of its repudiation of the gospel, Israel is hated by God, and therefore salvation can also come to the Gentiles; but as Israel is the elect people, it is God's beloved for the sake of the patriarchs (verse 28), since the gifts of grace entrusted to Israel (cf. 9:4–5) and the call of God are irrevocable (verse 29). The Gentiles who were once disobedient to God have come to have a share in salvation as a result of the present disobedience of Israel (toward the gospel); in precisely the same way, God will also show mercy to Israel in the future (verses 30–31); indeed, despite its disobedience in the present, God's mercy is extended to Israel in the present.

Verse 32 sums up verses 30–31: In order finally to show his mercy to both Jews and Gentiles, God has caused them both to be disobedient: the Gentiles in the past and the Jews in the present.

In verses 33–36, Paul's remarks on Israel culminate in a hymn of praise to God's wisdom.


## EVALUATION OF PAUL'S CONTRADICTORY ANSWERS ABOUT THE FATE OF UNBELIEVING ISRAEL

Paul says different, indeed contradictory things about the fate of unbelieving Israel. We meet various statements of total rejection that run like a scarlet thread through all letters of Paul. It is noteworthy that even the first and second answer in Rom. 9–11 (see above, pp. 157–58) assume this, and of course 1 Thess. 2:14–16 is notorious in that respect (see above, pp. 151–54). On the other hand, Paul reversed such a jugdment and concluded in the third answer of Rom. 9–11 that God will save Israel whether its members become believers in Jesus Christ or not.

The contradictory wording of these passages notwithstanding, their statements may still stem from a unitary starting point, once we note that they are conditioned by the situation. While in 1 Thessalonians the mission to the Gentiles is in danger, Rom. 11:25–26—the third answer—reflects the possible loss of Jewish Christianity. Both letters are based on Paul's immutable postulate that the church must consist of both Jews and Gentiles together.

However, this explanation of the different wording does not solve the contradiction. And yet the special importance here assigned to the Jews appears all the more artificial, since Paul obviously finds it impossible not to assign a special role to his own people whether or not they believe.[22] While this assignment may be difficult to justify on Paul's premises, it should not be surprising, for deep in his heart he was a Jew to the very end—even though in reality he had become a Christian. In other words, Paul tried to have it both ways. Nietzsche's acute characterization of the phenomenon is worth recalling:

Christianity can be understood only in terms of the soil out of which it grew—it is *not* a counter-movement to the Jewish instinct, it is its very consequence, one inference more in its awe-inspiring logic. In the formula of the Redeemer: "Salvation is of the Jews."[23]

Paul the Christian was still in some measure Paul the Jew, and despite his radical redefinition of Jesus the Jew as the redeeming Son of God, important ancestral features marked this new form of Judaism called Christianity.[24]

## NOTES

1. See also the occurrence of the name "Christians" along with the term "the third race" in the fragments that have survived from *The Preaching of Peter* (early second century). See the English translation in Montague Rhodes James, *The Apocryphal New Testament, Being the Apocryphal Gospels, Acts, Epistles, and Apocalypses* (Oxford: Clarendon Press, 1924), p. 17. The passage in question is from Clement of Alexandria *Stromateis* 6.5.39.

2. The best account in English is still the book by Arthur Darby Nock, *Early Gentile Christianity and Its Hellenistic Background* (New York: Harper & Row, Torchbooks, 1964).

3. See Rudolf Bultmann, *Theology of the New Testament*, vol. 1 (New York: Charles Scribner's Sons, 1951), p. 64.

4. The best book on the subject is still Marcel Simon, *St. Stephen and the Hellenists in the Primitive Church* (London/New York/Toronto: Longmans, Green and Co, 1958). Disappointing is the recent work by Craig Hill. In his *Hellenists and Hebrews: Reappraising Divisions within the Early Church* (Minneapolis: Fortress Press, 1992), he does not see any division between the two groups. See my comments in "Das Urchristentum," *Theologische Rundschau* 65 (2000): 178f.

5. Bultmann, *Theology of the New Testament*, vol. 1, pp. 55–56.

6. See Johannes Weiss, *Earliest Christianity: A History of the Period* A.D. *30-150*. English translation edited with a new introduction by Frederick C. Grant, 2 vols., 1937. Reprint, Gloucester, Mass.: Peter Smith, 1970, vol. 1, pp. 175–77.

7. See the survey by Hans Dieter Betz, *Galatians: A Commentary on Paul's Letter to the Churches in Galatia* (Philadelphia: Fortress Press, 1979), pp. 197–200.

8. The passages in John 3:22, 26; 4:1 (diff. 4:2) have no historical

value. The assertion that Jesus himself baptized was a counterreaction to a charge by the rival Baptist community that with the baptism that Christians practiced they were dependent on John. It is similarly possible that after Jesus had become the center of the cult, the view arose that he himself had baptized. See my *Jesus After Two Thousand Years: What He Really Said and Did* (Amherst, N.Y.: Prometheus Books, 2001), pp. 443–45.

9. Tacitus *Histories* 5.5.

10. See as an analogy Rev. 12:7–17 and in addition Job 1–2, where the fate of the patient is predetermined in heaven. Cf. Dan. 10:13/11:1: Here the battle of the nations runs parallel to the battle of the archangel Michael against the "princes" of Persia and Greece. In 2 Macc. 5:2–3 the angels join in the fight in the clouds when Antiochus goes against Egypt.

11. Either the possibly authentic Thomas 65:1–7 or the oral tradition behind it was allegorized by Mark (12:1–12).

12. The verb "to hinder" is also found in Rom. 1:13; 1 Cor. 14:39. The verb "to speak" is found fifty-two times in Paul (see especially 1 Thess. 2:2, 4). "Gentiles" is used by Paul forty-five times and "to save" nineteen times.

13. E. P. Sanders, *Paul, the Law, and the Jewish People* (Philadelphia: Fortress Press, 1983), p. 173.

14. Ibid.

15. Adolf von Harnack, *The Mission and Expansion of Christianity in the First Three Centuries* (New York: Harper & Row, Torchbooks, 1962), vol. 1, pp. 300–335.

16. E. P. Sanders, *Paul* (Oxford/New York: Oxford University Press, 1991), p. 119.

17. In Paul's writings this formula always introduces something new: thus in 1 Thess. 4:13 the teaching that despite their death those who have died will participate in the fellowship of Christ (cf. 4:14–17, see above, p. 50); in 2 Cor. 1:8 the report of the deadly danger to Paul in Asia; and in Rom. 1:13 the fact that Paul has often wanted to come to Rome (cf. further 1 Cor. 10:1; 12:1).

18. "In Rom. 11:25–26a the salvation of the Gentiles is intimately connected with the salvation of Israel, and the connection is causative. Part of Israel is hardened until the full number of Gentiles come in and thus—in that manner—all Israel will be saved as a consequence of the Gentile mission, as Paul had already said (11:13–16). The same point is repeated in 11:31" (Sanders, *Paul, the Law, and the Jewish People*, pp. 193ff.).

19. Ibid., 195.

20. Cf. Isa. 59:20–21.

21. Cf. Isa. 27:9.

22. Therefore Bultmann has said about Rom. 11:25–27, "the history of salvation mystery in Rom 11:25ff. is derived from speculative fantasy" (*Theology of the New Testament*, vol. 2 [New York: Charles Scribner's Sons, 1955], p. 132).

23. The Antichrist sec. 24 (quoted from Walter Kaufmann, ed., *The Portable Nietzsche* [New York: Viking Press, 1954], p. 592).

24. See James D. G. Dunn, "Who Did Paul Think That He Was? A Study of Jewish-Christian Identity," *New Testament Studies* 45 (1999): 174–93 (with a helpful survey of previous research).

# 7

# PAUL THE APOSTLE
# OF JESUS CHRIST

**"A**postle" (in Greek, *apostolos*) is the designation of someone who is sent out. In modern English "messenger" or even "missionary" would be an appropriate rendering. For Paul, an apostle is endowed with more authority than any one else in the church. At one place in 1 Corinthians he arranges a list of leaders in the church in descending order: apostles come first, then prophets, and after that teachers, workers of miracles, healers, helpers, administrators, and eventually speakers in tongues (1 Cor. 12:28).

Paul was absolutely certain that God had called him to be an apostle (1 Cor. 1:1: "Paul, called by the will of God to be an apostle of Jesus Christ"). It was even more than a call, for Paul had been consecrated for that purpose (Rom. 1:1: "Paul a servant of Jesus Christ, called to be an apostle, set apart for the gospel of God"). Indeed, Paul claims that his apostolic standing is the result of an appointment not by human beings but by God. This can be well illustrated by two passages from his letter to the Galatians:

*Gal. 1:1:*

> Paul an apostle not from men nor through man, but through Jesus Christ and God who raised him from the dead.

*Gal. 1:12:*

> For I did not receive it [the gospel] from man, nor was I taught it,
> but it came through a revelation of Jesus Christ [effected by God].

Most of the passages mentioned so far stem from the beginnings of various letters where, as in the address of a modern letter, the writer identifies him- or herself. At the same time, as will become clear, this assertion of dignity carries through into the main section of various letters.

One of the most important of the passages in Paul's letters that shed light on the origin, context, significance and real reason of Paul's claim to be an apostle is 1 Cor. 15:1–11:[1]

> (1) And now, brothers, I must remind you of the gospel that I preached to you; the gospel which you received, in which you stand, (2) by which you are saved, if you hold fast—unless you believed in vain. (3) For I delivered to you as of first importance what I also received, **that Christ died for our sins *in accordance with the scriptures*, (4) and that he was buried, that he has been raised[2] on the third day *in accordance with the scriptures* (5) and that he appeared to Cephas, then to the Twelve.**
>
> (6) Thereafter he appeared to more than five hundred brothers *at one time, most of whom are still alive, though some have fallen asleep.* (7) Thereafter he appeared to James, then to all the apostles.
>
> (8) Last of all, as to one untimely born, he appeared also to me. (9) For I am the least of the apostles, indeed unfit to be called an apostle, because I persecuted the church of God. (10) But by God's grace I am what I am, and his grace toward me was not in vain. On the contrary, I worked harder than any of them, though it was not I, but the grace of God which is with me. (11) Whether then it was I or they, so we preach and so you believed.

## PAUL'S INTENTION

The position of 1 Cor. 15 at the end of the letter is self-explanatory: the instruction about the end-time always comes at the end (cf. 1

Thess. 4:13–5:11; Mark 13; Didache 16; Barnabas 21:1). 1 Cor. 15 is a well-rounded unit on the resurrection of the dead. However, this does not become clear immediately, but only as a result of verses 12–34 ("the fact of the resurrection") and verses 35–49 ("the manner of the resurrection").

In verses 1–11 Paul takes up the confession of faith which he communicated on his founding visit to the community: this spoke of Christ's death and resurrection and appearance to Cephas and the Twelve (1 Cor. 15:3b–5), and adds the other appearances of Christ that he asserts had been reported to him: the appearance to more than five hundred brothers at one time and the appearance to James, then to all the apostles. This probably had the purpose, *first*, of providing historical proof of the resurrection. Paul underlines this by adding verse 6b (printed in italics) implying that anyone who was still skeptical about what they had heard could ask the witnesses directly, since most of them were still alive. In addition, the expression "at one time" in verse 6a (set in italics) on the redactional level is probably meant to intensify the objectivity, because more than five hundred witnesses could hardly all have been deluded. *Second*, Paul was evidently concerned to place himself within the tradition which he had proclaimed to the Corinthians on his founding visit, which already included Jesus' appearance to Cephas. That being the case, it was necessary for him to add appearances of the same kind which chronologically preceded his own. Thus it is clear that in verse 8 Paul is claiming to have received the same vision as all the other people listed in this sequence. In this way the statements in verses 5–7 are used by Paul to support the assertion that Christ appeared also to him.

## PAUL DEFENDING HIMSELF

Why does Paul place his experience within a successive pattern of appearances? Why does he stress the identity of his vision with that of all the people mentioned earlier? One cannot avoid the assumption that this was to defend his apostolic authority. Verses 8–10 clearly have an apologetic character. How else are we to understand the reference to his own work (verse 10b)? How else are we to understand the surprising length of his comments about himself, the designation of himself in verse 8 as "one untimely born" (in relation to those mentioned previously)? Note that the statement in verse 7 that Christ appeared to James, then to *all the apostles*, strictly speaking, excludes a further appearance to another apostle. In other words, at least the group of the apostles around James who were at home in Jerusalem would strongly object to the claim that Christ appeared to the apostle Paul. As if aware of this, Paul points out that the appearance to him happened as to one who was untimely born. (The Greek word *ektroma* alludes to Paul's sudden and unexpected "birth" into the apostolic family.)

Furthermore, it emerges quite plainly from 1 Cor. 9:1b–18 that his apostolic authority was doubted by some people in Corinth. They questioned his status as an apostle on the basis of his refusal to accept the support which is an apostle's due (cf. 1 Cor. 9:3–7).[3] And in 1 Cor. 15:8–10 he notes that he had from the first claimed the necessary credentials for the teaching which follows, all the more so since he understands himself (as in 1 Thess. 4:14) as an authorized expounder of the Christian confession of faith which he summarizes once again in verse 12a ("since Christ is preached as being raised from the dead"), and from which, unlike some Corinthians, he concludes a future (bodily) resurrection of Christians.[4] For him, the one is inconceivable without the other: "If the dead are not raised, then Christ has not been raised" (verse 16).

## THE TRADITION CONTAINED IN 1 COR. 15:3–7

It is evident that the tradition in verses 3b–5 (printed in boldface) is different in structure from the elements of appearance-tradition that follow in verses 6–7. (Another sentence construction begins after "then to the Twelve," employing a different conjunction.)

Verses 3b–5 offer a twofold proof, (a) from the scriptures (we know them as the Old Testament), and (b) from confirmation by facts. Accordingly, verses 3b–5 consist of two parts and are to be read as follows:

*Line 1*: Christ died for our sins in accordance with the scriptures and was buried.

*Line 2*: He has been raised on the third day in accordance with the scriptures and appeared to Cephas, then to the Twelve.

## THE ORIGIN OF THE TRADITION 1 COR. 15:3b–5

There are different views about the origin of this piece of tradition. One branch of scholarship derives it from the Greek-speaking communities around Antioch to whom Paul had particularly close ties. A primary reason for this contention is the observation that "Christ" here is already a name and no longer a title. (Otherwise one would have expected to find "*the* Christ.") Another contingent of scholars derives it from the Aramaic-speaking community of Jerusalem, in which case we must presuppose a translation into Greek. On the whole, the dichotomy of "Jerusalem or Antioch" seems to be an exaggeration, for even if Christians in Antioch mediated the tradition to Paul, they would only have reproduced what they had received from Jerusalem.

## THE FIRST APPEARANCE OF CHRIST TO CEPHAS

We now must address the question of the first appearance of Christ to Cephas (verse 5) and its relationship to the appearance of Christ to James (verse 7).

The statement in verse 5, "he appeared to Cephas, then to the Twelve," can be detached as an independent unit from the tradition handed down by Paul on the visit during which he founded the community. This is suggested first by the parallel to Luke 24:34 ("the Lord was really raised and appeared to Simon") and Mark 16:7 ("tell his disciples and Peter"), and second by the structural parallel of the formula in verse 7 ("he appeared to James, then to all the apostles") to that in verse 5 ("he appeared to Cephas, then to the Twelve"). This parallelism could be explained in two ways: (a) here Paul was modeling his language in verse 7 on verse 5, which employed a tradition about an appearance to James and to all the apostles; (b) Paul was reproducing two independent traditions. In the latter case either the one formula had already been modeled earlier on the basis of the other or the two formulae have a common origin. At all events, it is clear that there is an earlier tradition in both verse 5 and verse 7.

## WHAT IS THE FUNCTION OF SUCH FORMULAE?

The formulae handed down in verses 5 and 7 contain the brief report that the risen Christ had appeared to a particular group of believers. The possible function of such a formula becomes clear from an examination of Paul's writings. Note how in the following cases Paul asserts his authority over that of his "opponents" by referring to his "vision" of the risen Christ. In 1 Cor. 9:1 he asks, "Have I not seen the Lord?" In Gal. 1:16 he claims that God "chose to reveal his son to (or, in) me in order that I might proclaim him among the Gentiles," and in Phil. 3:8 he stresses "the surpassing worth of knowing Jesus Christ, my Lord." In short, Christ's appearance to Paul bestowed upon him apostolic authority. It put him on equal footing with the community of Jerusalem apostles around Peter and James.

## HISTORICAL ELEMENTS BEHIND THE TRADITIONS

What really happened when Christ "appeared" to various persons, including Paul?

The verb "to appear" is the English rendering of the Greek *ophthe*, i.e., the third-person aorist passive of *horan*, to see. That means the Greek phrase *ophthe Kepha* could be translated either "he appeared to Cephas" or "he was seen by Cephas."

Furthermore, it should be observed that in 1 Cor. 15:3–7 Paul lumps together such very different phenomena as individual encounters and mass manifestations under the single bracket of *ophthe*. The appearances exhibit other differences, too: For Cephas the experience denoted by *ophthe* does not depend upon a previous process of communication, nor is it contingent upon the consolidation of a community (and thus other members of a chain of witnesses), but is first of all an immediate event, a *primary* experience. The latter also applies to Paul (see below, this page). But a difference between Peter and Paul lies in the fact that Peter saw Jesus *again*, whereas Paul had not previously seen Jesus. Indeed, he saw him for the first time. In other words, the appearance to Peter and others is at least based on their acquaintance with Jesus during his lifetime, but the vision of the later apostolic witnesses is based on the proclamation of Jesus as the risen Christ by the earlier ones. And the appearance to Paul must be further distinguished from those to the "later" figures, because it affects the persecutor of a community. (Though for this reason it is a primary experience.)

On the other hand Paul uses "he appeared" with reference to himself (verse 8), thus putting his encounter with Christ in parallel with the appearances of Christ to the other witnesses, and moreover in other places uses different verbs to express the same thing. Therefore one may legitimately employ these passages to clarify the phenomenon mentioned in 1 Cor. 15:5–8.

## OTHER PASSAGES IN PAUL ON HIS "ENCOUNTER" WITH CHRIST

*1 Cor. 9:1:*

> Am I not free? Am I not an apostle? Have I not seen Jesus our Lord? Are you not my own handiwork in the Lord?

Here, in the form of a rhetorical question, Paul claims to have seen Jesus. He uses the first person perfect of the verb *horan*, i.e., a form of the active (*heoraka*). Thus he is expressing the same substantive content as in 1 Cor. 15:8 as his own active sensory perception, and thus asserts the visual nature of the appearance mentioned in 1 Cor. 15:8. This is not surprising, for as noted above, the phrase "he appeared" could also be translated by "he was seen." 1 Cor. 9:1 is then the active perception of Christ which the "appearance" stated in 1 Cor. 15:8 presupposes.

In my view it must be that in both places the apostle is reporting a vision of Christ in his transformed spiritual resurrection corporeality. Otherwise it is hard to understand why Paul would employ the phrase "he appeared" in 1 Cor. 15:5–8 to argue for the certainty of the bodily resurrection. The statements about the future resurrection bodies of the believers (1 Cor. 15:35–49) must also be derived from the resurrection body of Christ, all the more so since Paul's principle is evident: as Christ, so Christians.

*Gal. 1:15–17a:*[5]

> (15) But when he who had set me apart from birth, and had called me through his grace, (16) chose to reveal his Son to [or, in] me, in order that I might proclaim him among the Gentiles, I did not confer with flesh and blood, (17a) nor did I go up to Jerusalem to those who were apostles before me.

Since this passage stands in the framework of an account of the pre-Christian and earliest Christian activity of Paul, the "revelation" must refer to a *particular* event. Here verse 12 ("I did not receive [the gospel] from man, nor was I taught it, but it came through a revelation of Jesus Christ") combined with verse 16 (cited above) makes it clear that the content of the event was a revelation either the object (objective genitive) or author (subjective genitive) of which was Christ. The theme of revelation fits the seeing in 1 Cor. 9:1 and its presupposition, the appearance in 1 Cor. 15:8. Note that in Gal. 1:15–17 Paul interprets his own calling in the light of callings of Old Testament prophets: Isa. 49:5; Jerem.1:5. Such an interpretation is the result of his reflection on the Damascus event. It corresponds to the fact that as a rule visionaries pondered about their visions and not infrequently believed they were granted visions based on earlier visions; hence their ability to give new interpretations to earlier visions.

*Phil. 3:8a:*

> Indeed, I count everything as loss because of the surpassing worth of knowing Christ Jesus my Lord.

In this verse Paul returns to a discussion of the "Damascus event." Here he is speaking of the knowledge (in Greek, *gnosis*) of Christ which has led him to see his life hitherto as "refuse." The context of verse 8a, in verses 2–11, is strongly stamped with polemic. As we saw in Gal. 1:15–17a and possibly 1 Cor. 9:1, he is responding to opponents from Jerusalem; here he stresses his blameless life in Judaism (verses 4–6) and distinguishes it from the righteousness that comes from faith as was revealed to him by the knowledge of Christ (verses 8–10). It is worth noting that the phrase "righteousness . . . through faith" appears in verse 9.

In this section we again have a theological interpretation of the "Damascus event" and no more than an intimation of what actually happened. Hence those scholars who think that there is no visionary element in Phil. 3 are overlooking the historical context. It is not that the visionary element has been excluded here, but that it has been set within the historical framework: 1 Cor. 9:1, Paul's statement that he has seen Jesus, provides the key for a historical understanding of the polemical statements of Phil. 3:4–11.

*2 Cor. 4:6:*

> For it is the same God who said, "Let light shine out in darkness," who has shone in our hearts to give the light of knowledge of the glory of God in the face of Christ.

This text may also reflect the "Damascus event," in which Paul is reported to have seen Christ in the form of light at his conversion; this would fit his remarks about the heavenly man (1 Cor. 15:49). But more than this, Paul would be putting his vision of Christ in parallel with the dawning of light on the morning of creation to express what had happened to him before Damascus.

## RESULT

Specifically, "Christ appeared to Paul" means that Paul saw the risen Christ in his glory. In and of itself the statement could signify either an inner vision or an outward vision, but clearly it reports an extraordinary event and a revelation. In other words, in it the visionary received insights into an otherworldly sphere of reality, which had an esoteric character and therefore represented secret knowledge. The whole event had a character of light and happened, like the vision of John (Rev. 1:10), in the spirit, i.e., in an ecstasy. In it, seeing and hearing were probably not mutually exclusive.

Thus the most apt description of what happened to Paul near Damascus is that he had a vision of a kind that occurs in the Hebrew Bible (cf. Job 4:12–16; Isa. 6; Dan. 10:4–21; Ezek. 1:1–3:15; Amos 7:1–9), in other Jewish sources (e.g., 1 En. 14; 4 Ezra 3:1–9:25), in numerous parallels from the Hellenistic and Roman environment of the New Testament, and in the New Testament itself (e.g., Acts 7:55–56; Rev. 1:13–16).[6] On 2 Cor. 12:2–4 see below, pp. 178–81.

## WHAT IS A VISION?

"Visions" are usually understood to be appearances of figures, things, or events, or perceptions of voices and sounds which have no external reality. As such they are, like dreams, initially neural phenomena. They happen *inside* the human mind or soul, though visionaries regularly describe them differently. They claim to perceive images and hear sounds *from outside*. So too, Paul certainly never doubted that he had seen Christ near Damascus. The vision had no less impact and influence on him than an objective fact would have had. However, the objectivity of the mode of expression cannot be used to impugn the fact that this is a religious expression of the subject.

A vision is a primary phenomenon, a religious experience abrogating both the limitations of space and time and the subject-object relationship, and occurring within a nonrational modality. It cannot be otherwise.

PAUL

## HOW MANY VISIONS DID PAUL HAVE?

This raises the question of whether Paul experienced anything similar at a later date. Could it be that the apostle continued to experience visions and revelations analogous to the one near Damascus?
In the interest of emphasizing the unique nature of Paul's Damascus
experience, many a Protestant scholar has rejected this. But let me
hasten to ask: After seeing Christ in his heavenly glory before Damascus would not Paul experience something similar if he saw Christ
again after his conversion? And if that is the case, is there a text in
which Paul talks about such a vision of Christ during his life as a
Christian? Not only is there, but since Paul even gives a date for this
vision—fourteen years before writing it down—we can date it to
within a decade of Paul's conversion vision. I refer, of course, to the
account in 2 Cor. 12.

*2 Cor. 12:1–10:*

> (1) I must boast; there is nothing to be gained by it, but I will go on
> to visions and revelations of the Lord.
>
> (2) **I know a man** in Christ who fourteen years ago **was caught
> up** *to third heaven*—**whether in the body or out of the body I do
> not know, God knows.**
>
> (3) And <u>I know this man—whether in the body or out of the
> body I do not know, God knows</u>—(4) that he **was caught up** *into
> Paradise* and he heard things that cannot be told, which man may
> not utter.
>
> (5) On behalf of this man I will boast, but on my own behalf, I
> will not boast, except of my *weaknesses*. (6) Though if I wish to boast,
> I shall not be a fool, for I shall be speaking the truth. But I refrain
> from it, so that no one may think more of me than he sees or hears
> me to be. (7) And therefore <u>to keep me from being too elated</u> from the
> abundance of revelations, a thorn was given me in the flesh, a mes-
> senger of Satan, to harass me, <u>to keep me from being too elated</u>. (8)
> Three times I begged the Lord to rid me of it; (9) but he said to me,
> "My grace is sufficient for you, for the (its) power is made perfect in
> *weakness*." I will all the more gladly boast of my *weaknesses*, that the
> power of Christ may rest upon me. (10) For the sake of Christ, then,

I am content with *weaknesses*, insults, hardships, persecutions, and calamities; for when I am weak, then I am strong.

Apparently, the substance of the charge which led Paul to write 2 Cor. 10:12 through 12:18, the unit of which the present text is a part, was that his endowment with the spirit of God was defective. Note the anti-Pauline slogan implicit in 2 Cor. 10:1: "He is weak when face to face with you (plural), but bold to you when he is away" (I have changed the first person singular into the third person singular). The charge recurs in a different form in 2 Cor. 11:6: Paul is "unskilled in speaking." This theme is taken up again in 2 Cor. 13:1–3:

(1) This will be my third visit to you. The evidence of two or three witnesses must sustain any charge. (2) To those who sinned in the past and to all the others I give the warning now while absent, as I did when present on my second visit, that if I come again I will show no leniency. (3) Then you will have the proof you seek of the Christ who speaks through me. He is not weak in dealing with you, but is powerful in you.

The last sentence shows that those addressed are "pneumatics," i.e., those empowered by Christ's spirit. They are calling for proof that the same applies to Paul. Until it is given they question his spiritual empowerment and authority.

In 2 Cor. 12:1b, "but I will go on to visions and revelations of the Lord," Paul is taking up a new topic in the current discussion. By means of 2 Cor. 12:2–9 he is seeking to prove that he too can boast of visions and revelations of the Lord. Evidently these have been denied to him in Corinth. It was probably part of the charge of weakness (2 Cor. 10:10: "His letters . . . are weighty and powerful; but when he appears he has no presence, and as a speaker he is beneath contempt") that Paul could not point to any visions or revelations. The section, then, stands in the context of an argument, and we must be very cautious in any attempt to ascertain Paul's intention in it or to derive historical information from it.

*Verse 1a:* "I must boast" repeats 2 Cor. 11:30a, where he has justified his boasting of weakness. There after an oath (verse 31) Paul tells of his flight from Damascus (verses 32–33), which is evidently intended as an illustration of his weakness. So in 2 Cor. 12 the apostle is giving an account of an event which is similarly meant to show his weakness (verses 5b, 9).

*Verse 1b:* "Visions" and "revelations" are almost synonymous. Because of what follows, the genitive "of the Lord" is likely to be an objective genitive, i.e., the Lord is the "object" envisioned or revealed (see below, p. 181).

*Verses 2–4:* Paul writes in the third person, although he is talking about himself. In verses 7–10 he speaks of the temptation to be elated because of this special experience. So he was promptly given a "thorn in the flesh" to remind him of his mortality. By using the third person when talking about himself, Paul gives the statements an objective character and at the same time maintains a modesty of style, which becomes particularly clear in verses 5–6. The note "fourteen years" emphasizes the real character of the events described in what follows. The dating of the call visions of the Old Testament prophets has a similar function: cf. Isa. 6:1; Jer. 1:1ff.; Ezek. 1:1, etc.

Verse 2 and verses 3–4 exhibit a parallel structure. I have set verse 2 in bold face and the corresponding part of verses 4–5 in underlined bold font. Either verses 3–4a are a variation of verse 2—third heaven would be identical with paradise—or verses 3–4a contain a second heavenly journey into the paradise which lies beyond the third heaven. Because of the careful parallel stylization, preference is to be given to the former possibility, especially since in Judaic tradition paradise could be located in the third heaven (otherwise it is the seventh heaven). Furthermore, in the case of two different events a single chronological setting is hardly comprehensible, and yet the note "fourteen years ago" applies both to verse 2 and to verses 3–4a. So in verses 2–4 Paul is depicting a *heavenly journey*[7] which has many parallels in the world of early Christianity and its environment. The repetition of the narrative stresses the extraordinary nature of the event, and the dating asserts the historicity of the account. To be sure, it would also be possible to regard the event described by Paul as rapture, but it is not always possible to make a clean distinction between ascension and rapture.

The journey to heaven or rapture described by Paul anticipates for a moment the "going home" to the Lord which he so ardently hopes for in Phil. 1:21 (cf. 2 Cor. 5:1–2, 6–8). Both his claim not to know whether he was "in the body or outside the body" and the immediate addition of "God knows" interpret this event as caused by God in a gift of grace (verse 9; see also 2 Cor. 5:13). Although Paul does not describe the circumstances more closely, we may assume that the heavenly journey or rapture involved an experience of ecstasy. The way in which he speaks of himself in the third person fits this. One in ecstasy customarily distinguishes himself from normal people and speaks of himself as though he were someone else. Visionaries often have the awareness of experiencing their ecstasy in the form of a bodily rapture; in many other instances it is not clear to them whether their rapture is only in the spirit or also in the body. Since for Paul the result of this ecstatic experience is a temporary communion with the heavenly Christ—anticipating the eschatological communion—and since he elsewhere identifies "the Lord" with "the Spirit" (2 Cor. 3:17; Rom. 8:9–10), it can reasonably be concluded that in 2 Cor. 12 Paul is describing ecstasy as a "pneumatic" experience, that is, a spiritual encounter with the divine.

## EXCURSUS: CHRIST AND THE SPIRIT ACCORDING TO PAUL

The statement just made on the close relationship of Christ and the Spirit needs some substantiation. Let us therefore look at a central Pauline text, Rom. 8:9–11:

> (9) But you are not in the flesh, you are in the *Spirit*, if the *Spirit* of God really **dwells in you**. If someone does not possess the *Spirit* of Christ, he does not belong to him. (10) But if Christ [**dwells**] **in you**, then although the body is a dead thing <u>because of</u> sin, yet the spirit is life itself <u>because of</u> righteousness. (11) If the *Spirit* of him who raised Jesus from the dead dwells in you, he who raised Jesus from the dead will give life to your mortal bodies also through his *Spirit* which **dwells in you**.

In verse 9 the Spirit of God and the Spirit of Christ are used interchangeably to describe what dwells within Christians. Indeed, Christ abides in Christians (verse 10) and the Spirit of the One who raised Jesus from the dead dwells in them (verse 11). However, in thus binding the Spirit to God—just as he bound ecstasy to God in 2 Cor. 12—Paul is preventing any autonomy of those who bear the Spirit and thus understands the gift of the Spirit as sheer grace. That does not alter the fact that Spirit (of God) and Christ stand in parallel and are ultimately identical. In the same way the formulae we find elsewhere correspond; cf. "in Christ" (Gal. 3:28, etc.) and "in the Spirit" (Gal. 5:25, etc.).

This coalescing of the Spirit and Christ in Paul confirms what has been said about the Damascus event, in which Paul saw Jesus as a spiritual heavenly being. Against this it might be argued that Paul never designates "the Risen One" who appeared to him and to the other apostles explicitly as Spirit or attributes the vision to the working of the Spirit. But is not 1 Cor. 15 with its reference to the spiritual body of "the Risen One" (verse 45) an answer to the question of what figure of "the Risen Lord" Paul saw before Damascus?

In further confirmation of this, let me adduce the connection between Spirit and Christ in the Revelation of John and in the Gospel of John: The author of Revelation introduces his writing as a revelation of Jesus Christ which God gave him to show his servants what would happen soon. But then it is "in the Spirit" that he sees all his visions. It is Christ who orders him to send the seven letters in which the following formula constantly occurs, "He who has an ear, let him hear what the Spirit says to the churches" (Rev. 2:7, 11, 17, 29; 3:6, 13, 22; cf. 13:9).

The two notions also run side by side in the farewell speeches of the Gospel of John: The Lord promises to return to his disciples and to show himself to them (14:3, 18–19, 21, 23, 28; 16:16), and on the other hand he promises to send the Paraclete to them instead of himself (14:16–17, 26; 15:26; 16:17–25).

Thus the question is not whether appearances of Christ and appearances of the Spirit are explicitly identified in a theological, didactic way. The question is rather whether, from a historical and phenomenological perspective, in the earliest period of the Church the experience of Christ was an experience of the Spirit, and being touched by the Spirit was being moved by Christ.

## CONTINUATION OF THE ANALYSIS OF 2 COR. 12:1–10

"He heard things which cannot be told" (2 Cor. 12:4) can mean either that the words cannot be recalled or that they may not be repeated. Because of the continuation, "which man may not utter, . . ." the second possibility is to be preferred.

In Jewish and Greek accounts of ascensions, what the persons concerned saw and heard is often reported in greater or lesser detail. By contrast, Paul merely states that he "heard things that cannot be told, which man may not utter" (verse 4). He does not say whether he saw anything or, if he did, what it was. However, his use of the word "paradise" offers a strong hint. He felt the place where the "journey" ended to be paradise and "knew" where he was—probably by recognizing what he saw. Above all, in addition to angels and the righteous he may be presumed to have seen the Lord himself on his throne (cf. Acts 7:55–56; Rev. 1:9–11).

The following instances show that seeing and hearing often occur together in such heavenly journeys and revelations:

IV Ezra 10:55–56: "Go in and _see_ the splendor and the glory of the building. . . . Then you will _hear_ as much as your ears can grasp and _hear_."

Rev. 1:2: John "bore witness to the _word_ of God, and to the testimony of Jesus Christ, even to all that he _saw_."

Rev. 1:12: "I turned _to see_ the _voice_ that _spoke_ to me."

Verse 5: Paul argues that the vision given by God justifies his boasting of the one who received the vision, but as for himself, he will boast only of his weakness. According to Paul the grace of God is visible on this earth only in weakness, even if communion with Christ is real in the present. It should be noted that later (verse 10)

Paul will say that in weakness he is strong, i.e., he is even stronger than the Corinthians who similarly boast of visions. To the Corinthians this most likely sounded like false humility: "I was exalted by God, but remain a humble fellow who proclaims only his failings: See how modest and noble I am."

*Verse 6a*: This verse takes up verse 5a and emphasizes Paul's right to boast of his journey to heaven. The theme of being a fool harks back to 2 Cor. 11:1, 16, 19; and 2 Cor. 12:11 shows that Paul regards 2 Cor. 12:1–10 as a compulsion to speak as a fool, for only a fool boasts. To understand "boast" better, we need to supplement it with either "about the visions" or "about weakness": "Though I boast about weakness I shall not be a fool, for I speak the truth."

*Verse 6b*: The phrase "than he sees or hears me to be" means what it says, namely that Paul is not going to boast because he does not want to make himself look good—i.e., other than what they see and hear for themselves.

*Verse 7*: I suggest the following understanding of this difficult verse: To keep me from getting too swelled-headed because of the visions, God decided to give me a dose of reality to remind me of my mortality. This verse contains a *mythical* description of an illness of Paul. The expression "angel of Satan" presupposes that the angels which serve Satan are subject to him (cf. Matt. 25:41; Rev. 12:9, etc.) and that Satan, his angels, and evil demons cause sicknesses (cf. Job 2:7, etc.). *Thus in Paul the vision and sickness are related.* The revelations are accompanied by a sickness so that Paul does not exalt himself above others. The sinfulness of self-exaltation is an ancient Jewish theme: note the fall of Adonijah in 1 Kings 1–2 and Ezek. 29:15. Those who exalt themselves will be punished or brought down. At this point Paul is evidently rationalizing (despite the mythological language) the juxtaposition of revelations and sicknesses in his own person.

*Verses 8–9a*: These verses tell of Paul's request for remission and Christ's assurance that his power is at work in weakness. Verse 8 contains clear evidence of prayer to Jesus, which is elsewhere rarely attested in the letters of Paul (cf. 1 Cor. 1:2, "call on the name of the Lord"; 1 Thess. 3:11–12). Verse 9a contains the negative answer to Paul's prayer, for the healing is refused. It is the only word of the

Lord that Paul cites in 2 Corinthians. One may assume that he received such an answer through a revelation, especially since revelations have been mentioned previously.

Probably the event described in verses 8 and 9 is another ecstatic experience (note the audition in verse 9a), which is either part of the same event found in verses 2–4 or one which in Paul's memory has become fused with the prior event. In any case, it is clear that Paul understands an inherent relation between the exaltation and the interpretation of his weakness by the heavenly Christ.

*Verse 9b*: In this clause Paul paraphrases verse 9a, now as a remark of his own. In so doing he claims the word of the Lord as a meaningful interpretation of the situation.

*Verse 10*: Verse 10a builds a bridge to the context (the specific sufferings epitomize 2 Cor. 11:23–27), and verse 10b ("for when I am weak, then I am strong") provides a weighty conclusion.

## THE VISION NEAR DAMASCUS
## AND THE VISION BEHIND 2 COR. 12

One important result of the previous section is the conclusion that in 2 Cor. 12 Paul describes a journey to heaven or a rapture that is combined with an audition and perhaps also a vision of paradise and the heavenly Lord. It resulted in, or was combined with, an illness. That brings us to the point of attempting to identify the relationship between Paul's first vision of Christ "near Damascus" (cf. 1 Cor. 9:1; 15:8; Gal. 1:17) and the vision behind 2 Cor. 12. The location "near Damascus" for Paul's first vision follows from Gal. 1:17 (see above, p. 31).

In terms of the psychology of religion the conversion vision and the heavenly journey seem to be two different events: in the first instance Christ descended and appeared to Paul; in the second Paul ascends to the Lord in heaven. However, both consist of a vision, and here 2 Cor. 12 is richer. Both events culminate in a hearing of the Lord, but the content is different. The reason why Paul did not simply tell the Corinthians about his vision near Damascus in 2 Cor.

12 may be that they already knew about it from Paul himself when he founded the community. But note that Damascus is mentioned (2 Cor. 11:32) in the section immediately preceding 2 Cor. 12.

It is important to observe that in both the vision near Damascus and the one behind 2 Cor. 12, an illness is part of the event (2 Cor. 12:7/Acts 9:8). According to Acts Paul became blind, whereas 2 Cor. 12 does not allow any closer definition.

But is Acts reliable at this point? To answer this we must examine the pertinent text, Acts 9:3–19a:

(3) While he (Saul) was still on the road and nearing Damascus, suddenly a light from the sky flashed all around him. (4) And he fell to the ground and heard a voice saying to him, *"Saul, Saul, why do you persecute me?"* (5) *And he said, "Who are you, Lord?" And he said, "I am Jesus, whom you are persecuting; (6) but rise and enter the city, and you will be told what you have to do."* (7) The men who were traveling with him stood speechless; they heard the voice but could see no one. (8) Saul got up from the ground; and when he opened his eyes, he could not see; so they led him by the hand and brought him into Damascus. (9) *And for three days he was without sight, and took no food or drink.*
(10) There was a disciple at Damascus *called* Ananias. The Lord said to him in a vision, "Ananias." And he said, "Here I am, Lord." (11) And the Lord said to him, "Rise and go to Straight Street, and inquire in the house of Judas for a man of Tarsus *called* Saul. You will find him at prayer. (12) He has had a vision of a man *called* Ananias coming in and laying his hands on him so that he might regain his sight." (13) *But Ananias answered, "Lord, I have heard from many about this man, how much evil he has done to your saints at Jerusalem; (14) and here he has authority from the chief priests to bind all who invoke your name." (15) But the Lord said to him, "Go, for he is my chosen instrument to bear my name before the Gentiles and kings and sons of Israel; (16) for I will show him how much he must suffer for the sake of my name."* (17) So Ananias departed and entered the house. And laying his hands on him he said, "Brother Saul, the Lord Jesus who appeared to you on the road by which you came, has sent me that you may recover your sight and be filled with the Holy Spirit." (18) And immediately something like scales fell from his eyes and he recovered his sight. Then he rose and was baptized, (19a) *and took food and his strength returned.*

*Outline*

Verses 3–9: The christophany to Saul near Damascus
    3a: Travel note with information about the location
    3b: Appearance of light
    4a: Saul falls down
    4b–6: Conversation between Jesus and Saul
    7: The reaction of the companions
    8–9: The effect of the phenomenon on Saul

Verses 10–19a: Ananias's vision of Christ with the commission; he
    carries it out
    10a: Introduction of the figure of Ananias with information
        about locality
    10b: Information about the form of perception (vision)
    10c–16: Conversation in the vision and command
    17–19a: Laying on of hands, which leads to the regaining of
        Saul's sight and his baptism by Ananias

## LUKE'S INTENTION

At the redactional level this is the second of three conversion stories
narrated in Acts. The account is connected with the previous peri-
cope (8:26–40) about Philip and the Ethiopian eunuch and the subsequent story of Cornelius (10:1–11:18) in that each time the actions
of two people are connected and coordinated. In the Cornelius story
this comes about through duplicate visions, as it does in the present
story. A significant difference is that Saul's encounter occurs in an
emotionally charged context (see 9:1), involves Jesus, and constitutes a conversion experience; Ananias receives a traditional Old
Testament vision from God which commissions a specific action (cf.
Gen. 22:1). By contrast 8:26–40 simply reports the appearance of an
angel of the Lord to Philip, who is sent by this angel to the eunuch.
Unlike the second figure in the narratives in Acts 9 (Ananias) and
Acts 10–11 (Peter), the eunuch himself has not received a corresponding vision. This makes it clear that the three stories in ques-

tion belong together and have been arranged by Luke toward a climax, for the first story is the most simple and the third the most developed story with the Saul-Ananias story belonging rightly in the center. This suggests that Luke was the first to give narrative status to the vision of Ananias in order to incorporate the story into the wider narrative.

## THE INFORMATION AVAILABLE TO LUKE AND ITS HISTORICAL VALUE

The tradition behind verses 3–19a reports, in agreement with the letters, that a particular event made the persecutor a preacher, an enemy of Christ a disciple of Christ (cf. Gal. 1: 15–16a, 23b). Furthermore, the information that the conversion took place near Damascus is likely historically accurate (cf. Gal. 1:17c). The tradition further agrees with Paul's own testimony in reporting an appearance of Christ.

I am inclined to regard the existence of a disciple Ananias who healed Paul as historical. First, the name Ananias is almost certainly not an invention since there was already another Ananias, the hostile high priest (Acts 23:2), and yet another Ananias who was struck dead for fraud (Acts 5:1–6). Second, an illness as the concomitant of a vision was previously documented (see above, pp. 182–83) and that would easily stand in accord with the blindness resulting from Paul's first encounter with Christ.

## PRELIMINARY RESULT

Paul was convinced that it was God's call that made him an apostle. This calling had similarities with the calling of Old Testament prophets.

For Paul, his calling marked the beginning of the end time, for it was the calling to be an apostle of Jesus Christ, the Son whom God had raised from the dead.

The calling bestowed on Paul authority and put him on an equal footing with the apostles before him in Jerusalem (cf. Gal. 1:17).

Paul's call to be an apostle meant participating in the sufferings of Christ as well as the trials incident to apostleship (see the catalogues in 2 Cor. 11:23–27 and 2 Cor. 12:10).

## WHAT WAS THE REAL REASON FOR PAUL'S CONVERSION?

But why was it not enough for Paul simply to be a member of the Christian movement? Why did he have to be an apostle, even *the* apostle to the Gentiles? The answer to this is no doubt rooted in his character. Let me put it simply: As a Jew he claimed to have surpassed his Jewish contemporaries. The same was true for him afterward. As a Christian he claimed to have worked more than all the other apostles (1 Cor. 15:10) and to have a greater gift for speaking in tongues than any of the Corinthians (1 Cor. 14:18). A person like Paul always had to be "number one." Since at the time of his conversion the place of apostle to the Gentiles was still not filled, Paul was eager—of course subconsciously—to assume that exalted position.

But why did Paul change from Judaism to Christianity? Why didn't he remain within Judaism where he could have filled a very important post? I shall try to suggest a credible answer to this question by an analysis of Paul's complex—and no doubt largely subconscious—pattern of motivation. If anything can, it may explain his claim to be the apostle to the Gentiles.[8] Paul's pre-Christian period, which lasted until he was around thirty, had been characterized by a great zeal for the law (Phil. 3:6), which expressed itself in the persecution of Christians (Gal. 1:23). The reason for this lay in the proclamation of the crucified Messiah and, even more, the *de facto* disregard of the Torah which resulted from social dealings with Gentiles (Gentile Christians) from the time of the Hellenists around Stephen onward. Paul actively persecuted Christians, whereas other Jews like "Gamaliel" counseled waiting (Acts 5:38–39). In other words, the preaching of the early Christians did not automatically generate persecution; rather, the persecution came from a particular Jewish group of which Paul was a leader.

The sources tell us little about the change in Paul from persecuting the Christians to proclaiming Christ, apart from the fact that it was a sudden upheaval. Reference should be made especially to Gal. 1:23 ("He who once persecuted us is now proclaiming the faith he once tried to destroy") as part of a thanksgiving to God (on this text see above, p. 151) for the sudden change in the persecutor of Christians.

The once popular use of a passage from Paul's letter to the Romans (Rom. 7:7–25a) to understand the shift in his life story is now generally repudiated. In this chapter Paul purports to describe his mental turmoil before he turned to Christ. Three objections have been made to a biographical understanding of his "ego-analysis": (a) The ego is a rhetorical or stylistic form, as for instance in the Psalms of the Hebrew Bible; (b) Rom. 7 is to be understood in the context of the letter: its retrospective form indicates a theological, not historical, description of the pre-Christian self; (c) in other passages, like Phil. 3:6, where the apostle claims to have been blameless in the observation of the Jewish law, Paul does not give any indication of conflict in his pre-Christian life.

Against the first two points it has to be said that a biographical understanding is certainly not ruled out here. Indeed, a reference to the theological form of this retrospective does not necessarily rule out the historical question of how far Paul's theological interpretation of his own life has a biographical nucleus.

In defending the third point, quite a few scholars affirm that the solid self-confidence that is reflected in Phil. 3:6 excludes any split in the personality of the pre-Christian Paul. "Paul believed that he could live up to the high demands of perfect observance of the Torah of a Pharisaic kind, without any qualifications."[9] However, such a reference to Phil. 3:6 takes too little account of the argumentative character of the text, in which the apostle was concerned to bring out his perfection in the fulfillment of the law (cf. Gal. 1:13–14). Moreover, one can be proud in the awareness of one's nomistic achievements and at the same time be unconsciously coping with a conflict.

This brings me to an attempt at an explanation in terms of depth psychology, which considers explanation the key to understanding. It seeks on the one hand to increase our knowledge about Paul's conversion and on the other hand to grasp its significance.

The need to ask psychological questions must be stressed. If, for example, one studied primitive Christianity or another religious group like the Mormons in an exclusively historical and source-critical way, one would simply skirt the problem of personal dynamics and not penetrate into the mystery of these groups and the persons attached to them. It is not enough to study the reports from and about these groups and persons. The faith of the first Christians, for example, derives from emotions, assumptions, and goals we can at least begin to identify and understand. And surely a historical study of the resurrection of Jesus or the belief of individual Christians that they "saw" Jesus after his death has to be supplemented by the enhanced understanding of the human mind and personality that modern psychology has afforded us. This is nothing but the consistent extension and deepening of the historical investigation of the life of the individual by pursuing it into the subconscious sources of perception and motivation.

As I have already indicated above, the source texts indicate that the pre-Christian Paul was a committed, zealous persecutor of Christians. This vigorous reaction on Paul's part indicates that the basic elements of the preaching of Christians had had a powerfully disturbing effect on him. The encounter with Christians and their preaching and practice took place not only at a cognitive level but also at an emotional and unconscious one, as is probably true of all social and religious experiences. Behind Paul's vehemently aggressive antagonism to Christians there must have been an inner build-up in his person of the kind that depth-psychology has ascertained in other cases to be the basic motivation for aggressive behavior; it is also something that has been described in art and literature. It is not difficult to imagine that the basic elements of Christian preaching and practice unconsciously attracted Paul, and that, recoiling against his subconscious but all-consuming needs for acceptance and self-importance, he projected them onto the Christians so as to justify attacking them all the more savagely.

Sometimes another explanation of Paul's excessive zeal for the law is introduced, namely that his fanaticism sprang from an authoritative belief that the teachings of the Christians whom he persecuted sullied God's honor and destroyed the divinely willed purity of the Jewish community, and therefore had to be exterminated. But such a view makes it difficult to understand the sudden change from persecutor to preacher, unless one writes it off to a miracle, in which case there would be an end to any effort to arrive at a historical understanding.

Of course, fanatics often suppress the very doubts that define and commission their views of life and the ends they strive for. Paul shows clear evidence of conflicting emotions: a radical sense of guilt and unworthiness combined with an exalted self-image which results in the need to be an authority figure. Likely enough, the latter was an overcompensation for the former. At any rate, caught up in an intellectual and emotional maelstrom which can only have been intensified by his growing familiarity with the sect he was harrassing, he seems at last to have discovered the resolution of his problems. This humble and self-sacrificing Jesus represents a new vision of the Almighty: no longer a stern and demanding tyrant intent on punishing even those who cannot help themselves, but a loving and forgiving father who offers rest and peace to imperfect humans who accept his grace. Besides, by transforming this Jesus into a mythic Christ-Redeemer, Paul could become the Apostle-in-Chief of a new program of salvation with a culture-wide appeal. Something of that nature was in all likelihood the dynamic that impelled the persecutor turned proclaimer (dare one say promoter?) whose religious zeal was a measure of his inner tension, and was powerfully released in a vision of Christ.

Ironically, the Christians whom he persecuted may have brought the simmering yet unconscious yearning toward a Christ-figure to a boil. Paul wanted to find release by fighting an external enemy. That became his "destiny." But, of course, given his nature, he had to claim for himself the most important post that was vacant in primitive Christianity: the apostleship to the Gentiles.

What may we suppose the source of this inner revolt to have been? *First*, it must have had to do with the law. Romans 7 is too authentic, too "loaded with experience" and too alive, for Paul to have developed it as a purely theoretical construct. In other words it reflects real life. However, it was formulated in retrospect and describes the unconscious conflict which Paul endured before his conversion. *Second,* this conflict could have been sparked by the proclamation of a crucified Messiah (a crucified Messiah could not be the real Messiah). *Third,* it could have stemmed from revulsion at the universalistic tendencies of the preaching of the Hellenists whom Paul persecuted. When Paul approached Damascus, there was a catastrophic breakthrough. Paul fled from his painful situation into the world of hallucination from which he soon returned to make himself the apostle of Jesus Christ and finally the apostle to the Gentiles, commissioned by Christ himself.

## NOTES

1. For the analysis of 1 Cor. 15:1–11, see my book *The Resurrection of Jesus: History, Experience, Theology* (Minneapolis: Fortress Press, 1994), pp. 33–109, which I have freely used and revised.

2. In verse 4b I have translated the verb "has been raised" instead of "was raised" because the Greek has a perfect form whereas the other three verbs (died, was buried, appeared) are in the aorist. Perhaps this reflects a deliberate emphasis on the present and continuing significance of the resurrection in Paul. Cf. Paul's use of the perfect participle in "Christ crucified," which seems to indicate the existential presence of Christ for the apostle: 1 Cor. 1:23; 2:2; Gal. 3:1.

3. See my *Opposition to Paul in Jewish Christianity,* pp. 65–78.

4. On the bodily resurrection see above, pp. 123–25.

5. See the analysis of this passage and of Gal. 1–2 above, pp. 28–33, 39–46.

6. The most recent work on "Paul the visionary" is the one in German by Bernhard Heininger, *Paulus als Visionär: Eine religionsgeschichtliche Studie* (Freiburg: Herder, 1996). For older studies see my *Resurrection of Jesus,* pp. 54–79. See also Alan F. Segal, *Paul the Convert: The Apostolate and Apostasy of Saul the Pharisee* (New Haven and London, 1990), pp. 34–71 (chapter 2: "Paul's Ecstasy"). After a rich discussion of various Pauline and Jewish texts that stretch from the prophets of the Hebrew Bible to Kabbala, Segal comes to a somewhat negative conclusion and writes: "We shall never know Paul's experience. But we can see how Paul reconstructs it. In retrospect, Paul

construes his first Christian experience as (ecstatic) conversion" (p. 70). *Against this* I would assert that to some extent we do know what Paul's experience was in the same way that we do know about the content of our dreams last night. Whether we can know its actual content is, of course, another problem. However, I do not want to go into epistemology here. Segal's book like so many learned books today ends up in skepticism. Yet it deserves full support when it stresses that "Paul is the only mystic to report his own personal identifiably confessional mystical experience in the fifteen hundred years that separate Ezechiel from the rise of Kabbala" (p. 52).

7. See Alan F. Segal, "Heavenly Ascent in Hellenistic Judaism, Early Christianity and Their Environment," *Aufstieg und Niedergang der Römischen Welt* II 23.2 (Berlin/New York: Walter de Gruyter, 1980), pp. 1333–94.

8. For the following section see my *Heretics: The Other Side of Early Christianity* (Louisville: Westminster John Knox Press, 1996), pp. 67–76.

9. Martin Hengel, *The Pre-Christian Paul* (Philadelphia: Trinity Press International, 1991), p. 79.

# 8

# PAUL AND JESUS[1]

Many Christians think of Paul as one of the greatest disciples or followers of Jesus.[2] But such a claim is from the start beset with historical difficulties, for Paul did not know Jesus personally. Furthermore, Paul never calls himself a disciple or a follower of Jesus, nor does he claim to follow the example or the teaching of Jesus in the same way as those who followed the Lord during his lifetime. Therefore some contend that Paul founded a religion centered on Christ which has to be distinguished from the religion of Jesus the Jew. Yet other scholars continue to proclaim that Paul was one who truly understood the master and continued his work. The famous church historian Adolf Harnack (1851–1930) affirms this by making the statement:

> This opinion is borne out by the facts. Those who blame him for corrupting the Christian religion have never felt a single breath of his spirit . . . those who extol or criticise him as a founder of religion are forced to make him bear witness against himself on the main point, and acknowledge that the consciousness which bore him up and steeled him for his work was illusory and self-deceptive. As we cannot be wiser than history, which knows him only as Christ's emissary, and as his own words clearly attest what his aims were and what he was, we regard him as Christ's disciple, as the apostle who not only worked harder but also accomplished more than all the rest put together.[3]

*Against this an objection must be raised:* Of decisive importance in this connection is the fact that Paul's theology proper, with its theological, anthropological, and soteriological ideas, is in no way either a recapitulation of Jesus' own preaching or a further development of it. It is especially significant that he *never* adduces any of the sayings of Jesus on the Torah in favor of his own teaching about it.

## "REIGN OF GOD"—CENTRAL TO JESUS BUT MARGINAL FOR PAUL

One should note that the "Reign of God," a concept central to Jesus' gospel, is so marginal for Paul that it appears only in Rom. 14:17; 1 Cor. 4:20; 6:9–10; 15:50; and Gal. 5:21 (but see 1 Thess. 2:12). Conversely, Paul's repeated emphasis on "the righteousness of God" as a sine qua non of salvation has no parallel in Jesus' teaching. For Paul, God's righteousness is revealed in the gospel about Christ (Rom. 1:17); for Jesus, living by the "gospel" message means expecting and experiencing the kingdom of God.

It is of the utmost importance to address this doctrinal dissonance; for as the first Christian theologian, Paul not only defined primitive Christianity but propounded a call to faith and an orthodoxy of belief that still remains normative for most modern Christians. Whether one accepts Paul's testimony on faith or seeks to refine or strengthen a commitment to Christ, it should be of vital concern whether and to what degree the Pauline message of Jesus Christ is consonant with the life and teachings of the historical Jesus. The Christian who accepts the apostolic message of the resurrected Christ finds included within it the assertion that the risen Lord is the same Jesus of Nazareth who in his lifetime was known by a number of those who are reported to have been witnesses to his resurrection.

Thus the faith that seeks to explain itself in theological terms must somehow resolve the apparent disparity between the Jesus revealed by historical study and the Christ proclaimed by faith. If only in the interest of intellectual honesty, the Christian whose faith is rooted in the New Testament message is duty bound to learn as much as possible about the Jesus on whom his faith is based. Surely an informed acquaintance with the historical Jesus must be the first step in the achievement of a genuine and therefore critical faith.

The task just described, like Caesar's Gaul, can be divided into three parts:

(1) We must determine whether the life of the earthly Jesus from his birth to the cross mattered for Paul, and if so, in what way? And in order to answer this question we must ask another: What was Paul's view of Christ?

(2) If the first elicits a positive answer one has to ask another: What traditions of Jesus, if any, did Paul use in his letters and during his missionary activity?

(3) After dealing with those two problems we will have to present a systematic evaluation of Paul's relation to Jesus. This section will include a comparison of the historical place of Paul and that of Jesus.

## THE RISEN JESUS IS THE EARTHLY JESUS

The previous chapters have made it clear that for Paul the Risen Christ was of primary, indeed of the utmost importance. He had appeared to Paul near Damascus calling him to be his apostle. Moreover, he was present in the community of the saints who confessed him to be Lord, and would come back on the clouds of heaven to establish his kingdom. Though when confessing Christ as the **Lord**, Paul is thinking in the first place of the resurrected One, still he repeatedly uses this title also to speak of Jesus between his birth and death. The following passages will serve to illustrate this:

> "To the married I give this ruling, not I but the **Lord**, that the wife must not separate from her husband . . . and that the husband must not divorce his wife" (1 Cor. 7:10–11).

> "The **Lord** gave charge to those who proclaim the gospel that they live by the gospel" (1 Cor. 9:14).

> "The **Lord** Jesus on the night he was handed over took bread . . ." (1 Cor. 11:23–25).

> "[The Jews] who killed the **Lord** Jesus and the prophets . . ." (1 Thess. 2:15).

". . . God has raised the **Lord** and will also raise us . . ." (1 Cor. 6:14).

". . . the cross of our **Lord** Jesus . . ." (Gal. 6:14).

". . . the brothers of the **Lord** . . . James, the **Lord's** brother" (1 Cor. 9:5/Gal. 1:19).

"For you know the grace of our **Lord** Jesus Christ, that he, being rich, yet for your sakes became poor . . ." (2 Cor. 8:9).

Therefore it seems inescapable that in speaking of "God's Son, Christ Jesus whom we proclaimed among you" (2 Cor. 1:19) he refers to both the man Jesus *and* the Risen Lord. Clearly the Jesus of Paul's proclamation *included* his human existence, his work, and his message. In view of Paul's emphasis on the birth of God's son (cf. Gal. 4:4: "But when the time was fulfilled, God sent his Son, born of a woman, born under the law") and the heavenly preexistence of the divine son who was of woman born (see the text below from Philemon) this is beyond any doubt. At the same time the passage in Gal. 4:4 seems to exclude Paul's knowledge of the virgin birth.[4]

In referring to Jesus as "Lord" he has taken a title belonging to the Resurrected One and assigned it retroactively to the earthly Jesus, and then to the Preexistent One. This characteristically Pauline merging of personae is indisputable evidence that when Paul speaks of the resurrected Lord, the man Jesus is at the same time in his mind, and that for Paul the man Jesus and the preexistent and risen Lord are one and the same.

Still it was important to Paul that Jesus was born a Jew (Rom. 1:3; 15:8) and lived under the law (Gal. 3:1). When the apostle refers to Jesus as somebody to imitate or as an example, he thinks of both the preexistent *and* the earthly Jesus (see Rom. 15:2–3; 1 Cor. 11:1; 2 Cor. 8:9; 10:1; 1 Thess. 1:6) who serves as the main figure in a cosmic drama. His sonship is to be seen in his obedient fulfillment of God's will. Not only is his obedience the key quality adduced in the early hymn Paul records in Phil. 2:6–11, specifically in verses 7–8,

(7) [He] emptied himself taking the form of a servant, being born in the likeness of man. (8) And being found in human form he humbled himself and became obedient unto death, even unto death on the cross,

but the Apostle also contrasts it with Adam's disobedience: "As through the *disobedience* of the one man the many were made sinners, so through *obedience* of the one the many will be made righteous" (Rom. 5:19).

## THE PROBLEM OF 2 COR. 5:16

In view of these facts it is strange that some have drawn the conclusion that Jesus' life was of no significance whatever for Paul. They have amplified this with the statement in 2 Cor. 5:16:

Henceforth we know no one according to the flesh; if indeed we had known Christ according to the flesh, we no longer know him thus.

But this is clearly a misconstrual and a misapplication of 2 Cor. 5:16, for therein Paul is not denying interest in the real-life Jesus. He is not talking about "Christ in the flesh," but about knowing Christ "from a human point of view" (RSV). What Paul rejects is a relation to Jesus that is limited to empirical, this-worldly cognition. In short, while Paul is far from a systematic biographer, it is incorrect to say that the man Jesus was of no interest to him.

As noted above, Paul seldom quotes Jesus; still he occasionally refers or alludes to sayings of Jesus—or so attributes sayings—often without direct citation (on this see further on pp. 201–208). This is not so difficult to understand when we recognize that while he presents Jesus as the authority (cf. 1 Cor. 7:10), Paul can always claim for himself, as one commissioned by Christ, the mantle of present authority. Note, for example, 1 Cor. 7:40: "But I think that I, too, have the spirit of God."

## DEATH AND RESURRECTION OF JESUS
## AS THE MAIN FOCUS IN PAUL

In short, Paul appeals to Jesus' life and teachings when doing so suits his agenda, but the unchanging focus of his proclamation is Jesus' death and resurrection. For only thus have sin and death been conquered, and God's plan of salvation at last actualized (Rom. 8:3; cf. Col. 1:22; 2:14–15). Herein rests the dynamic appeal of Paul's message, and hence he can unequivocally pronounce the crucified Christ as the essence of his gospel: "But we preach Christ crucified, a stumbling block to Jews and folly to Gentiles" (1 Cor. 1:23); "You foolish Galatians . . . before whose eyes Jesus Christ has been proclaimed as crucified" (Gal. 3:1). Since this man is of central importance to the apostle's proclamation, it seems strange indeed that the epistles so seldom make reference to his life and teachings.

## THE EXTENT AND THE ROLE OF
## JESUS' SAYINGS IN PAUL

Having concluded that Jesus' earthly ministry did figure into Paul's formulation of Christianity, we must, as our task description demanded, determine the extent and the role of Jesus' teaching in Paul's thinking. I want to propose that the *first* step should be to consider those places where Paul explicitly cites sayings of Jesus. In these, at any rate, there is a reasonable likelihood that Paul is quoting a saying that came down to him in the tradition as a word of the Lord. But then in a *second* step we should examine the possibility that the letters might contain allusions to or echoes of Jesus' sayings. Hand in hand with these two tasks we must continually ask whether these quotations and/or allusions go back to the historical Jesus, or only reflect a proclaimed Christ.[5]

## QUOTATIONS OF SAYINGS OF JESUS

*1 Cor. 7:10–11:*

> (10) To the married I give this ruling, not I but the Lord, that the wife must not separate from her husband, (11) but if she does, let her remain single or else be reconciled to her husband, and that the husband must not divorce his wife.

The prohibition of divorce has parallels in Mark 10:1–12 and Q (Matt. 5:32/Luke 16:18). Note, however, that the earliest stratum of the tradition is reflected by Q, where only the husband's right to divorce his wife is presupposed. In both Mark and Paul the wife has the right to initiate a divorce, a provision clearly derived from Greco-Roman law. And not only that: Paul's is the earlier mention of this case, for he has obviously met women in his communities who availed themselves of a right familiar to their culture. In other words, although he quotes the Lord, the historical Jesus cannot possibly have spoken the words that Paul attributes to him because he had said nothing about women initiating a separation. Either Paul's prescription is a developed form of the saying or he has applied an earlier, less developed saying to the situation in Corinth. The same can be said for the first evangelist, who in Matt. 5:32 (cf. Matt. 19:9) uses the Q-saying on divorce but, no doubt because of cases of fornication in his community, has Jesus allow divorce in such instances.

*1 Cor. 9:14:*

> The Lord gave charge to those who proclaim the gospel that they live by the gospel.

Paul refers to the Lord here because he wants to build up a strong case for the support of missionaries even though it is a perquisite he repudiates in his own case. (He had on purpose not accepted any support from the Corinthians.) So far is he from applying to himself the words of the Lord as a new tradition. In 1 Cor. 9 he adduces the following points in asserting the right to support: reason and common experi-

ence (verse 7), the Old Testament (verse 9), universal religious practice (verse 13), and the teaching of Jesus himself (verse 14). All these
support the custom by which apostles and other ministers are maintained at the expense of the church built up by their ministry.

Presumably the saying Paul has in mind is the one contained in
Q: ". . . The laborer deserves his food/his wages" (Matt. 10:10/Luke
10:7). It does not go back to the historical Jesus but has been
ascribed to him later (cf. Deut. 24:15; Jer. 22:13, et al.)

(On *1 Cor. 11:23–25* see above, pp. 148–51.)

*1 Cor. 14:37:*

> If any one thinks himself to be a prophet or spiritual person, let him
> recognize that what I am writing to you is the command of the Lord
> (in some manuscripts, "comes from the Lord").

There can be no doubt that some in Corinth thought themselves to
be prophets or spiritual persons. Against their authority Paul insists
that he, too, has the mind of Christ, i.e., the authority of Christ (cf. 1
Cor. 7:25, 40). Thus the above text cannot be used as an instance of
a word of Jesus.

*2 Cor. 12:9:*

> My grace is sufficient for you, for the (its) power is made perfect in
> *weakness.*

On this saying see above, p. 182.

*1 Thess. 1:8:*

> For not only has the word of the Lord sounded forth from you in
> Macedonia and Achaia, but your faith in God has gone forth every-
> where, so that we need not say anything.

Here, of course, the "word of the Lord" refers not to a saying of Jesus
but to the success of Paul's missionary efforts in Thessalonica.

*Acts 20:35:*

Jesus said: "It is more blessed to give than to receive."

This purported saying of Jesus is part of Paul's speech at Miletus to the church elders of Ephesus. It has a certain affinity to a Persian maxim reconstructed from Thucydides 2.97.4: "to give rather than receive." There is another parallel in 1 Clem. 2:1, but not as a saying of Jesus.

## ALLUSIONS TO SAYINGS OF JESUS

*Rom. 12:14:*

Bless those who persecute you; bless and do not curse them.

This is a likely echo of Jesus' command in Matt. 5:44, "Love your enemies, and pray for those who persecute you." But Luke 6:27, the Q-parallel to Matt. 5:44, shows that Rom. 12:14 constitutes a more developed form of Jesus' command. In Luke 6:27 we read simply, "Love your enemies." It appears that Paul must have known a later version of Jesus' command to love one's enemies that included the reference to persecution like the Matthew version of Q.

*Rom. 12:17a:*

Never pay back evil for evil.

This verse echoes Matt. 5:39a ("Do not resist evil"). A dependence of Paul on Jesus at this point is excluded because Matt. 5:38–39a derives from the author of the first gospel.[6]

*Rom. 12:21b:*

Conquer evil with good.

While finding no precise parallel in the synoptic Gospels, we naturally think of Jesus' advocacy of nonresistance (see Matt. 5:39b–42).

Still, the fact of Paul's affinity for this repeated theme hardly justifies seeing this verse as an allusion to Jesus' words. For further evidence of this, note the parallel in Testament of the Twelve Patriarchs, Benjamin 12: "Doing good he conquers evil."

*Rom. 13:7:*

> Pay all of them their due: taxes to whom taxes are due, revenue to whom revenue is due, respect to whom respect is due, honor to whom honor is due.

This verse bears some resemblance to Mark 12:17: "Give to Caesar what is Caesar's and to God what is God's." Since the second half is absent from Paul, however, a direct relation cannot be claimed.

*Rom. 13:8–10:*

> (8) Owe nothing to anyone except to *love* one another; for he who *loves* someone other than himself has fulfilled the law. (9) The commandments—You shall not commit adultery, You shall not kill, You shall not steal, You shall not covet, or any other commandment—are summed up in this one saying: You must love your neighbor as yourself. (10) love does no wrong to a neighbor that is why love is the essence of the law.

This statement of the central importance of love might be taken as a reprise of Jesus' teaching as reported in the synoptics (Mark 12:28–34; Matt. 22:34–40; Luke 10:25–28. But their two-part commandment is apocopated in Rom. 13 (cf. Gal. 5:14) to the single injunction to love one's neighbor. To be sure, this does not involve a contradiction, but the difference in form argues against direct derivation from Jesus. Of course Paul's animus against Judaism might be adduced to explain his omission of any clear reference to the Shema (Deut. 6:5), a thrice-daily recitation by observant Jews. Yet even if we admit that possibility, parallels in the Rabbinic literature indicate that Rom. 13:8–10 is not a demonstrable case of Paul quoting Jesus.

*Rom. 14:10a:*

> Why do you judge your brother?

Naturally we hear in this verse an echo of "Do not judge lest you be judged" (Matt. 7:1). But here again one can cite a number of parallels from the rabbinic literature. There is, for example, the famous saying of Hillel (early first century C.E.): "Do not judge your neighbor until you have gotten into his condition." When we note that the same injunction appears in Rom. 2:1 and James 4:11, we recognize that it would be much safer to assume that all these passages are variations on a common Jewish theme.

*Rom. 14:13:*

> Let us no longer judge one another, but rather decide never to put
> a stumbling block or an obstacle in a brother's way.

First of all, we must note that verse 13a is a clear echo of verse 10a ("Why do you judge your brother?"). Besides, the mere use of the "stumbling block" (*skandalon*), an image or motif which is similarly employed in synoptic sayings (Mark 9:42–47; Matt. 5:29–30; 18:6–9; Luke 17:1–2), is insufficient evidence that Paul here reflects these or similar Jesus traditions. Further, the appearance of the symbolic stumbling block in Lev. 19:14 suggests that Paul may be dependent on a much older tradition.

*Rom. 14:14:*

> As one who is in the Lord Jesus, I know and am convinced that
> nothing is unclean in itself; but it is unclean for any one who con-
> siders it unclean.

This, of course, has a familiar ring: "There is nothing that goes into a person from outside which can make him unclean: but those things that come forth from a man, they are what make people unclean." (Mark 7:15; cf. Matt. 15:11). In this passage, however, Paul is dealing with a particular issue involving the Roman community, and the phrase "in the Lord Jesus" is not in any way an attribution, but simply a formula by which he avows his association with the risen Lord as a basis for the correctness of his opinion. While Mark 7:15 is likely authentic, the reason for Paul and Jesus' agreement is uncertain; at any rate, whether this pronouncement of Paul comes from Jesus remains an open question. (Cf. also 1 Cor. 8:4 as a background of Rom. 14:14.)

*1 Thess. 4:8:*

> Therefore, whoever rejects this [God's call to holiness] rejects not man but God.

Some try to read into this verse a reference to Luke 10:16: "Whoever hears you hears me, and whoever rejects me rejects the One who has sent me." Unfortunately, their primary evidence, namely that the two passages contain the same verb, "reject" (*athetein*), is rather shaky support for the notion that Paul may have derived the saying from Jesus.

*1 Thess. 4:9b:*

> You are yourselves taught by God to love one another.

This has no direct synoptic parallel, but some have suggested that it shows a clear though unspecific affinity with the spirit of Jesus which, it is purported, Paul's thinking amply and consistently reflects. This may be a lovely sentiment, but it falls far short of being evidence.

*1 Thess. 4:15–17:*[7]

> (15) *This we say to you in a word of the Lord, that we who are alive, who are left until the Lord's coming, shall by no means precede those who have fallen asleep.* (16) For *the Lord himself* will descend from heaven with a cry of command, with the archangel's call, and with the sound of the trumpet of God. And the dead *in Christ* will rise *first;* (17) then we who are alive, who are left, shall be caught up

together with them in the clouds to meet *the Lord* in the air; *and so we shall always be with the Lord.*

The view that a saying of the Lord is contained in this section is supported primarily by verse 15a ("For this we say to you in a word of the Lord") which stands as an introduction to verses 15b–17. This conclusion is not undisputed. Some contend that verse 15a is not the introduction of a direct quotation, but a reference to Jesus using prophetic modes of discourse (cf. Sir. 48:3: "By the word of the Lord he [Elijah] shut up the sky and three times called down fire"). Moreover it is not clear whether the postulated quotation is to be found in verse 15b or in verses 16–17. Linguistic analysis indicates that phrases untypical of Paul appear specifically in verses 16–17. Moreover, an awkward fit between the terminology and the redactional context supports the assumption of an independent tradition in verses 16–17. Whereas Paul uses "those who have fallen asleep" for the dead in verse 13, verse 16 speaks of "the dead." Originally the saying in verses 16–17 may have referred to the descent of the "Son of Man," which Paul has replaced by "the Lord himself" in view of the understanding of the community in Thessalonica. The Pauline "in Christ" may also be an addition, as may also be verse 17b as a whole (cf. the we-style as in verse 15b).

Many scholars regard verses 16–17 as an authentic Jesus-tradition, which was perhaps spoken by Jesus forecasting the persecution of his disciples (Matt. 10:16–23). Their death will not put them at a disadvantage at the return of Jesus on the clouds of heaven. In terms of content, scholars have also cited some analogies in verses 16–17 to such sayings of Jesus as Matt. 10:39; 16:25, 28; 24:31, 34; 25:6; 26:64; Luke 13:30. However, none of these instances, including 1 Thess. 4:15–17, is really convincing. To discover in these verses an oblique reference to Jesus' teachings requires a vivid imagination indeed.

Rather, in 1 Thess. 4:16–17 we seem to have a Jewish "miniature apocalypse" which has been put into the mouth of Jesus—like the synoptic apocalypse in Mark 13 and parallels. The imagery used in verses 16–17 recalls the ancient Near Eastern ceremonial reception of the king and works with similar motifs and ideas, many of which are to be found in Jewish apocalyptic. Alongside the report of the Son of Man (4 Ezra 13:13), reference can be made to the notion, also attested elsewhere, that the dead take part in the eschatological salvation (4 Ezra 7).

Paul inserts this Jewish miniature apocalypse—which, however, he presents as a saying of the exalted Lord—into a wider appeal (1 Thess. 4:13–18) that he develops in view of the critical situation in Thessalonica. There the fate of members of the community who have already died is becoming a divisive issue. The death of some members of the community obviously led to hopelessness and mourning in the community—probably because the notion of the resurrection of Christians was unknown in Thessalonica. How can they attain the eschatological salvation at the return of Jesus if they have died?

Before tracing Paul's train of thought any further, let us examine the text of the two verses that precede verses 15–17 printed above:

*1 Thess. 4:13–14:*

> (13) But we do not want you to be ignorant, brothers, concerning those who have fallen asleep, that you may not grieve as others who have no hope. (14) For since we believe that Jesus died and rose again, even so, through Jesus, God will bring with him those who have fallen asleep.

Paul attempts to combine the notion of the return of Jesus with faith in the resurrection. After an exposition in verse 13, he makes use of the traditional creed of the death and resurrection of Christ, through which he confirms that the dead Christians will also have future communion with Christ (verse 14). Since Jesus died and rose again, the dead, too, will have a share in paradise. This statement, which is new to the Christians in Thessalonica, is explained further by what we earlier argued was a Jewish miniature apocalypse avowed by Paul to be a saying of the Lord (verses 16–17a). Verse 15 applies this in advance to those to whom Paul is writing and sums it up for them. The dead will not be at a disadvantage upon Christ's return, because through their resurrection they will be put in the same situation as the living. Both will experience communion with Christ as the result of being transported in order to meet the Lord in the air (verse 17b).

Verse 18 ("Therefore comfort one another with these words") serves as a concluding admonition.

*1 Thess. 5:2:*

> The day of the Lord comes like a thief in the night.

This uses the same image as the Q-parallel in Matt. 24:43/Luke 12:39. Cf. also Thomas 21:5; 2 Pet. 3:10a; Rev. 3:3b. The images used reflect common Jewish tradition (cf. Job 24:14; Hos. 7:1) and cannot be used as an instance of Paul's dependency on a saying of Jesus.

*1 Thess. 5:3:*

> When people say, "There is peace and security," then sudden destruction will come on them as the pangs that come on a woman with a child, and there will be no escape.

The suddenness of God's coming in judgment at the end of the world is, to be sure, also an element in the traditions of Jesus' sayings (cf. Luke 12:39; 21:34), but there are also many similar passages in the literature of Jewish apocalyptic. Nothing in the present text justifies a reference to synoptic traditions.

*1 Thess. 5:6:*

> So we must not sleep, as others do, but keep awake and sober.

Cf. Matt. 24:42: "Therefore be awake, because you do not know on what day your Lord is coming" (cf. Mark 13:35; Luke 21:36). However, admonitions to watchfulness and sobriety are frequent in Jewish apocalyptic literature.

*1 Thess. 5:13b:*

> You must live at peace among yourselves.

This is very close to Mark 9:50: "Be at peace with one another." However, the phrase in Mark reflects the editorial work of the second evangelist and, apart from that, is simply too general to serve as evidence for Paul's dependency on a saying of Jesus.

*1 Thess. 5:15:*

> See that none of you pays back evil for evil, but always seek to do good to one another and to all.

See above, p. 201 (on Rom. 12:17a).

*1 Thess. 5:16:*

> Rejoice always.

This admonition is sometimes regarded as an echo of Luke 6:23 ("Rejoice in that day . . . your reward is great in heaven") and Luke 10:20 ("Rejoice that your names are inscribed in heaven"). However, one must certainly exercise great imagination to see an allusion to Jesus' teachings here.

## PRELIMINARY RESULT

*First,* the specific citations make it certain that Paul was familiar with traditions about Jesus' teaching and knew certain specific elements of that teaching. However, it goes without saying that Jesus' ethic was inadequate as a moral guide for the church in a Hellenistic society. This point receives unambiguous support in 1 Cor. 7:25, where Paul expresses disappointment that, "concerning those who are not married," no word of the Lord is available to him. Not only that observation, but also the apostle's care to distinguish his own opinion from the charge of the Lord (1 Cor. 7:12), demonstrate both the value and importance Paul could ascribe to sayings of Jesus and his readiness to issue advice and commands on his own authority.

But of Paul's familiarity with *some* traditions of Jesus' sayings in *some* form, there should be no doubt.

*Second,* one must nevertheless concede the infrequency of either explicit or implicit references to Jesus' teachings to be found in the Pauline letters. The argument that he could assume his readers' familiarity with these because he had already passed them on in his missionary preaching is not convincing. He could and does presume some familiarity with the Greek translation of the Scriptures, the Septuagint, which was mediated to his converts either by himself or earlier by the local Jewish community. For this reason he is constantly and specifically citing it in the course of his ethical teaching. (See above, pp. 102–103.) Moreover, when Paul himself summarizes the content of his missionary preaching in Corinth (1 Cor. 2:1–2; 15:3b–5), there is no hint that a narration of Jesus' earthly life or a report of his earthly teachings was an essential part of it. The only exception is the tradition about the Last Supper (1 Cor. 11:23–25), which he must have transmitted to the Corinthians at the time he founded the community. This is evident from the fact that he had to correct the Corinthians' abuse of the Eucharistic meal, a ritual he had introduced (cf. 1 Cor. 11:17–22).

In the letter to the Romans, which cannot presuppose the apostle's missionary preaching and in which he attempts to summarize its main points, there is not one direct citation of Jesus' teaching. One must record with some surprise the fact that Jesus' teachings seem to play a less vital role in Paul's religious and ethical instruction than the Old Testament does.

*Third,* not once does Paul refer to Jesus as a teacher, to his words as teaching, or to Christians as disciples. In this regard it is of the greatest significance that when Paul cites "sayings of Jesus," they are never so designated; rather, his references in such instances are, without a single exception, to "the Lord."

*Fourth,* the term "Law of Christ" should not be taken to mean a summary of Jesus' teaching; rather, it designates the law of love. In other words, the phrases "under the law of Christ" (*ennomos Christou*) in 1 Cor. 9:21 and "the law of Christ" in Gal. 6:2 cannot be used to support the hypothesis that Paul conceived of the traditional words of Jesus as constituting a new Torah or a Christian Halakah.[8]

## PAUL AND JESUS: HOW DIFFERENT, YET HOW ALIKE!

In our attempt to understand Paul it is essential that we see him both in comparison and in contrast to Jesus on the basis of what we know about their lives. Jesus came from a village, Paul from a city. Even if all the existing evidence did not make this plain, it is clearly attested by the images they habitually employed.

The world of Jesus' parables is a rural one. Jesus knows the sower in the field (Mark 4:3–8) and the mustard plant in the garden (Mark 4:30–32); he sees the shepherd with his flock (Mark 6:34), the birds of the sky (Matt. 6:26), and the lilies in the field (Matt. 6:28). Even the sparrow which falls to the ground (Matt. 10:29) makes Jesus, the man from the village, think of the omnipotent activity of God.

In contrast, Paul's letters reflect city life with the stalls of traders (2 Cor. 2:17), past which the tutor (Gal. 3:24–25) goes to school holding the hands of his little charges, and the street through which the solemn triumphal procession moves (cf. 2 Cor. 2:14). Paul takes his imagery from the life of soldiers (2 Cor. 10:3–5). Similarly, he uses parallels from the legal sphere (Gal. 3:17), from the theater (1 Cor. 4:9), and from athletic competitions (1 Cor. 9:24) for his arguments. Jesus, however, never mentions the theater or the arena and likely never attended either, though the city of Sepphoris, stamped with Greco-Roman culture, where he may well have worked as a craftsman, was barely three miles from Nazareth. In contrast to Jesus, Paul was highly literate, having received both a Jewish and a Greek education. Unlike Jesus, who spoke Aramaic and perhaps a little Greek, Paul had a good command of Aramaic in addition to his native Greek. As a Roman citizen he was endowed with numerous privileges Jesus lacked. In origin and education, Paul was cosmopolitan, while Jesus was provincial.

But despite all the differences, the two would have had things in common. Paul and Jesus were committed Jews, devoted to their God, who had created heaven and earth and chosen Israel. Paul and Jesus shared this basic framework of religious convictions with most other Jews.

Paul also shared with Jesus a powerful hope for the future and his own role in bringing it to pass. Paul called on the members of the

Corinthian community not to sue one another, since in the heavenly world they themselves would judge angels (1 Cor. 6:3). In addition, he implied that the incorporation of the Gentiles into the future kingdom of God was solely up to him (cf. Rom. 11:13–36). Jesus' hope was no less fantastic: that he could inaugurate among the oppressed underclass a movement based on and empowered by love that would overcome the imperial power of Rome and that God will establish his kingdom very soon.

Yet it must be pointed out that, along with such rash and exaggerated hopes for the future, Paul and Jesus both founded their preaching on timeless wisdom. While the evidence for this is undisputed in the case of Jesus, it has to be argued again for Paul. The apostle himself was at one time convinced that he would live to experience the coming of the Lord on the clouds of heaven and almost obsessively wanted to carry on his mission throughout the Roman Empire before the return of Jesus. But at the same time we find in his writings such timeless truths as the foolishness before God of human wisdom (1 Cor. 1–2), and he has left to posterity the magnificent hymn to a kind of love which knows no expectation of an imminent end. In 1 Cor. 13 he writes that love is greater than hope (for God's final victory) and greater also than faith (in Christ who first made possible the expectation of that victory). It follows from this that in the minds of both Paul and Jesus, contrary to modern logic, the expectation of God's future triumph over evil stood side by side with wisdom teaching, ethics, and religious reform.

To be sure, both Paul's epistles and the gospel accounts of Jesus fail to afford a complete picture of either man's life and teaching, but one ineradicable and crucial difference remains. Paul's postulation about salvation history and mankind's changed situation with respect to it point to the fact that Christology, instead of the kingdom of God, stands at the center of Paul's system. This cannot be explained by saying that in Paul's time the gospel tradition was as yet hardly known anywhere in Christendom, nor by suggesting that a lack of interest in the Jesus tradition or a reluctance to profane it caused Paul to refer to this tradition so rarely.

The unavoidable conclusion is that these two men had very different visions of the role and function of religion in human life. For Jesus, faith was primarily a spiritual posture that would enable people to live together in mutual respect and support. For Paul, it was the way to ensure personal salvation. Naturally, the religion he propounded was shaped by that attractive promise. How like that of Jesus, yet how different!

## NOTES

1. See the useful collection by A. J. M. Wedderburn, ed., *Paul and Jesus: Collected Essays* (Sheffield: Sheffield Academic Press, 1989).

2. As does David Wenham, *Paul: Follower of Jesus or Founder of Christianity?* (Grand Rapids, Mich.: Wm. B. Eerdmans Publishing Co., 1995).

3. Adolf Harnack, *What Is Christianity?* (New York: Harper & Row, Torchbooks, 1957), p. 176.

4. See my *Virgin Birth? The Real History of Mary and Her Son Jesus* (Harrisburg: Trinity Press International, 1998), pp. 43–44.

5. For the following see Victor Paul Furnish, *Theology and Ethics in Paul* (Nashville: Abingdon Press, 1968), pp. 51–59 (still basic as is the whole book). In "The Pauline Epistles and the Synoptic Gospels: The Pattern of the Parallels," *New Testament Studies* 28 (1982): 1–32, Dale C. Allison Jr. argues that Paul was actually acquainted with collections of Jesus' sayings. He thus finds many more references to sayings of Jesus in Paul than Furnish and I do.

6. See my *Jesus After Two Thousand Years: What He Really Said and Did* (Amherst, N.Y.: Prometheus Books, 2001), pp. 142–43.

7. On this text see above, pp. 49–51.

8. See Furnish, *Theology and Ethics in Paul*, pp. 59–65.

# 9

# PAUL THE FOUNDER
# OF CHRISTIANITY

At the outset, some reflections on the terms "founder"[1] and "Christianity" are appropriate. *First*, identifying Paul as the founder of Christianity is polemical, for it denies that Jesus initiated the tradition that bears his title "the Christ."[2] This denial is based in part on the widely accepted evidence that the title was not assigned to him nor was the movement so designated during his lifetime. It arises also from the truth of the droll but accurate observation that Jesus was looking for the Kingdom of God, but the church arrived instead.[3] *Second*, it was not until the Jesus movement was identified externally and internally as something new that the term "Christianity" arose. In the following we have to ask whether these two points—the external and the internal one—apply to the movement in question.

Chapter 5 (see above, pp. 113–37) and the related appendix (pp. 259–82) show that groups founded by Hellenists were given the name "Christians" by outsiders, and my conclusion is that the same was true of the Pauline communities. These groups perceived themselves as fellowships in which all previously recognized differences between human beings had been canceled: "There is neither Jew nor Greek, there is neither slave nor free, there is no male and female" (Gal. 3:28). Instead, all are now "one in Christ" (ibid.). Indeed, they are now part of a new creation, "for neither circumcision counts for anything, nor uncircumcision" (Gal. 6:15). Thus the name "Christians" that was applied to them from outside corresponded to the self-definition of the members of these groups.

Against this classification of Christianity as a new and distinct religion it cannot be objected that many of its members, including Paul, drew heavily on the Old Testament and defined themselves as the true Israel, the Israel of God, or the Israel according to the flesh. Since all these persons were born Jews and acculturated primarily within the Jewish tradition it could hardly have been otherwise.

## THE REAL REASON FOR THE HELLENISTS' DEPARTURE FROM THE JEWISH RELIGION

Let me hasten to add that it was not belief in Jesus as the Messiah that made them depart from their Jewish religion. Rather it was the consequence of that belief—that members experienced a new birth in Christ—which led them to adopt a new Christian identity. Furthermore, since Gentiles were welcomed as members of Christian groups, and males did not have to undergo circumcision, the covenant between Israel and God became an irrelevancy. By taking this step, the leaders of the Christian movement clearly departed from Israel notwithstanding the many ties which bound them to it. This opening up to the Gentiles had other serious consequences for Jewish Christian members of these communities. *First,* by observing open table fellowship and thus admitting their fellow Gentile Christians to participate without dietary prerequisites, Jewish Christians radically compromised their Jewish identity. *Second,* within a decade or so, Gentiles comprised a majority in these communities. This created a further erosion of identity for the Jewish Christian members; indeed, critics report that soon they no longer circumcised their male newborns (cf. Acts 21:21). At this point, little was left of their inherited Jewishness.

Since the apostle Paul received his early Christian education from members of the very groups that he had but lately persecuted, it was ironically he who ensured that their tentative beginnings were nurtured, brought to fruition, and translated to the Greco-Roman world. Indeed, his unflagging missionary efforts and the raising of a new generation of fellow workers clearly mark him as the real founder of Christianity, all the more so since the Jerusalem mother church was eradicated in 70 C.E., leaving Pauline Christianity the dominant paradigm.

But should one not regard the Hellenist Jews as the real founders of Christianity if both terms are defined as above? The answer is yes and no. Yes, for they were the ones who not only preached to Gentiles but also gave them equal status in their own communities. No, for when being challenged by James of Jerusalem (see above, pp. 44–46) they immediately gave in to his demands and withdrew from table fellowship with the Gentiles. Their faith was, in the long run, too shaky a foundation for a Christianity that became predominantly Gentile. The new religion required a doctrinal unity and the authority to enforce it; that in turn called for vision (and perhaps *a* vision) and the supreme self-assuredness to insist on its truth; and those, of course, were the spark and the fuel which powered the immense missionary effort that made Paul the founder of Christianity.

The center of the new religion that he founded was the Christ who had appeared to him before Damascus and who continued to give him instructions. Indeed, Christ lived in Paul, as he did in all the Christians, and the life that the apostle lived in the flesh, he lived as he himself writes, "by faith in the Son of God, who loved me and gave himself up for me" (Gal. 2:20b). Finally, he expects Christ to return in the near future so that *all* the believers may live with him. "For God has destined us not for wrath, but to obtain salvation through our Lord Jesus Christ, who died for us so that whether we wake or sleep we might live with him" (1 Thess. 5:9–10).[4]

It is one of the many unsolved questions in Pauline research why and how the apostle relates the Jewish law to Christ.[5] On the one hand he claims that were we able to fulfill the law—which we are not—then Christ would have died in vain (cf. Gal. 2:21). At the same time he claims that grace, properly understood, leads to the fulfillment of the law. And he goes even further than that in Rom. 2:6 and especially 2:13 ("For it is not the hearers of the law who are righteous before God, but the doers of the law who will be justified") which he then contradicts in Rom. 3:28 ("a man is justified by faith [alone] apart from works of the law"). Last but not least, Paul himself enforces the will of God, the sanctification, in his predominantly Gentile Christian communities as if he had never talked about grace by faith, but always insisted on proper conduct in Christ (see above, pp. 100–102).

It should be noted that the above is hardly an unprecedented critique of Paul; once again we find in Porphyry a very early censure of
the apostle, vituperative as it is perceptive.

> The same man who writes, "The law is spiritual"[6] to the Romans,
> and "The law is holy and the commandment holy and just"[7] . . .
> puts a curse upon those who obey what is holy.[8] Then, as if to con-
> fuse the point further, he turns everything around and throws up a
> fog so dense that anyone trying to follow him inevitably gets lost,
> bumping up against the gospel on one side, against the law on the
> other, stumbling over the law and tripping over the gospel—all
> because the guide who leads them by the hand has no idea where
> he is headed.
>
> Look again at this charlatan's record. Following any number of
> references to the law which he used to find support (for his case),
> he nullifies his argument by saying "The law entered so that the
> offense might increase"[9] and previous to this, "The goad of death
> is sin and the power of sin is the law."[10]
>
> With a tongue sharp as a sword, he [Paul] mercilessly cuts the
> law into little pieces. But this [nevertheless] is the man who tends
> to keep the law and finds it virtuous to obey its commandments. By
> clinging to inconsistency, as he does apparently by habit, he over-
> turns his judgment in all other cases.[11]

To be sure, the complex web of corroboration and contradiction
is puzzling. One thing, however, seems to be certain. Some of Paul's
Jewish Christian contemporaries claimed that his doctrine of grace
by faith led to libertinism: In Rom. 3:8 we have a statement, formally
in the style of an objection in the diatribe, a statement directed
against the apostle, which he quotes: "Some people charge us with
saying, 'Let's do evil that good may come.'" Paul can only describe
such a view as "slander" and indignantly throw it back at those who
say it. "Their condemnation is just" (Rom. 3:8c).

Assuming that the quotation in Rom. 3:8 is located in the proper
context with regard to its subject matter, it seems clear that the anti-
Pauline reproach had been sparked by Paul's doctrine of justification
by faith alone, the negative counterpart of which was the invalida-
tion of the law as a means of salvation. For since in Paul's view the

righteousness of God convicts everybody as being under the power of sin (cf. Rom. 1:18–3:20), the question arose for Paul's opponents whether Paul's theology did not mislead people directly to libertinism. They thus attributed to Paul their conclusion: that he taught that people should do evil in order that good, that is salvation in Christ, might come. They must have seen in Paul's doctrine of the law a fatal error, and then a self-contradiction if Paul also advocated the keeping of the (moral aspects of the) law. Therefore they are almost surely identifiable as Jews loyal to the law, who had taken note of Paul's doctrine and practice. We can also consider them to be Jewish Christians, for not only do we know for certain of hostility to Paul from Jewish Christians in Jerusalem, Antioch, and Galatia, but also the line of argument in Romans is closely related to that of Galatians, which had been formulated in response to Jewish-Christians actions and arguments (see above, p. 29). Thus the declaration in Galatians apparently provoked allegations such as those which become visible in Rom. 3:8. That the refutation of such objections was a central concern of Paul's is seen in Rom. 6:1, 15, where again, using the diatribe style of argument, he rejects inferences similar to that in the quotation of Rom. 3:8.

Paul, then, asserted that the opposite is true: that being saved by grace alone, Christians would walk in the newness of life, all the more so since they had died with Christ in baptism and consequently would translate Christ's resurrection into proper ethical behavior (cf. Rom. 6:4).

While there can be no doubt about Paul's ethical teaching and his criticism of improper conduct in the Corinthian community (1 Cor. 5:1–5, etc.), it must be said that Paul's doctrine of justification by faith alone did not automatically lead to ethics.[12] Rather it seems to be the fragment of a doctrine created largely for the purpose of relieving Gentile Christians and potential converts of the requirement of circumcision. No wonder that almost nobody in the first two centuries seems to have understood Paul on this point, and the one who did, Marcion, obviously misunderstood the apostle on other matters, for Paul would never have granted that the God of the Hebrew Scriptures is different from the God of Jesus Christ (see above, p. 17).

Thus although "justification by faith" did not become the foundation of Paul's Christianity, his ministry certainly included the mysteries of baptism and the Lord's Supper and redemption provided by Christ's atoning sacrifice.

The notion of God who had sent his Son into this world in order to save people was a core element of the Christianity that Paul founded. As Jewish as this notion was, given the exclusivity and the zeal of the God of Israel who was now on Paul's side, it could quickly turn anti-Jewish if Jews were to reject the salvation plan conceived by the apostle. He believed himself commissioned by God, remember. And certainly it became anti-Jewish once Paul's Gentile Christian followers began to claim the Hebrew Bible as their Holy Scripture and referred to it as a book that had prophesied Christ's coming and basically contained all the Christian doctrines outlined by Paul.

## ON THE EXPLOITATION OF
## JEWISH SCRIPTURE BY CHRISTIANS

It was Paul who began to exploit the Holy Scripture of the Jews for his own purposes. For example, in 1 Cor. 10:1 he refers to the Israelites crossing the sea as "our fathers" and goes on to write in 1 Cor. 10:2–4:

> (2) They *all* received baptism into Moses in the cloud and in the sea, (3) and they *all* ate the same supernatural food (4) and they *all* drank the same supernatural drink; for they drank from the supernatural Rock that accompanied them; and that Rock was Christ.

In this text Paul not only implies that the Israelites were the forefathers of the Gentile Christian Corinthians but also claims that Christ was present and that the Israelites shared the same sacramental gifts that the Corinthians enjoyed: baptism and eucharist. So Paul in effect paved the way for the Gentile Christian exploitation of the Holy Scripture of the Jews and withdrawal of its promises from the latter unless they joined the Christian Israel.

Friedrich Nietzsche again aptly commented about what he called a "philological farce":

In the end, however, what are we to expect of the aftereffects of a religion that enacted during the centuries of its foundation that unheard-of philological farce about the Old Testament? I refer to the attempt to pull away the Old Testament from under the feet of the Jews—with the claim that it contains nothing but Christian doctrines and *belongs* to the Christians as the *true* Israel, while the Jews had merely usurped it. And now the Christians yielded to a rage of interpretation and interpolation, which could not possibly have been accompanied by a good conscience. However much the Jewish scholars protested, everywhere in the Old Testament there were supposed to be references to Christ and only to Christ, and particularly to his cross. Wherever any piece of wood, a switch, a ladder, a tree, a willow, or a staff is mentioned, this was supposed to indicate a prophecy of the wood of the cross. . . . Has anybody who claimed this ever *believed* it?[13]

## ON THE REAL REASON FOR ANTI-JUDAISM

The consequence of this phenomenon is commonly called anti-Judaism. It is directly bound up with the claim of Christian communities that salvation is only in Christ and in no one else. In addition to the aforementioned Pauline texts two other exemplary passages from the New Testament, Acts 4:12 and John 14:6, contain the same assertion.

In Acts 4:12 "Peter" says, "And there is no salvation in anyone else at all, for there is no other name under heaven given among men by which we may receive salvation." In other words, Christology leads to a claim which excludes all other ways of believing, and if it is not acknowledged, it immediately vilifies any such way. In John 14:6 "Jesus" says about himself, "I am the way and the truth and the life; no one comes to the Father but by me."

Now the two texts mentioned are rooted in particular situations and are not meant to be judgments which apply in all situations and at all times, nor were they meant to be accepted into a canon of sacred writings. Rather, they must be explained historically. Given their content, the only possibility is to understand them in the light of the claim to exclusiveness of the groups concerned or by the Christianity which handed down these judgments. Any other understanding would go against their literal content. In other words, in their view there is no getting around an acknowledgment of Jesus Christ as the salvation of the world—either for Jews or for Gentiles—regardless of whether their author was still a member of a Jewish community or already outside it. And if, as often happened, Jews and/or Gentiles did not assent to this judgment about Jesus as salvation of this world, they had to be assigned to the realm of darkness. *So anti-Judaism is the other side of "Christ alone."* There is consequently no way of liberating Christianity from its anti-Judaism without finally repudiating its Christological hermeneutic.

## JEWS AND CHRISTIANS CLAIM ELECTION FOR THEMSELVES

At the same time, for honesty's sake it must be said that Christianity and Judaism will never be able to remove their lasting differences. Notwithstanding their claim to worship the same God, the Jewish confession of the one God cannot be detached from its awareness of being the chosen people, nor can the Christian confession of the one God be detached from the one Son in whom God has reconciled the world to himself. Though one religion had to be opposed to the truth claim of the other religion, from an outsider's perspective their structure of thought remained identical in that the election of a specific group of people was claimed.

Such matters had to come under attack as soon as Christianity reached the educated classes of the Roman Empire. The second-century Platonic philosopher Celsus wrote an attack against Christianity in which he tells his readers about Christian missionaries: They take advantage of the lack of education of gullible people and lead them wherever they wish, demanding nothing else but faith.

> Do not ask questions; just believe. Your faith will save you. The wisdom of this world is an evil, and foolishness a good thing.[14]

The specific doctrine of election also comes under attack. Celsus writes the following parody about Jews and Christians:

The race of Jews and Christians is similar to a cluster of bats or ants coming out of a nest, or to frogs holding council round a marsh, or to worms assembling in some filthy corner, quarrelling with one another as to which of them were the worse sinners. They say:
"God shows and announces to us all things beforehand; and he has even deserted the whole world, and the motion of the heavens, and disregarded the vast earth to give attention to us alone; and he sends messengers to us alone and never stops sending them and seeking that we may be with him for ever." And in his fictitious representation, he [Celsus] compares us to worms who say: "There is God first, and we are next after him in rank, since he has made us entirely like God, and all things have been put under us, earth, water, air, and stars; and all things exist for our benefit, and have been appointed to serve us and ordained to be subject to us."[15]

As this second-century philosopher rightly observed, it requires only a modicum of education to subvert many specific Jewish and Christian doctrines. To mention only one, the idea of one special group being elected by God is both repulsive and self-defeating. Indeed, the Christian claim to be elected by God is the most severe counterclaim against the equivalent Jewish claim and necessarily led to hostility and acts of aggression.

## THE POSSIBLE DEVELOPMENT OF THE JESUS MOVEMENT

Let us imagine for a moment how the Jesus movement and the Hellenistic groups might have developed in the absence of the Pharisee Paul. I shall deal first with the Jesus movement and then with the Hellenists.

The Jesus movement was a reform movement within Judaism and did not show any inclination to reach out to Gentiles. The life of Jesus and the history of the Jerusalem church illustrate this. Despite the various appearances of the risen Lord to leaders of the Jerusalem church, a mission to Gentiles was beyond their imaginative horizon. It was not until the Gentile mission was in full force that Luke, in order to connect his hero Paul with the Jerusalem church, in Acts

10–11 (on this see below, p. 277) makes Peter, the leader of the Jerusalem church, start the mission to the Gentiles. (The appearance-story in Matt. 28:16–20 with the command to go to the Gentiles stems from the second or third Christian generation.) Rather, the Gentile issue was forced upon them by the Hellenists and by Paul, and as a result of this, some members of the Jerusalem community such as their previous leader Cephas seem to have later opened up to the issue of a mission to Gentiles.

To a certain extent the Jerusalem church's association with other groups that were engaged in a mission to the Gentiles was the reason why its members had no chance of contributing to the reorganization of Judaism after the destruction of Jerusalem in 70 C.E. Indeed, they had already lost the confidence of many Jews prior to that disaster. Their leader James the Just, a brother of Jesus and an opponent of Paul, had succeeded Cephas in the leadership of the Jerusalem church but was executed in 62 C.E. for his alleged transgression of the law.[16] The religion that he and his followers espoused was the same common Judaism as that of Jesus.[17] Since all of them wanted to remain within Israel, and would have been very surprised at what happened afterward, they should *not* be regarded as representatives of Christianity.


## THE POSSIBLE DEVELOPMENT
## OF THE HELLENISTS (WITHOUT PAUL)

The Hellenists were forced out of Jerusalem and, "driven by the spirit," opened their table to Gentiles. One can only speculate about the specific motives behind this. How conscious was that step? What role did the martyrdom of their leader Stephen play? In what way was the mission to the Gentiles integrated into their belief? Let me emphasize that in the confession of faith in 1 Cor. 15:3–5 which the Hellenists transmitted to Paul there was no mention of any mission to the Gentiles.

In all probability the practice preceded the theory in this specific case. At first, it seems, Gentiles were admitted to the meals, and afterward people insisted that their presence was a God-given decision. It was not until Gentiles were part of the community that reasons were given for their presence. In this process, enthusiasm seems to have been a chief factor. Further, earlier acculturation in Hellenism should not be underrated. There was among many of them, I suppose, a deeply rooted longing for a unity of mankind. Why not reenact with the new Gentile converts what they had experienced with Jesus and with the spirit?

It all looked so promising, the more so since a powerful new convert was added to their flock, Paul of Tarsus. But this convert, who associated his conversion with a call from God and who read all his former longings and messianic ideas into the Damascus event, demonstrated to the Hellenists that they were not yet ready to put the new experience into reality. The incident at Antioch (Gal. 2:11–14) revealed the limits of their vision and made clear that they still belonged to Judaism, for in a moment of crisis their solution was to incorporate Gentiles into a new form of that old dispensation. Hence one should not consider the Hellenists the founders of Christianity. With this judgment I am in the company of Paul, who addresses Peter in the following way: "If you, though a Jew, live like a Gentile and not like a Jew, how can you force the Gentiles to live like Jews?" (Gal. 2:14). Thus Paul himself attests that the Hellenists in Antioch retreated from Christianity to Judaism and therefore cannot be regarded as the founders of Christianity. My guess is that the Hellenists, without the work of their convert Paul, would not have survived the catastrophe of 70 C.E., or else would have become just another one of the several Jewish groups which survived the destruction of Jerusalem.

## HOW PAUL BECAME THE FOUNDER OF CHRISTIANITY

Still, Paul would never have become the founder of Christianity—his Jewish bias remained simply too strong (see above, pp. 108–109)—had he not raised up gifted pupils who transmitted his preaching to coming generations. Some of them indeed composed letters in his name thus presented his message in a different situation. In chapter

2 (pp. 22–64) it became evident that reactions to Paul both among his pupils and among other Christians were notably diverse. Let us now sketch what happened to his letters and how his heritage was preserved in order to be able to serve as the foundation of Christianity.

Paul's letters were read aloud in the worship services of the communities that he had founded, as is evident from the earliest extant letter (1 Thess. 5:27: "I adjure you by the Lord to have this letter read to all the brothers"). The communities probably also exchanged the letters among themselves after a certain time (cf. Col. 4:16), though it is unlikely that Paul himself made a collection of them. However, as was noted previously (see above, pp. 223–24), he had a number of colleagues with whom he constantly exchanged ideas, and pupils who must have had some share in the composition of the letters (indeed Paul often mentions cosenders). At all events, the influence of Paul continued after his death, and with it that of his letters, as far as they have been preserved. A detailed history of them is, of course, beyond our knowledge. But they lived on in the original theology of Colossians; and Ephesians, which builds on Colossians, is also eloquent testimony to the activity of a circle of pupils going back to Paul himself.[18]

Whether a collection of Paul's letters was made by the author of Ephesians is disputed. There is, however, much to suggest that Bishop Onesimus of Ephesus assembled a collection of the apostle's letters at the beginning of the second century, which he arranged by length, putting Ephesians, which he had written, at the beginning, and Philemon, in which he himself appears as a runaway converted by Paul (verse 10), at the end. At any rate, this would be as good an explanation as any for how the little letter of Paul to Philemon found its way into the canon: with it the former runaway Onesimus would have created a memorial to himself.[19] Marcion then made use of this collection, put Galatians at its head and set Ephesians in place of Galatians. Marcion in turn was successfully attacked by the pupil of Paul who wrote the Pastorals (1 and 2 Timothy; Titus).[20] As we all know, these three letters became documents of the New Testament, while none of Marcion's works were allowed to survive. To some extent the author of the Pastorals along with the authors of 2 Thessalonians and of Acts ensured Paul's acceptance into the New Testament canon, though as we saw they grossly misunderstood the apostle. Again I am reminded of a passage from Friedrich Nietzsche which brilliantly illuminates this by introducing the term "blind disciples":

> The disciple . . . who has no eye for the weaknesses of the doctrine, the religion, and so forth, dazzled by the aspect of the master and by his reverence for him, has on that account usually more power than the master himself. Without blind disciples the influence of a man and his work has never yet become great. To help a doctrine to victory often means only so to mix it with stupidity that the weight of the latter carries off also the victory of the former.[21]

A little later Nietzsche continues:

> For the greatest achievements of the people who are called geniuses and saints it is necessary that they should secure interpreters by force, who *misunderstand* them for the good of mankind.[22]

## NOTES

1. See Hans Dieter Betz, "Paul's Ideas about the Origins of Christianity," *Paulinische Studien. Gesammelte Aufsätze* III (Tübingen: J. C. B. Mohr [Paul Siebeck], 1994), pp. 272–88.

2. Martin Hengel and Anna Maria Schwemer, *Paul Between Damascus and Antioch: The Unknown Years* (Louisville: Westminster John Knox Press, 1997). Therefore Hengel and Schwemer, *Paul*, prefer to speak of Paul as "the second founder of Christianity" (p. 309). Notwithstanding the apologetic tone in this designation, their conclusions are sound: "Christianity would rather have remained a messianic sect on the periphery of Judaism and gradually have disappeared from history like other Jewish sects of antiquity. . . . As a theologian and missionary he put it on the way by which it became a world religion—the first" (pp. 309ff.).

3. Alfred Loisy, *The Gospel and the Church* (London: Ibister and Co., 1903), p. 166.

4. In this text "we wake" means "are alive at the Second Coming of Jesus" and "we sleep" means to have died before the Second Coming of Jesus.

5. See the impressive summary by E. P. Sanders, *Paul* (Oxford/New York: Oxford University Press, 1991), pp. 84–100.

6. Rom. 7:14.

7. Rom. 7:12.

8. Cf. Gal. 3:10.

9. Rom. 5:20.

10. 1 Cor. 15:56.

11. R. Joseph Hoffmann, *Pophyry's against the Christians: The Literary Remains*, edited and translated with an introduction (Amherst, N.Y.: Prometheus Books, 1984), pp. 62ff.

12. See the convincing argument by E. P. Sanders, *Paul and Palestinian Judaism: A Comparison of Patterns of Religion* (Philadelphia: Fortress Press, 1977), pp. 474–523.

13. *The Dawn* sec. 84 (Walter Kaufmann, *The Portable Nietzsche* [New York: Viking Press, 1954], pp. 80ff.).

14. *Contra Celsum* 1.9 (Henry Chadwick, *Origen Contra Celsum* [Cambridge: University Press, 1965], p. 12).

15. *Contra Celsum* 4.23 (Chadwick, *Origen*, pp. 199ff.).

16. Josephus *Jewish Antiquities* 20.199-203. See my *Heretics: The Other Side of Early Christianity* (Louisville: Westminster John Knox Press, 1996), pp. 49–51.

17. E. P. Sanders, *Judaism: Practice and Belief 63* B.C.E.*–66* C.E. (Philadelphia: Trinity Press International, 1992).

18. See my *Heretics*, pp. 120–30 ("Left-wing Paulinists" [Colossians/Ephesians]).

19. Cf. John Knox, *Philemon among the Letters of Paul: A New View of Its Place and Importance*, 2d ed. (New York and Nashville: Abingdon Press, 1959).

20. On the origin of the New Testament canon see my *Heretics*, pp. 193–208.

21. *Human, All-Too-Human* sec. 122 (based on the translation in my *Heretics*, p. 293n.495, for there is no translation of this passage in Kaufmann, *Portable Nietzsche*).

22. Ibid., sec. 126 (translation based on my *Heretics*, p. 293n.495, for the same reason as in the previous footnote).

# 10

# PAUL'S RELEVANCE
# FOR TODAY

If Paul then is the real founder of Christianity, it is incumbent upon us to assess both the historical impact and the contemporary significance of his work.

By way of introduction I would like to draw the reader's attention again to Nietzsche, whose analysis has greatly helped me to understand Paul as the founder of Christianity. Without Paul, Nietzsche writes,

> there would be no Christianity; we should scarcely have heard of a small Jewish sect whose master died on the cross. Of course, if this story had been understood in time: if Paul's writings had been read not as revelations of the "Holy Spirit" but with an honest and free spirit of one's own, and without at the same time thinking of all our personal troubles, if they had *really been read*—and for a millenium and a half there were no such readers—then Christianity would have been done for long ago: so much do these pages of the Jewish Pascal expose the origins of Christianity, just as the pages of the French Pascal expose its destiny and that of which it will perish.
>
> That the ship of Christianity threw overboard much of its Jewish ballast, that it went, and was able to go, among the pagans—that was due to this one man, a very tortured, very pitiful, very unpleasant man even to himself. He suffered from a fixed idea—or more precisely, from a fixed, ever present, never resting question: what about the Jewish law?[1]

## A LOOK AT PAUL FROM A JEWISH PERSPECTIVE

First, I shall look at Paul from a Jewish perspective.[2] As all of us know, Judaism survived not only the Jewish War of 66–70 but also the Bar Kochba War of 132–135 and even Christianity. It survived Christianity although Christian writers, from the New Testament on to the tractates of church fathers, claimed that the destruction of Jerusalem by the Romans was the just punishment for the crimes against Jesus and his apostles, and that Jews would be shortly removed from the face of the earth.

In the year 312 the Christian historian Eusebius wrote the following account about the unbelieving Jews:

> (2) After the ascension of our savior the Jews, in addition to their crime against him, had devised innumerable plots also against his apostles: first they put Stephen to death by stoning; and then, after him, James, who was son of the Zebedee and the brother of John, was beheaded, and finally James, who was the first, after the ascension of our savior, to receive the throne of the episcopate there, departed this life in the manner we mentioned above (i.e., by being stoned). As for the other apostles, countless plots were laid against their lives, and they were banished from the land of Judaea; but they sojourned among all the nations to teach the message, in the power of the Christ who said to them, "Go and make disciples of all the nations in my name." (3) Moreover, the people of the church at Jerusalem, in accordance with a certain oracle that was vouchsafed by way of revelation to approved men there, had been commanded to depart from the city before the war, and to inhabit a certain city of Peraea. They called it Pella. And when those who believed in Christ had removed from Jerusalem, as if holy men had utterly deserted both the royal metropolis of the Jews itself and the whole land of Judaea, the justice of God then visited upon them all their acts of violence to Christ and his apostles, by destroying that generation of wicked persons root and branch from among men.[3]

Indeed Paul himself had paved the way for such an attack on the nonbelieving Jews, for in his earliest letter, 1 Thessalonians, he could go so far as to write that God's wrath had come upon them forever (1 Thess. 2:16).

However, it must also be said that near the end of his life Paul had somewhat modified the general Christian view on the fate of the unbelieving Jews. When he realized that Gentile Christians might despise Jewish Christians, he claimed to have received as "a mystery from the Lord" the knowledge that after the fullness of the Gentiles had found salvation, Israel would be saved (Rom. 11:25–26). And although this in effect retracted all that he had earlier written about salvation by faith, it could not undo what he had said and done before and what he probably said and did afterward. Still, it makes him a more sympathetic figure, for it reveals an abiding love for his own people. Indeed, we might reasonably conclude that Paul remained in his heart of hearts a Jew although he was the real founder of Christianity.

Having said this, some serious charges must be lodged against Paul. At the foundation of Paul's teaching lay Jewish beliefs and opinions which took on a new, half-pagan complexion from foreign influences, and thus became non-Judaism and anti-Judaism. *Paul himself was not aware of this.* He considered his teaching as true Judaism, as the fulfillment of the promises and assurances of authentic Judaism. So of course it gave him great pain that his people Israel did not accept his teaching, which he did not consider essentially new but based largely on the Scriptures. Hence arises the difficult problem which every serious student of Christianity must face sooner or later: How is it that Christianity grew directly out of Judaism and yet, although adopted by half the world, was emphatically rejected by Judaism itself?

The answer has to be given: In spite of the fact that the *foundations* of Paul's doctrines are Jewish, his teaching entails both the contradiction of the Jewish religion and the rejection of the Jewish nation.

Although Paul freed his Christian converts from the bondage of hundreds of rules and ritual observances, he shackled them with dogmas whose collective effect was even more stultifying: belief in Jesus as the Messiah and the bodily risen Son of God, and the proposition that grace, atonement, and salvation are gifts available only through his sacrificial death. There is yet a further difficulty: Paul's teaching denies freedom of the will, and replaces it with the foreordained gift of grace. Thus not only does it substitute faith for deeds, and make the Kingdom of Heaven a mystical concept rather the reconstitution of society ordained by the prophets, but it makes a mockery of Jesus' clarion call to active and concerted personal reform. No doubt, however, Gentiles found attractive the considerable similarity of Paul's Christianity to the pagan mystery religions.

Paul's interest in the Jesus tradition was to derive from it elements from which he could create a salvation myth that would prove attractive to Gentiles. His system is a syncretism formed by fitting Jesus (what little he knew of him) into the mystery-religion format. Same old story with a new real, historical hero. It sold like hot cakes.

## A LOOK AT PAUL FROM A SECULAR PERSPECTIVE

Second, let me try to assess Paul's work from a modern perspective. (It goes without saying that some of the following points reinforce the objections of the Jewish side and that others are objections to the Jewish perspective.) It has to be said plainly at the outset that Paul's religious claims about God and his plan belong in a museum and cannot be accepted by modern man in the light of today's knowledge. I am thinking primarily of his notions of salvation and the consummation of this world at the return of Christ. In the light of today's knowledge it is impossible to believe as Paul did that Jesus rose bodily from the dead. In all likelihood his body rotted away in a tomb or was even devoured by vultures and jackals. But I would insist that those who understood Jesus' resurrection in a symbolic way are *not*, like the Corinthians and later the various kinds of Gnostics, "of all men the most to be pitied" (see 1 Cor. 15:19). On this point Paul deceived himself and shares the weakness of many religious people by claiming to know what he does not. He should perhaps have been more modest, although the consequence of such a seemly reticence would doubtless have been the early disappearance of the traditions that eventually coalesced to form the dogmatic Christianity that shaped Western culture.

Further, Paul's thinking cannot withstand the challenge of theodicy, which looms ever larger the more we know about this universe. What are we to make of a creation in which the routine activity is for organisms to tear each other apart with teeth and claws? Creation is a nightmare spectacular taking place on a planet that has been soaked for hundreds of millions of years in the blood of all its creatures.

Along with this, Paul's arguments against philosophy as opposed to faith sound suspiciously like the propaganda of someone who suffered that resounding defeat at Athens. All that Paul says about the foolishness of wisdom is dangerous, and throws away one of the most important gifts that human beings have left. Nietzsche's evaluation of this matter should be taken seriously:

> A religion like Christianity, which does not have contact with reality at any point, which crumbles as soon as reality is conceded its right at even a single point, must naturally be hostile against "the wisdom of this world," which means *science*. . . . "Faith" as an imperative is the *veto* against science—in practice, the lie at any price. Paul comprehended that the lie—that "faith"—was needed; later the church comprehended Paul. The "God" whom Paul invented, a god who "ruins the wisdom of the world" (in particular philology and medicine, the two great adversaries of superstition), is in truth merely Paul's own resolute *determination* to do this. . . . Paul wants to ruin the "wisdom of the world"; his enemies are the good philologists and physicians of Alexandrian training.[4]

When Paul talks about Jesus' death as atonement for the sins of others, I cannot help shuddering. Although I have heard noted theologians say that by Jesus' death all subsequent sacrifices were rendered superfluous, I insist on asking why the death of Jesus was necessary at all. Indeed I would emphatically urge that Jesus' death was a crime and should never have served as an object of speculation.

Here is one of the two greatest Pauline ironies: The religion he founded was based on several grievous misrepresentations, yet it became the spiritual core and prime mover of what is probably the greatest civilization in human history. The other is that he grossly distorted the religion of Jesus, but except for him we would never have heard about Jesus.

Let me hasten to add that Albert Schweitzer's way of dealing with the factual evidence about Paul stands in contradiction to his own hermeneutical agenda that I quoted as an ideal of my own (see above, p. 10). Schweitzer recommends Paul as "the patron-saint of thought in Christinanity" and continues, "And all those who think to serve the faith in Jesus by destroying freedom of thought would do well to keep out of his way."[5] Furthermore, according to Schweitzer, "From a truly historical point of view the teaching of Paul does not diverge from that of Jesus, but contains it within it."[6] To me all this is wishful thinking, for neither claim of Schweitzer can be confirmed by the evidence. The following quotation from Schweitzer's work shows that he is not talking about historical evidence, but rather a matter of hope which sustains his belief:

[W]hen our belief attains to clearness, and relates itself to the true Jesus and the true Paul, we find that for it, too, they belong together. It thenceforth neither permits an unauthentic or incomplete Paul to obscure for our religious life the fundamental Gospel of Jesus, nor does it continue to cherish the delusion that it must free itself from Paul in order really to give allegiance to the Gospel of Jesus. Henceforward Paul is for it, as he so often designated himself, the "minister of Jesus Christ."[7]

Thus it has to be said frankly that Schweitzer, in spite of his impressive agenda, deceived himself when formulating the relevance of Paul for his time, for the Paul that he talks about here never existed.

## ATTEMPTS BY OTHER LIBERAL THEOLOGIANS TO INTERPRET PAUL WHILE REMAINING HONEST

I shall now turn for help to other modern theologians who, while like Schweitzer denying a bodily resurrection of Jesus, still appeal to Paul in order to claim that Christ's death and resurrection must be regarded as "salvation-occurrence." Of course, I have in mind Rudolf Bultmann's attempt to use Paul's writings as a model to speak of the Bible as the word of God even in a modern world. Since many pupils of his and an even larger number of liberal theologians today still hope to combine veracity in historical matters with adherence to Christian faith by adopting such an approach, it demands a careful analysis. Bultmann writes:

> The deed of divine grace consists in the fact that God gave Christ up to die on the cross. . . . Christ is preached as "the crucified. . . ." Therefore, the gospel can be called "the word of the cross. . . ." But the death and the resurrection of Christ are bound together in the unity of one salvation-occurrence: "he who died" is also "he who was raised up. . . ." *The salvation-occurrence, then, includes the death and the resurrection of Jesus.* Such was the tradition that Paul had received (1 Cor.15:1–4), and such was the tradition that he passed on. . . . Jesus' death-and-resurrection, then, is for Paul the decisive thing about the person of Jesus. . . . The salvation-occurrence, viz. Christ's death and resurrection, is the deed of the prevenient grace of God; and . . . the various expressions which describe this deed intend to describe its unprecedented nature and its might which so radically transformed the human situation.[8]

A few pages later Bultmann continues:

> *How can the salvation occurrence* be understood *as an occurrence directed at man, reaching him, and happening to him?* It takes place in the word, which accosts the hearer and compels him to decide for or against it. . . . The union of believers into one *soma* (body) with Christ . . . has its basis . . . in the fact that in the word of proclamation Christ's death-and-resurrection becomes a possibility of existence in regard to which a decision must be made, and in the fact that faith seizes this possibility and appropriates it as the power that determines the existence of the man of faith.[9]

A little later Bultmann explains this as follows:

> Nothing preceding the faith which acknowledges the risen Christ can give insight into the reality of *Christ's resurrection*. The resurrection cannot—inspite of 1 Cor. 15:3–8—be demonstrated or made plausible as an objectively ascertainable fact on the basis of which one could believe. But insofar as it or the risen Christ is present in

the proclaiming word, it can be believed—and only so can it be believed. Belief in the resurrection and the faith that Christ himself, yes God Himself, speaks in the proclaimed word (2 Cor. 5:20) are identical. For in the proclamation Christ is not in the same way present as a great historical person is present in his work and his historical after-effects. For what is here involved is not an influence that takes effect in the history of the human mind; what does take place is that a historical person and his fate are raised to the rank of the eschatological event. The word which makes this proclamation is itself part of the event; and this word, in contrast to all other historical tradition, accosts the hearer as personal challenge. If he heeds it as the word spoken to him, adjudicating to him death and thereby life, then he believes in the risen Christ.

Any counter-questioning as to the proclamation's right to its claim means that it is already rejected. Such questioning must be transformed into the question which the questioner has to ask himself—whether he is willing to acknowledge the Lord-ship of Christ which is putting this decision-question to his self-understanding.[10]

I have quoted Bultmann extensively to let the reader participate in his train of thought. This is necessary, for his position is often caricatured or misrepresented. *First*, full support must be accorded to his plain statement that, historically speaking, Jesus did not rise from the dead. *Second*, he correctly emphasizes that the statement, "Christ rose" does not belong to the same category as any statement about the influence or impact of any other historical person, as for example, "George Washington rose." For in the latter case, it would be a historical judgment, whereas in Jesus' case, we assert an eschatological event, something that transcends history.[11]

*Third*, this "event" must be preached; indeed the proclamation itself is part of the eschatological event. Concretely put, resurrection is the believing interpretation of the death of Jesus. *Fourth*, any questioning of this event is already a rejection of it.

The last two points invite intensive criticism, for they reflect the dogmatic basis of Bultmann's statement. For one thing, we may ask, why does he take such pains with demythologizing the message of the New Testament if he ends up with such a strategy of immunization against criticism? The other question that arises is why Bultmann invites readers to misunderstand him by using "death and resurrection of Jesus" in a parallel way as if the two were parallel occurrences? Such a careless use of terminology has a parallel in the statement that the Bible contains the Word of God *and* the word of man. In both cases the paired terms—cross and resurrection, human word and the word of God—are, to use Ludwig Wittgenstein's terminology, parallel in surface grammar, but different in depth grammar. The cross and the human word denote historical facts, the resurrection and the word of God their interpretations. Accordingly the two expressions "cross and resurrection" and "human word and Word of God" suggest a parallel which simply does not exist, for resurrection is an interpretation of the cross and Word of God an interpretation of human words.

When the Bultmann school and their fellow theologians today continue to make ingenuous and careless predications about the actions of God, they willfully overlook the fact that in the humanities outside theology—for example in history and philology—no one speaks any longer of God's action in history. And this is a good thing, since in any case God was too often introduced as a "God of the gaps," who served to defend one's own views against those of others.

It cannot be said often enough that God cannot be an object of historical or scientific research unless the entity designated God is falsifiable. Therefore the attempt to understand both the human word of the Bible as Word of God and Jesus' death as the eschatological event of God raising him from the dead is apologetic through and through. It can never be refuted on the interpretive side of the argument.

Regarded from this angle, Bultmann's enterprise of demythologizing also serves the purpose of making what Bultmann calls the *kerygma* (preaching) unassailable, namely immune from all criticism. Thus he wants to rescue the alleged core of Christian faith by an interpretation which harmonizes it with the present worldview. What is problematical, however, is that Bultmann interprets the "salvation-occurrence" as an act of God. But a historical act of God is possible only in the context of the *kerygma*. Therefore his talk of God's action is devoid of any objective reference when he interprets the cosmological picture of the world that corresponds to the *kerygma*—the only picture in which a historical action of God is plausible—in existentialist terms and replaces cosmology with anthropology.

Now in this context the notion of resurrection which is destined for rescue or dogmatization is so completely empty of meaning that it can no longer clash with any possible fact. It has become a hollow shell with no trace of empirical content.

As an example of a crude and forced way of raising the notion of resurrection into the cloudy spheres of dogma one might draw attention to the conversation between Werner Harenberg of the well-known magazine *Der Spiegel* and the former Göttingen New Testament professor Hans Conzelmann, on which Hans Albert comments.[12] Concerning the question of whether or not Jesus is risen, Conzelmann replies:

> Anyone who asks this sort of question . . . is in reality not asking but already knows in advance what resurrection is.

On this Albert comments:

> What an . . . astonishing statement! If one asks whether Spartacus led a revolt, one presumably also "knows in advance what a revolt is," i.e., how the word "revolt" is to be used.

Conzelmann continues:

> The question whether the resurrection is an historical fact, whether it is an event in time or space, is completely meaningless. Only one thing is of essential importance, namely that the crucified one is not annihilated, that he is there . . . that he is the Lord, and that the world thus stands under the determination of the cross. For the risen one is the crucified one. We can see him only as such.

Again Albert comments:

> The arrogance with which the question is rejected is striking. In the end it could be dictated by a simple interest in determining what one should believe as a Christian today. What may be a reasonably specific though naive notion, similar to that which presumably

Christians have held down to the present day, is also associated with "resurrection." And it is then dismissed by an expert on the grounds that the question is meaningless. . . . What then is defined as being of essential significance is certainly no clearer than the question of the resurrection. But really the only person who can claim that this is not significant is someone who is completely indifferent as to whether the statements of the Bible have any truth-value in the usual sense. From the semantic perspective Conzelmann's answer is at least as naive as the question which he so arrogantly dismisses. Extremely painful questions are associated with each of his statements, and can be suppressed here only because the sloppiness which has crept in under the influence of hermeneutical irrationalism seems to exclude them.

In short, the attempt of Bultmann and his followers to understand Paul by combining radical historical criticism with a theological approach must be regarded as a failure. There seems to be no way thereby to translate Paul's message into today's world and at the same time sustain his theological claim that cross and resurrection have a universal cosmological importance. Therefore such an approach must be abandoned.


## OTHER ATTEMPTS TO REVITALIZE PAUL

A similar objection must be raised against any approach that seeks to keep Paul's message alive by promoting his *doctrine of justification by faith*. For it has become clear not only that this doctrine involves a caricature of Judaism but also that it is only one fragment of a larger set of teachings on salvation. Surely it would be unwise to revitalize something that is both flawed in content and incomplete in scope. I shall therefore look at Paul from another perspective.

Though he claimed to be weak, he thought of himself as being strong, indeed the strongest and wisest of his age. I simply refuse to countenance this sort of dialectical false modesty. In fact, I would suggest that whether expressed or implied, all pretensions of strength or importance should be viewed with skepticism and alarm in view of mankind's well-attested propensity for hubris and its natural consequence, tragedy. It corresponds to this insight that reason—our only hope for survival—is never loud and always aware of its limitations.

## PAUL—MOST WRETCHED OF ALL HUMAN BEINGS?

Judged by his own claim Paul is the most wretched of all human beings, his faith being vain, for Jesus did not rise from the dead. In other words, he deceived himself. A rather pitiable development took place when pupils of Paul and with them the rest of Christianity, in view of the unfulfilled Second Coming of Jesus, claimed the doctrine of personal immortality for themselves.

Again Nietzsche's acute observations are worth recalling at this point:

> That everyone as "an immortal soul" has equal rank with everyone else, that in the totality of living beings the "salvation" of *every* single individual may claim eternal significance that little prigs and three-quarter-madmen may have the conceit that the laws of nature are constantly broken for their sakes—such an intensification of every kind of selfishness into the infinite, into the *impertinent,* cannot be branded with too much contempt. And yet Christianity owes its triumph to this miserable flattery of personal vanity; it was precisely all the failures, all the rebellious-minded, all the less-favored, the whole scum and refuse of humanity who were thus won over to it. The "salvation of the soul"—in plain language: "the world revolves around *me.*"[13]

## PAUL—MADE HUMAN AGAIN

These objections notwithstanding, let me try to formulate some positive results from the study of Paul. In spite of my severe criticism of him, he has also offered some insights that are worth pondering, even in a context that is completely different from his, and that from the very start repudiates Paul's claim to absolute truth.

*First,* he insists on the need and the preference for understandable speech in matters related to one's faith. See 1 Cor. 14:19: "In church, I would rather speak five words with my mind, in order to instruct others, than ten thousand words in a tongue." Such a statement is all the more important because Paul himself knows of the temptation to indulge in religious emotions. Indeed, he claims to be more gifted in tongues than all the Corinthians who did not care to translate their emotions into understandable language (1 Cor. 14:18).

*Second,* Paul taught that religion is not an exclusively individual concern, but has important social dimensions (see 1 Cor. 8–10, 12–14, etc.).

*Third,* Paul held the conviction that life is a gift (1 Cor. 4:7b). Paul naturally saw God as the giver of life, but even in a world where this claim is no longer generally agreed upon, the concept of life as a gift seems to be a useful guard against any ideologically rooted arrogance that treats human beings as garbage or advocates some form of social Darwinism.

*Fourth,* Paul's conviction that love is preferable even to faith and hope is noteworthy and could serve as a useful preventive against any future dogmatism.

In sum, though most of what Paul advocated is ancient history, there remain elements that deserve to be preserved. However, they do not belong to the Christian heritage but to the Jewish one. This is quite ironic, for Paul believed that Christianity had replaced Judaism—though in the end he was no longer so sure of it as in his early days.

As a consequence of my research, I am not suggesting that we should repudiate Paul and focus exclusively on Jesus. This would only repeat mistakes of the past when a slogan of that sort has been no more than a tacit shibboleth to distinguish between those still attached to the Christian tradition and those alienated from and hostile to Christianity.[14]

Furthermore, such a step would still face the hermeneutical dilemma that we encounter in dealing with Paul: as modern human beings we would have to rewrite the received tradition, considerably diminish his message, and eliminate or redefine his unfulfilled hope for the future.

Research on Paul can afford us the same benefits as research on Jesus. Transporting both from the church of today into their proper first-century setting can have a liberating function. Such a freeing from the past is all too necessary because dogmatic images of normative Christian origins are not only reinforced every Sunday during worship but are also subconsciously lodged in the minds of scholars. They are like demons that lurk in dark corners to reproach us when we are critical of the Christian creed.

There is another advantage that historical reconstruction can offer. By showing that in the process of interpretation both Paul and Jesus have been twisted to suit the interests of the various interpreters, it admonishes the contemporary interpreter not to abuse either of them for his own purposes, but to let them remain in the first century. The next step, then, must be a constructive one, namely to formulate one's own vision in the context of our own culture. Working toward a better understanding of Paul is thus a way to set one part of the historical record straight in order to move ahead with a good conscience and an enthusiasm that both springs from and enhances the fullness of life in the present world.

Last but not least a rather painful issue has to have the last word: If Paul's message is based on a self-deception, how can we who live in a world that was so much shaped by Pauline Christianity escape from self-deception, the more so since nobody can base his or her life on a lie? I have two answers to that dilema: *First*, the truth can never be hidden forever, it will ultimately come out. So if Pauline Christianity is based on self-deception, this has to be spelled out with the utmost clarity. *Second*, most of today's Christians do not take Christianity seriously anyway and have already departed from Paul, but for the sake of a good conscience they continue to ascribe to him a major definitive influence. Therefore it is time to draw aside that curtain in order to gain a new and clearer vision of the way ahead. That would not be the least service that my book could provide.

## NOTES

1. *The Dawn* sec. 68 (Walter Kaufmann, *The Portable Nietzsche* [New York: Viking Press, 1954], pp. 76ff.).

2. I have learned most from Joseph Klausner, *From Jesus to Paul*

(London: Allen & Unwinn, 1943), and Leo Baeck, *Judaism and Christianity*, essays by Leo Baeck, translated with an introduction by Walter Kaufmann (Meredian Books. Cleveland/New York: World Publishing Company and Philadelphia: Jewish Publication Society of America, 1961), especially from Baeck's essay on "Romantic Religion" (pp. 187–292).

3. Eusebius *Ecclesiastical History* 3.5.2–3.

4. *The Antichrist* sec. 47 (Kaufmann, *Portable Nietzsche*, p. 627).

5. Albert Schweitzer, *The Mysticism of Paul the Apostle* (New York: Seabury Press, 1968), p. 377.

6. Ibid., p. 394.

7. Ibid.

8. Rudolf Bultmann, *Theology of the New Testament*, vol. 1 (New York: Charles Scribner's Sons, 1951), pp. 292–94.

9. Ibid., p. 302.

10. Ibid., p. 305f.

11. Note Bultmann answers the question whether Jesus has risen in the same way as Goethe. He says: "One can say that Jesus has risen in the same way as Goethe if one regards the person and work of Jesus as a phenomenon of intellectual history. For in intellectual history the persons and works of great men continue to have an influence, and that is also true of Jesus. But if one understands Jesus as an eschatological phenomenon, and that means as the end of history, insofar as its course is open to an objectifying consideration, then his present does not consist in his influence on intellectual history, but it comes about only on occasion in Christian proclamation of faith. . . . In that case, to believe in the resurrection of Jesus means to allow oneself to be encountered by the proclamation and to respond to it in faith." (The text is based on my *The Resurrection of Jesus: History, Experience, Theology* [Minneapolis: Fortress Press, 1994], pp. 185–86n.5.)

12. The following section is based on my book *The Unholy in Holy Scripture: The Dark Side of the Bible* (Louisville: Westminster John Knox Press, 1997), pp. 21ff.

13. *Antichrist* sec. 43 (Kaufmann, *Portable Nietzsche*, pp. 618ff.).

14. Even Nietzsche could regard Jesus as a Christian (cf. *Antichrist* secs. 31–39) only to distance himself from Christianity. See further Hans Dieter Betz, "The Birth of Christianity as a Hellenistic Religion: Three Theories of Origin," *Journal of Religion* 74 (1994): 16–24.

# EPILOGUE

In this book we have looked at Paul through a number of different lenses, and have perforce created a somewhat impressionistic portrait, composed as it is of overlaid and somewhat disparate images. This should not be surprising. Just as the light from distant galaxies appears to shimmer because it has passed through the vast and dusty expanse of space, so after two thousand years we must not expect a perfectly focused picture of so complex, creative, and controversial a man living in such turbulent times.

For one thing, we all too easily overlook the fact that a view of reality radically different from our own mediated the world to people of that preempirical time. They took for granted a three-tiered universe: this flat world, with the place of the dead below and the residence of the divine high in the heavens. Thus they conceived of God as a being apart from this world, who nevertheless controlled all that happened in it, and whose ineluctable will was carried out in part through the ministrations of good and evil spirits who abounded and were seldom at rest. Those within the Jewish tradition understood that their God had created the world as they knew it a few thousand years earlier, and in the view of many, he had plans to replace it with an ideal form of existence in the not too distant future.

Such all but universally accepted modern notions as the heliocentric solar system, the long evolution of life on the planet, and the unconscious workings of the human mind were not available to explain any of a thousand daily occurrences they saw as riddles or wonders, but which we understand as part of the normal and ordinary

243

course of events. We on the other hand can no longer conceive of the universe as a divided reality defined in terms of a natural-supernatural dichotomy. No longer can we take literally the notion that we possess a dual nature, that we are a mysterious amalgam of body and soul.

Several additional factors especially test our mettle when we have Paul sitting for our portrait, and may cause us to experience a further cognitive dissonance in dealing with him.

1. His perception of himself and his relation to the world was highly subjective. He was racked by guilt, admittedly perplexed by the conflict between his convictions, desires, and behavior. Today we might say he was afflicted with an overpowering superego, a phenomenon which, in that unsophisticated age, he quite readily projected on the heavens and mistook for the voice of God. To further complicate the situation, his guilt and professed unworthiness were paradoxically accompanied by the stated conviction that he had been specially appointed and called to the apostolate, and that he had been specially favored with God's revelation of his divine son.

2. It is clear that he felt an intense personal involvement in his missionary activities and his theological doctrines. He must be all things to all people. If the arguments fail to persuade, the teaching is true because he says it is. Anyone who will not accede to his belief or practice is to be cast out of the church. That a fine line divides conviction and fanaticism can perhaps be seen in his claim to have been divinely appointed to a role for which he was no doubt uniquely qualified. After all, every believer becomes a new person; his previous self has passed away.

3. The intensity of his self-involvement seems to have enabled him to blend myth with fact, to combine disparate ideas into a single vision, and to invest the resulting concept with ontological certainty. The crucifixion could not be understood simply as Jesus' self-sacrifice for a noble cause; by combining the scripturally attested but unrelated roles of the Messiah and the Suffering Servant, Paul was able to create a new mythic hero. And by assigning to this hero divine status, and to his death the power of atoning for the collective sins of mankind, he cre-

ated a cosmic myth and then declared it a historical fact. By a similar stroke of illogic he supported that declaration by identifying the man Jesus with the proclaimed Christ.

4. The attractive power of his message depended in considerable measure upon speculative doctrines and emotional responses. His spirituality was so grounded in mystical experiences that he was able to issue contradictory pronouncements on the status and validity of the Jewish Law with no apparent awareness of their palpable conflict. Highly trained in the Scriptures, and having found freedom from his inner demons in the Christian promise of God's unconditional love and forgiveness, and familiar with the powerful sway that pagan mystery religions exercised over the hearts and minds of many of his contemporaries, he was able to assemble—no doubt largely at an unconscious level of synthesis—a religion with a wide and powerful appeal.

Not only do these factors make him an elusive subject, but the inclination to minimize or even disregard the historical context of a great man's life commonly clouds our perception of him. We tend to forget not only the numerous uprisings and the two major rebellions of the first one and one-half centuries of the common era, but the *sturm und drang* of daily life for the vast majority. The purportedly halcyon world of the Pax Romana (Dominic Crossan incisively quips that it meant peace for Rome) ran on exploitation: some 5 percent of the population managed to live sumptuously by subjecting the other 95 percent to brief lives of drudging poverty. A less immediate but no less significant cultural phenomenon should also be noted: The republican ideals and institutions that had enabled Rome's rise to world prominence had given way to ever more authoritarian and repressive measures for dealing with the social, political, and economic problems that threatened the Empire. It is easy to miss the relevance of this for our understanding of Paul until we recognize that the intellectual freedom of ancient Greece was gradually succumbing to the increasing domination of the many by the few, just as the political vigor of Rome before the Caesars was giving way to the sort of "bunker mentality" that is commonly to be observed in the behavior of aristocrat and peasant alike when daily life is both harsh and insecure.

Increasingly the Hellenistic enlightenment was being repudiated, and faith-based spiritualities with other-worldly orientations and promises of personal salvation attracted those for whom the world and this life had lost their luster. Born in times of disaster and oppression, the idea of a just and righteous God rewarding the faithful in a future life had been slowly gathering currency in Judaism for some seven centuries. The promise of a messiah and the idea of a day of judgment had similar roots and obvious possibilities of relatedness. It was Paul, the cosmopolitan Jewish Greco-Roman who encountered the world on many fronts, and who was driven by some deep insecurity to find justification in acceptance, who put the pieces together.

If, as some have suggested, Jesus can be imagined as a superstar, then perhaps we may compare Paul to a supernova whose brilliance has considerably receded. Or, pursuing a slightly different metaphor, may we propose that Christianity as we know it began in the empty center of a red supergiant that imploded somewhere along the hot, dusty road to Damascus? It might prove a pregnant paradox to trace our faith to a spiritual void from which was born a new *gravitas*, a sense of purpose that sustained a deeply troubled but indomitable spirit through the trials and hardships of his missionary career, and that left behind him a handful of communities, a couple of thousand souls with a new vision, and a church planted far enough from Jerusalem to survive the cataclysm of 70 C.E. And it was Paul who gave shape and form and substance to the religion that became the dominant force of the culture that at length gave birth to the modern world. His was no small achievement.

Paul's instincts were often sound, as we see in his stress on ethical living, his insistence on the equal status of all believers, and the human equality of Jew and Greek, male and female. But his personal compulsion to be the original and the final authority, and his missionary zeal to retain the converts he had made and to add ever more by solving problems with ad hoc doctrinal solutions, led him to create a religion far different from that of Jesus. It is a measure both of his spiritual conviction and power, and of the frailty of the human condition, that it has taken us nearly two thousand years to recognize what he did—and what he failed to do.

# PAUL'S SECOND LETTER TO THE THESSALONIANS

## A COUNTERFORGERY

On the basis of a textual analysis, the following contains a full argument that 2 Thessalonians was composed as a counterforgery (see above, pp. 13–15).

*2 Thess. 2:1–15:*

(1) We beg you, brothers, concerning the coming of our Lord Jesus Christ and our assembling to meet him, (2) not to be quickly shaken in mind or alarm yourselves, either by spirit or **by word of mouth or by letter** purporting to be from us, alleging that the day of the Lord has come [or, "is imminent"].

(3) Let no one deceive you in any way whatever, for [that day will not come] unless the rebellion comes first, and the man of *lawlessness* is revealed, the son of perdition, (4) who opposes and exalts himself against every so-called god or object of worship, so that he takes his seat in the temple of God, proclaiming that he himself is God. (5) Do you not remember that when I was still with you I told you this? (6) And you know what is restraining him now so that he may be revealed in his time. (7) For the mystery of *lawlessness* is already at work; only he who now restrains it will do so until he is out of the way. (8) And then the *lawless* one will be revealed, and the Lord Jesus will kill him with the breath of his mouth and annihilate him by the radiance of his coming. (9) But the coming of the *lawless* one by the activity of Satan will be with all power and with a deceptive show of signs and wonders (10) and everything evil that can deceive those doomed to destruction, because they would not grasp

the love of _truth_ so as to be saved. (11) Therefore God sends on them a strong delusion, to make them believe what is false, (12) so that all be brought to judgment who did not believe the _truth_ but had pleasure in unrighteousness.

(13) But we are bound to give thanks to God always for you, brothers beloved by the Lord, because God chose you from the beginning to be saved, through sanctification by the Spirit and belief in the _truth_. (14) To this he called you through our gospel, so that you might possess the glory of our Lord Jesus Christ.

(15) So then, brothers, stand firm and hold fast to the traditions which you were taught by us, **either by word of mouth or by letter**.

_Verse 1:_ This verse designates the theme of the following section: the Second Coming of the Lord Jesus and the union of the faithful with him.

_Verse 2:_ "Purporting to be from us" is the translation of _hos di' hemon_. The Greek particle _hos_ introduces a fabricated or objectively false property and is meant to indicate that the letter does not come from Paul. Because of the position of _hos di' hemon_ immediately behind "letter" it in all likelihood refers to the letter. If it similarly referred to the other two members (spirit, word), this would not alter the reference to "letter." Verse 2 warns the community not to allow itself to be confused over the Second Coming, "either by spirit [i.e., an exclamation in the Spirit] or by word of mouth or by letter purporting to be from us, alleging that the day of the Lord has come [or, is imminent]."

As to the origin of the latter slogan one has to remember that the most striking characteristic of 1 Thessalonians is an ardent expectation of the coming of Jesus from heaven in the very near future (1 Thess. 4:15, 17). A synopsis of that passage would closely resemble the slogan which is rejected by the author of 2 Thessalonians. (For more on this see below, p. 250.) The letter referred to is most likely 1 Thessalonians, for the author knows it and imitates it.

_Verses 3–12:_ Now the recipients of the letter are given the correct teaching about the end: it will come only (in the indefinite future) when the adversary has revealed himself. The "Thessalonians" can rest assured that Jesus will kill the "lawless one" (verse 8) and that God will punish the sinners for their refusal to accept the truth (verses 11–12).

*Verses 13–14:* On the basis of 1 Thess. 2:13 a second thanksgiving is attached. Referring back to 1 Thess. 4:7 and 5:9, verses 13b–14, as a counterpart to verse 10, formulate the state of salvation in the community.

*Verse 15:* This antithetical echo of verse 2 admonishes the recipients of the letter to stand firm and to hold to the traditions that they were taught "either by word of mouth or by letter." The letter referred to here is not 1 Thessalonians but 2 Thessalonians, whose doctrine the recipients must observe and which is antithetically dissociated from a forged letter. The letter mentioned in verse 2 is likely to be identical with 1 Thessalonians. (For the reasons see below, p. 250).

Two indications from the time of the Roman presbyter Hippolytus (end of second century c.e.) give us an idea of how the events described in 1 Thessalonians may have been envisioned or how the expectation of an imminent end may have been expressed in practice.[1]

In his *Commentary on Daniel* (4.18), Hippolytus writes:

> I can also relate something which happened recently in Syria. For a certain leader of the church in Syria . . . was himself deceived and deceived others. . . . [H]e deceived many of the brothers so that they went out into the wilderness with women and children to meet [*eis synantesin*] with Christ. These also wandered around in vain in the mountains, so that they would likely have been seized by a centurion as robbers and executed. Fortunately his wife was a believer. She persuaded him to desist from his anger, thus averting a general massacre.

Immediately after that (4.19), Hippolytus gives another example:

> Similarly, [there was] another man in Pontus, who was also a leader of the church, a pious and humble man, but one who did not hold fast to scripture; rather, he believed more in the visions which he himself saw. . . . And then he once spoke in his error and said, "I want you to know, brothers, that the final judgment will take place after a year." They heard him saying that the day of the Lord was imminent (*enesteken he hemera tou kyriou*), and prayed to the Lord with weeping and lamententation day and night, having the

coming day of judgment before their eyes. And he led the brothers astray into such great anxiety and fearfulness that they left their lands and fields desolate, and most of them sold their possessions. And he said to them, "If what I have said does not happen, then no longer believe scripture, but let each of you do what he wills." So they waited for what was to come. And when a year was past and nothing of what he had said happened, he himself was ashamed that he had been wrong, even though the scriptures seemed truthful. The brothers, however, took offence, so that they married their virgins, and their men went to work on the land. But those who had sold their property in vain were reduced for begging for their bread.

The two examples cited attest two concrete instances of an imminent expectation and the way in which it was disappointed, and key vocabulary elements correspond word for word with 1 Thess. 4:17 and 2 Thess. 2:2. The expectation to meet the Lord is rooted in the conviction that the day of the Lord is imminent; the slogan behind 2 Thess. 2:2 corresponds to the expectation of 1 Thess. 4:13–17.

The author of 2 Thessalonians not only attacks such an expectation, but repudiates an appeal to Paul by labeling 1 Thessalonians as a forgery and putting his "authentic" letter to the Thessalonians into circulation (or introducing it to the community). Second Thess. 2:2 and 2:15 are to be understood as follows: those who are confusing the community (in Thessalonica) "by spirit or by word of mouth or by letter" are basing themselves on a *false* document, 1 Thessalonians. Rather, the correct tradition about the end-time is in 2 Thessalonians; moreover, the content of the whole letter forms the basis for Christian faith and applies unconditionally. Therefore the author of 2 Thessalonians remarks: "If anyone disobeys what we say in this letter, note that man, and have nothing to do with him, that he may be ashamed" (3:14). In other words, the right way to understand Paul is through acceptance of 2 Thessalonians.

How audaciously the forger acted is shown by the conclusion of the letter with its "sign of authenticity" in 3:17: "The greeting is in my own hand, signed with my name, Paul; this is my own writing." Here the author is even trumping the Paul of 1 Thessalonians, which notwithstanding 1 Thess. 5:27 has no sign of authenticity, and formally sealing the inauthenticity for his readers who knew it. At the same time he commended 2 Thessalonians by its echoes of 1 Thessalonians. In this ploy he was possibly guided by the sign of authenticity in 1 Cor. 16:21 and Gal. 6:11, two passages in which Paul adds something in his own hand, or the pseudo-Pauline letter to the Colossians where a similar ruse is employed (Col. 4:18).

Of course, the next question to be asked is this: How could the author of 2 Thessalonians come to regard 1 Thessalonians, which had been known and handed down for many years, as a forgery? Was he also *subjectively* convinced of this? What criterion did he use to deny authenticity? Evidently the author began by assuming that 1 Thessalonians in its existing form did not come from Paul. For him, that followed from the false teaching of opponents who had linked their theology closely to it. And because he had arrived at his conviction on dogmatic grounds, the end sanctified the means: He turned to forgery, a fact of which he may have been conscious for only a short time. Moreover, his memory may soon have played a trick on him; it would be neither the first nor the last time that memory yielded to pride (Friedrich Nietzsche).

The observations on the relationship of 2 Thessalonians to 1 Thessalonians and the conclusions which followed from it no doubt shed light on a conflict among the followers of Paul in Macedonia and beyond, a battle between orthodoxy and heresy. (Chronologically we may think of the end of the first century, but a later date is also possible.)

One tradition appropriated the Pauline legacy of 1 Thessalonians by accepting indisputably Pauline statements about the nearness of the end. That could have taken place in the same way as in the two examples from Hippolytus quoted above. In that case we would have a flaring up of the expectation of an imminent end: the day of the Lord is immediately at hand. (However, the fact that there is no mention of their mistake in 2 Thessalonians tells against this.) The other and more likely possibility is that those followers of Paul who were attacked in 2 Thessalonians did in fact proclaim that salvation and the end were present: The day of the Lord had already dawned. They would no doubt be properly described as Gnostics or enthusiasts and may have had ties with the circles behind Colossians and Ephesians and the Pauline teachers attacked by 2 Tim. 2:18 who claimed that the resurrection had already taken place. In this case, not only is the statement *enesteken he hemera tou kyriou* in 2 Thess. 2:2 to be understood in the present, but the possibility recommends itself that the formulation derives from the author of 2 Thessalonians. (Similarly, the same statement in the second of Hippolytus's examples was probably formulated by Hippolytus himself.)

The other tradition, personified in the author of 2 Thessalonians, snatches Paul from the enthusiasts or Gnostics, interpreting him in accord with the time and thus keeping him useful for the church. The author may have been a churchman who resorted to such draconian measures out of a concern to care for and develop the legacy of Paul, but also in the face of the threat of confusion to ordinary people.

## NOTE

1. The two texts follow the (slightly modified) translation in my *Heretics: The Other Side of Early Christianity* (Louisville: Westminster John Knox Press, 1996), pp. 114–15.

# CRITICISM OF PAUL IN THE LETTER OF JAMES AND IN THE SECOND LETTER OF PETER

Acitation of and commentary on passages in which the authors of these two books deal with Paul will further clarify why Paul was a problem in primitive Christianity.

## CRITICISM OF PAUL IN THE LETTER OF JAMES

*James 2:14–26:*

> (14) *What good does it do*, my brothers, if a man says he has faith but has not **works**? Can that faith save him? (15) If a brother or sister is ill-clad and in lack of daily food, (16) and one of you says to them, "Go in peace, be warmed and filled," without giving them the things needed for the body, *what good does it do?* (17) So faith by itself, if it has no **works**, is dead.
> (18) But someone will say, "You have faith and I have **works**." Show me your faith apart from the **works**, and I by the **works** will show you my faith. (19) You believe that God is one? Excellent! Even the demons believe but shudder. (20) But can you not see, you quibbler, that faith apart from **works** is barren? (21) *Was not Abraham our father justified by* **works**, *when he offered his son Isaac upon the altar?* (22) You see that faith was active along with his **works**, and faith was completed by **works**, (23) and the scripture was fulfilled which says, "*Abraham put his faith in God, and it was counted to him as righteousness*"; and he was called the friend of God. (24) You see then that *a man is justified by* **works** *and not by faith*

*alone.* (25) And in the same way was not also the prostitute Rahab justified by **works** when she received the messengers and sent them out another way? (26) For as the body apart from the spirit is dead, so faith apart from **works** is dead.

This section contains the following points of contact (written in italics) between James and the Pauline letters.

(a) Cf. verse 21 with Rom. 4:2: "If Abraham was justified by works, he has something to boast about." Cf. verse 23 with Rom. 4:3b: "Abraham believed God, and it was reckoned to him as righteousness." A literary connection between these two texts is suggested by the observation that they agree verbatim with each other but agree in deviating from the Septuagint (Gen. 15:6) in two otherwise insignificant points which cannot be recognized in the English translation: in the spelling of *Abraam* rather than *Abram* and in the addition of the Greek particle *de* after "believed." This means that the author of James had accepted the example of Abraham but used it *against* Paul as proof for his view that faith is made complete by works (cf. verses 22b, 24).

(b) Cf. verse 24 with Gal. 2:16: "A man is not justified by works of the law but through faith in Jesus Christ," and Rom. 3:28: "We hold that a man is justified by faith apart from works of the law."

As in the texts discussed above, the verbatim agreements point to a literary connection. The hypothesis that James is dependent on Paul is further supported by the fact that the polar opposition of faith and works is not documented prior to Paul. It is interesting that the "alone" of James 2:24 does not appear in Rom. 3:28. Since "by faith" of Rom. 3:28 must, however, be understood in an exclusive sense, "alone" is thoroughly appropriate and cannot be used as an argument against a dependence of James on Paul.

In addition, James 2:24 has only "by works" instead of "by works of the law." However, this datum by no means weakens my hypothesis, but simply indicates that the author of James no longer perceived the function that the concept of law exercised in Pauline theology and therefore saw no difference between "works" and "works of the law."

If it is thus established that in the passages discussed above the author of James consciously presents a polemic against Paul, we may now look at another text in James. Though its polemical aim may be arguable, in light of our findings it might shed important light on James as an anti-Pauline document.

James 2:10 reads, "For whoever keeps *the whole law* but fails in one point has become guilty of all of it." Cf. with this the text Gal. 5:3: "I testify again to every man who receives circumcision that he is bound to keep *the whole law*," and Gal. 3:10b: "Cursed be everyone who does not abide by all things written in the book of the law, and do them."

Though the verbal agreements between James 2:10 and Gal. 5:3 (3:10) are only slight ("the whole law"), in terms of content the passages are practically identical.

Still, the different function of the statements is to be noted. Paul's adjurations are formulated to exclude the way of the law as an option for his congregations: Not only can no one fulfill the law, no one *should* fulfill it. The author of James, on the other hand, writes his sentence in order to challenge his congregation to keep the law. (Verse 10 stands in the unit of James 2:8–11, which deals with keeping the law.)

## RESULT

The upshot is that the author of James attacks passages from the Pauline letters and thereby Paul himself. Needless to say, the polemic exaggerates Paul's position. (Rom. 3:28 does not say "alone," but definitely implies it.) The apostle knows of no faith that is not at the same time obedience (cf. Rom. 1:5) and that is not active in deeds of love (cf. Gal. 5:6). Rather than accurately reflecting the historical Paul, the author's portrayal of the Pauline understanding of faith is something of a caricature.

An important parallel to the self-serving polemic in James is given by the apostle himself in Rom. 3:8 (cf. 6:1). Even during his lifetime Paul's opponents caricatured his doctrine of justification by claiming that it provoked an immoral life. Similarly, the author of James distorts key sentences from Galatians and Romans in such a way that the Pauline concept of faith seems to bear little or no relation to ethical conduct. (For at least a partial justification of such a criticism see above, pp. 215–17.)

## CRITICISM OF PAUL IN THE SECOND LETTER OF PETER

I shall now turn to the other writing from the New Testament that reflects misgivings about Paul, 2 Peter. The texts to be examined are 2 Pet. 3:3–10 and 3:15–16. For the sake of better understanding the argument in the letter, I will analyze them in the reverse order.

*2 Pet. 3:15–16:*

> (15) And count the patience of our Lord as salvation. So also our beloved brother Paul wrote to you according to the wisdom given him, (16) speaking of this as he does in all his letters. They contain some obscure passages, which the ignorant and unstable twist to their own destruction, as they do the other scriptures.

Three things are worth mentioning in this passage. *First,* the author has a very positive picture of Paul. *Second,* there is evidently already a collection of Paul's letters, otherwise it would not have been said that in *all* his letters Paul spoke of the "patience" of God. *Third,* the "patience" refers to the eschatological statements in the letters of Paul, that is to their underlying assumptions about the future. Here the author attributes to Paul his own idea, which he has developed in chapter 3.

*2 Pet. 3:3–10:*

> (3) Note this first: in the last days there will be people who scoff at religion, following their own passions (4) and they will say, "Where now is the promise of his coming? For ever since the fathers fell asleep, all things go on as they were from the beginning of creation." (5) They are choosing to forget that there were heavens and earth long ago, created by God's word out of water and with water; heavens existed long ago, and an earth formed out of water and by means of water, (6) and by water that first world was destroyed, the water of the deluge. (7) And the present heavens and earth, again by God's word, have been stored up for fire, being kept until the day of judgment and destruction of ungodly people.
>
> (8) But there is one thing, beloved, that you must not forget: that with the Lord one day is as a thousand years, and a thousand

years as one day. (9) The Lord is not being slow about his promise
as some suppose, but he is patient with you, not wishing that any
should perish, but for all to come to repentance. (10) But the day
of the Lord will come like a thief, and then the heavens will disap-
pear with a loud noise, and the elements will be dissolved with fire,
and the earth and all that it contains will be burnt up.

This section is directed at the question of the mockers, "Where is the
promise of his coming (*parousia*)?" (verse 4) that derives its force
from primitive Christianity's imminent expectation of the return of
Jesus on the clouds of heaven in. It is answered as follows:

Two arguments disqualify the opponents from the start: For one
thing, those who ask this kind of question are only following their
own passions (verse 3). In addition, the plan of salvation has
announced that such mockers will appear in the last time (verse 3).
Then the author introduces three arguments against the imminent
coming. (a) For the Lord, a day is as a thousand years (verse 8). (b)
The postponement has been given by way of patience (cf. verse 15),
so that all could still be converted (verse 9). (c) The day of the Lord
comes like a thief (verse 10).

The author of 2 Peter, however, knows Paul only as someone
who no longer has any expectation of an imminent return of Jesus.
This makes it all the more surprising that he refers to "some obscure
passages" (verse 16) in Paul; for he thus suggests that the opponents
whom he is attacking could precisely explain those difficult passages
in the letters of Paul, and put forward an interpretation of the eschatological statements different from that of the author of 2 Peter.

# THE HELLENISTS
# AS PRECURSORS
# OF PAUL

In order to substantiate the earlier profile of the Hellenistic church (see above, pp. 139–43), we shall now offer an analysis of the pertinent passages in Acts.[1] Although these passages cannot be checked against the Pauline letters for their historical accuracy, a total a priori skepticism is unwarranted. In such cases the methods of redactional and traditional analysis have to be applied, as I have done throughout the book (see especially the comment above, pp. 27–28).

"Hellenists" means Greek-speaking Jews. Though we do not possess primary writings from this group, we do have reliable items of information about them which stem not only from the letters of Paul—the apostle quite often quotes and interprets traditional pieces which most likely come from Hellenist circles—but also from the author of Luke-Acts, who dedicates Acts 6–8 and 11–14 at least in part to the Hellenists.

While there is general agreement on the first point, the second is often disputed because many doubt the possibility of deriving reliable historical information from Acts. In order to defend my hypothesis, let me *first* ask the reader to recall what was said about the use of Acts-tradition for a chronology of Paul (see above, pp. 26–27) and to recollect how plausibly the traditions of Acts were incorporated into the chronological framework which was based solely on the evidence of the letters. *Second*, it may be remembered that we have already shown—in connection with the name "Christian" in Acts 11:26d (see above, pp. 138–39)—how reliable information on the Hellenists can be derived from Acts. That should motivate us to continue our search for information about and traditions from the Hellenists that underlie much of Acts 6–14.

Remembering that a reconstruction and the resulting understanding of the Hellenists is essential for understanding Paul, let us analyze several texts from Acts in order to rediscover some basic elements of what the Hellenists said and did.

*Acts 6:1–15:*

> (1) *Now in those days when the disciples were growing in number, the Hellenists made a complaint against the Hebrews because their widows were neglected in the daily distribution.*
>
> (2) And the twelve called the body of the disciples and said, "It is not right that we should neglect the word of God in order to wait at table. (3) Therefore, brothers, pick out from among you seven men of good reputation, *full of the Spirit and of wisdom, whom we may appoint to this duty.* (4) *But we will devote ourselves to prayer and to the ministry of the word."* (5) And what they said pleased *the whole body,* and they chose Stephen, *a man full of faith and of the Holy Spirit,* and Philip, and Prochorus, and Nicanor, and Timon, and Parmenas, and Nicolaos, a proselyte of Antioch. (6) These they presented before the apostles, *and they prayed and laid their hands on them.*
>
> (7) *And the word of God continued to spread; and the number of the disciples multiplied greatly in Jerusalem, and very many of the priests were obedient to the faith.*
>
> (8) *And Stephen, full of grace and power, did great wonders and signs among the people.*
>
> (9) But some members of the synagogue called the Synagogue of the Freedmen comprising Cyrenians and Alexandrians, and people from Cilicia and Asia, came forward and disputed with Stephen. (10) But they could not hold their own against his *wisdom and the Spirit* with which he spoke. (11) Then they secretly instigated men, who said, "We have heard him speak blasphemous words against Moses and God." (12) And they stirred up the people and the elders and the scribes, and they came upon him and seized him and brought him before the council, (13) and produced false witnesses who said, "This man is forever saying things against this holy place and the law; (14) for we have heard him say, 'This Jesus of Nazareth will destroy this place, and will alter the customs handed down to us by Moses.'"

(15) *And fixing their eyes on him, all who sat in the council saw that his face was like the face of an angel.*

*Outline*

Verse 1: Exposition: The problem of neglect of the Hellenistic widows

Verses 2–6: Solution of the conflict: The choice of the Seven

Verse 7: Summary and note about priests joining the community

Verse 8: Summary description of the miracles of Stephen among the people

Verses 9–14: Two charges against Stephen
    9–10: The unsuccessful attack by the members of the Hellenist (synagogue) communities by means of disputations
    11–14: The attack by false witness, its impact on the people, the elders and the scribes and the proceedings before the Sanhedrin

Verse 15: Description of Stephen's face

## LUKE'S INTENTION

A new section in Acts begins with chapter 6. The narrative is introduced by the report in 6:1 of dissension within the community and its resolution by the appointment of deacons in 6:5–6. This continues the description of the communal organization of the congregation in Acts 2:44–45, and 4:32–5:11. But now—after the hints in 5:16—the mission which had previously been limited to Jerusalem reaches out to the surrounding areas through the preaching of the Hellenists. This section (6:1–8:3) centers on the person of Stephen, as does 8:4–40 on the figure of Philip.

*Verse 1:* The conflict reported here is intrinsically plausible. Many pious Jews settled in Jerusalem in the evening of their lives in order to be buried in the holy city. Therefore the care of their widows was a problem which came up relatively frequently. However, Luke creates an artificial conflict because members of the Jerusalem community were naturally involved in the Jewish community's care of the poor. We shall have to ask later what kind of real conflict Luke has papered over.

*Verses 2–6:* Verse 2a seems to presuppose the constitution of the Lukan church. Two groups are pictured in conflict: the leaders of the community—here the Twelve—and the full assembly. The leaders of the community summon the body and make proposals to it. The description of the task of the Seven, to see to the care of the widows, uses a phrase which recalls the summaries in Acts 2:45 and 4:35. While it was said there that the apostles (!) distributed the resources of the earliest community ("as any had need"), from now on the Seven (and no longer the apostles) will see to this task. Verse 4 reflects the Lukan conception that the Twelve were concerned with prayer and preaching the word (cf. Acts 2:42; 4:29—for the expression "ministry of the word" cf. Luke 1:2: the eyewitnesses as the servants of the Word means the twelve apostles). Verse 5 points back to verse 2, and like that verse reflects Luke's portrait of the constitution of the church; the proposal made by the Twelve, the leaders of the community, meets with the assent of the body of disciples, the full assembly. Luke is likely to be responsible for the order of the list in verse 5, which is from tradition. He puts Stephen at its head, for he will soon be the focus of events. Nor is it accidental that Philip occupies second place, as he will be the major figure from Acts 8:4 on. The proselyte Nicolaos occupies the last place. While the name goes back to tradition, his position at the end is due to redaction. Thereby Luke shows that he knows the difference between a (full) Jew and a proselyte. In *verse 6* the prayer and the laying–on of hands is redactional. The latter also appears in Acts 13:3, in the entrusting of someone with a special task.

*Verse 7:* This is a Lukan summary. By echoing verse 1 as well as 2:41, 47, and 4:4, verse 7a stresses the constant and rapid growth in the community. In verse 7b the report that many priests had joined the community indicates a further development, since previously only ordinary Jewish people had become Christians.

*Verse 8:* This verse, being redactional in terms of language, is a transition to the following episode. Stephen is not depicted "serving food" but speaking in public, nor in "serving the word," but being effective through miracles.

*Verses 9–14:* Verse 9 is a kind of prelude to the conflict which follows and which ends in Stephen's death. In verse 10 Luke points back to verse 3, and this links verses 1–7 to verses 8–15. The parallel between Luke 21:15 and verse 10 shows that the author of Acts sees Jesus' prediction in Luke 21:15 realized in the trial of Stephen. After the failure of the first attack against Stephen, verse 11 introduces a second, and verse 12 describes its success. Even "the people," who hitherto sided with the Hellenists (cf. also verse 8), are influenced, as are also—less surprisingly—the elders and scribes, who had already been involved in actions against the earliest Jerusalem community (Acts 4 and 5). Verse 13 says explicitly that the witnesses were false, whereas in verse 11 they were still described neutrally as "men." According to Luke, the statement made by the men/false witnesses is in any case wrong even though the accusation in verse 13 is not completely identical with that in verse 11. Verse 11 speaks of blasphemy against Moses and God, whereas verse 13 speaks of attacks on the holy place (the temple) and the law.

*Verse 15:* The language derives from Luke.


## THE TRADITION REWORKED BY LUKE

*Verse 1:* On the underlying conflict between the Hellenists and the Hebrews, which Luke tries to tone down, see above, pp. 261–62. In addition, the abrupt introduction of the dispute between the Hebrews and the Hellenists suggests the employment of tradition.

*Verse 5:* The bedrock tradition is the list of the Seven. That all of them have Greek names makes their Greek origin clear: Stephen, Philip, Prochorus, Nicanor, Timon, Parmenas, and Nicolaos. The sacred number *seven* was undoubtedly part of the tradition. The echo of this passage in Acts 21:8 (where Philip is called one of the Seven) need not tell against this.

*Verse 9:* This verse reflects the tradition that there were one or more such communities in Jerusalem. There is evidence of at least eleven such synagogues in Rome.

*Verse 10:* Stephen is portrayed as a preacher, in other words quite differently from what might have been expected from the share of work assigned to him in verse 2. If one thinks through Luke's account, one must ask whether the daily care for the widows could have improved at all under such conditions. It follows from this that the understanding of Stephen in verse 10 is quite different from that in verses 1–7. Therefore despite the Lukan peculiarities of language indicated in the translation by italics, verse 10 seems to have a traditional nucleus.

*Verses 11–14:* Verse 11 reflects elements of Stephen's preaching at the level of tradition as will verses 13–14.

## HISTORICAL ELEMENTS

There is almost universal consensus among scholars that the Hellenists are Greek-speaking Jews and the Hebrews Aramaic-speaking Jews of Jerusalem. This consensus is based on both the narrower and wider contexts of Acts 6. So the Seven have Greek names (verse 5) in contrast to the predominantly Semitic names of the twelve apostles (only Andrew and Philip are exceptions here). Further, Luke uses only one word etymologically related to "Hebrews," the adjective "Hebrais," which commonly connotes a linguistic reference. See the Greek phrase *Hebraidi dialecto* ("in the Hebrew language") in Acts 21:40 (cf. John 5:2; 19:13, 17, 20). There was some controversy between the parties of the Hebrews and the Hellenists in the early period of the primitive community, although no further information about the nature of the dispute is available on the basis of the tradition contained in verses 1–6. Since there is a genetic connection between the traditions behind verses 1–7 and verses 8–15, one can make a reasoned guess at the occasion of the conflict: Aramaic-speaking Christians who were strict observers of the law fell out with Greek-speaking Christians over the question of law, and the language barrier added a further element to the dispute. The dispute must have taken place in the early period of the primitive community in Jerusalem, since Paul was already persecuting members of this group of Hellenists outside Jerusalem, yet no longer found them in Jerusalem during his first visit.

## HELLENISTIC JEWISH COMMUNITIES IN JERUSALEM

The presence in Jerusalem of the groups named in verse 9 has a good deal to be said for it historically. It can be supported by the following evidence: A Greek inscription found in Jerusalem shortly before the First World War indicated, among other things, that the synagogue had been built by the priest and synagogue president Theodotus, son of Vettenus, and that a guest house and water supply for pilgrims had been connected with it. Perhaps this inscription is a reference to the *Libertini* (a Latin loanword that denotes freed Jews) mentioned in verse 9. The father of Theodotus has a Roman name, Vettenus, which he may have adopted after being freed because he owed his freedom to a Roman member of the *gens Vettena*. In that case his family may have belonged to the synagogue of the *Libertini* in Jerusalem.

## WHERE DID THE DISPUTE OVER STEPHEN ARISE?

It is historically improbable that all the Hellenistic Jews mentioned in verse 9 were involved in the disputation with Stephen, as Luke suggests at the redactional level. Rather, the dispute must have arisen in one Hellenistic synagogue to which Stephen belonged. The issue was that Stephen, a preacher filled with the Spirit, had a critical attitude toward the Law of Moses, a posture to which his opponents took offence. The dispute was, as in similar cases, initially verbal and then became physical. (How remote Luke already is from the historical Stephen is evident from the fact that, in verse 13a, he presents the information about Stephen's criticism of the law as untrue.)

We may assume that Stephen combined faith in Christ with an understanding of the law in a way that was unacceptable to the members of the Hellenistic synagogue. At any rate, it was regarded as blasphemous and led to the action hinted at in verse 12 and described in Acts 7:57–58 (see further below, pp. 266–69). Stephen's view of the law led not only to a fatal dispute in the Hellenistic synagogue(s) but also, as Acts 6:1f. indirectly depicts, to a split in primitive Christianity.

## STEPHEN'S UNDERSTANDING OF THE LAW

According to verse 11 Stephen spoke against Moses and God; i.e., he criticized the law. Furthermore, according to verse 14 he criticized the temple and the law with reference to Jesus. The formula that Jesus will alter the customs handed down by Moses does not suggest total abrogation of the law. (Such a step was not to be expected anyway unless a Jew deliberately became a Greek, something very unlikely in the case of Stephen.) Regardless of what the future tense means in verse 14, we must cautiously conclude that Stephen disparaged the law and the temple, that on the basis of God's will as revealed in or taught by Jesus he announced the destruction of the temple and censured at least some significant points of the law.

*Acts 7:54–8:1a:*

> (54) *Now when they heard these things they were infuriated, and they ground their teeth against him.*
>
> (55) *But he, full of the Holy Spirit, gazed into heaven and saw the glory of God, and Jesus <u>standing at God's right hand</u>; (56) and he said, "Look, I see the heavens opened, and the Son of Man <u>standing at God's right hand</u>."*
>
> (57) *But they <u>cried with a loud voice</u> and stopped their ears and rushed together upon him. (58) Then they cast him out of the city and* **stoned** *him; and the witnesses laid down their clothes at the feet of a young man named Saul. (59) And they* **stoned** *Stephen, while he was saying in invocation, "Lord Jesus, receive my spirit." (60) And he*

*knelt down* and <u>cried with a loud voice</u>, "Lord, do not hold this sin against them." And when he had said this, he died.

(8:1) *And Saul entirely approved of his murder.*

*Outline*

Verse 54: The Sanhedrin's reaction to Stephen's speech

Verses 55–56: Stephen's vision

Verses 57–60: The stoning of Stephen
    57–58a: The Sanhedrin's reaction to Stephen's vision:
        the stoning begins
    58b: The behavior of the witnesses: they lay down their clothes
        before Saul
    59–60: The stoning concluded; Stephen's behavior
        and his death

Verse 8:1a: Saul's approval of the murder of Stephen

## LUKE'S INTENTION

*Verse 54:* This verse is a redactional foreshadowing of verse 57.

*Verses 55–56:* The report of the vision in verse 55 and the announcement of the vision in verse 56 have been shaped by Luke, for the verses seem to depend on Luke 22:69: "From now on the Son of Man will sit at the right hand of the power of God." Note that in adapting Mark 14:62 to his passion account, Luke has omitted "you will see" from this sentence. In this case his purpose was to show that the vision of the exalted Christ was not granted to opponents, as in Mark 14:62; so here it appears only to Stephen, the believing witness.

*Verses 57–60:* "They cried with a loud voice" in verse 57 corresponds to the same expression in verse 60 (note underlines). The observation in verse 58b that the witnesses laid down their garments at the feet of the young man Saul serves to link the martyrdom of

Stephen with the story of Paul which follows. In this way the great missionary first appears on the scene as a bystander. That the witnesses laid down their clothes (as at some sport event) is presumably the result of a Lukan misunderstanding. The Jewish legal ordinance which Luke probably wanted to weave in here (Mishnah Sanhedrin 6:3) called for the condemned man to be stripped. Verse 59a resumes the thread of the narrative which was interrupted by verse 58a—as is visible from the repetition of "they stoned" (set in bold). The report of the death of Stephen in verse 59b is strikingly close to the narrative of Jesus' death and is therefore redactional. According to Luke 23:46 Jesus' last words are "Father, into your hands I commend my spirit." This corresponds almost word for word with Ps. 30:6 (LXX), a passage which in Judaism was used as an evening prayer. In contrast to Luke 23:46, Stephen's exclamation ("Lord Jesus, receive my spirit") is addressed to Jesus, whom he had seen as the exalted Lord. The introductory phrase "he knelt down" in verse 60a is Lukan in language and content (cf. Luke 22:41: in Gethsemane Jesus knelt down; Luke's source, Mark, differs here). In this way Luke has drawn a further parallel between the martyrdom of Stephen and that of Jesus. The calling out with a loud voice again recalls the passion of Jesus (Luke 23:46). Similarly, the petition, "Lord, do not hold this sin against them" is close to Jesus' saying, "Father, forgive them, for they know not what they do" (Luke 23:34— however, this verse may have been inserted into the gospel later).

*Verse 8:1a:* This is the work of Luke, who wants Saul to be involved in the execution; indeed it serves as climax to the remark in verse 58, where Saul functions as a guard for the clothes: in verse 1a he is already pleased by the killing of Stephen, and then 8:3 depicts him as an active persecutor).

The texts on the Hellenists and Stephen analyzed so far have been fully reworked by Luke so that a clean separation of redaction from tradition was impossible. Rather, here and there, we were able to recover traditional elements. Therefore I prefer to deal with the tradition that underlies the texts on Stephen and the Hellenists in a summarizing manner and shall simultaneously discuss the historical question.

## THE EXECUTION OF STEPHEN— THE RESULT OF A RIOT

The analysis of the redaction showed that Luke tried to make the trial and execution of Stephen an orderly procedure carried out by the Supreme Council (cf. 6:12b–14; 7:1, 58b). In so doing he made the mistake of describing the stoning as different from what was customary in Jewish legal ordinance (see above on verse 58b). If we assume that Stephen was killed in Jerusalem, it is probable that the account of a riot over Stephen has a basis in tradition, and that its consequence was that he fell victim to lynch law. There is no sentence, and Stephen is stoned without a verdict. The stoning is an act of popular justice. There is no sign of the Sanhedrin. It could not carry out capital sentences, only the Roman occupying force could, and there is no mentioning of them anywhere in the first part of Acts—this needs to be stressed. Stephen fell victim to a riot and there was no legal proceeding against him.

From this we must further assume that the tradition has been completely overlaid by Lukan language and shaping, particularly in the scene of the riot in verse 57. Stoning remains possible as a manner of his death, as lynch law often made use of it.[2] The report that supporters of Stephen had to leave Jerusalem following his martyrdom was probably also part of the tradition.

## THE EXPULSION OF THE HELLENISTS

Now it has to be asked whether there is a genetic connection between Acts 7:54–8:1a and 6:8–15. In support of an original connection is the fact that in verse 54 there is no further mention of the name Stephen. Otherwise a mention would have been expected after the long speech (Acts 7:2–53) which we left out as irrelevant for the historical Stephen and the Hellenists. This therefore supports the assumption that underlying Acts 6–7 is a tradition according to which the criticism of the temple and law by Stephen and the Hellenists caused a popular uprising in which Stephen suffered martyrdom and as a result his followers had to leave Jerusalem.

If this reconstruction is sound, a further assumption is at least possible, namely that the tradition lying behind 6:1–7 belongs to the block of tradition that has just been reconstructed. Indeed, it may have introduced it. The Stephen narrative might very well have been preceded by a report about the beginnings of the group on which Stephen made such a mark.

The death of Stephen is beyond dispute the clearest point in the history of Christianity before Paul. With this event we first find ourselves on undeniably historical ground. Evidence for that is the one decisive fact which was occasioned by the persecution of Stephen, namely the conversion of Paul—as if any further proof were needed of the fact of an event which according to all sides had such an indelible effect on the development of the Christian cause. As I explained in more detail earlier, Stephen's criticism of law and cult are to be regarded as historical. The expulsion of those of like mind from Jerusalem is the best reason for such an assumption.

*Acts 8:4–25:*

> (4) Now those who were scattered went about preaching the word.
> (5) Philip came down to the city of Samaria, and proclaimed the Christ to them. (6) And the crowds with one accord gave heed to what Philip said, when they heard him and saw the signs which he did. (7) For unclean spirits came out of many who were possessed, crying out with a loud voice; and many paralysed and crippled folk were cured. (8) So there was much joy in the city.
> (9) But there was a man *called* Simon who had previously practiced magic in the city and amazed the nation of Samaria, proclaiming himself to be someone great. (10) They all gave heed to him, from the least to the greatest, saying, "This man is that power of God which is called Great." (11) And they gave heed to him, because for a long time he had amazed them with his magic. (12) *But when they believed Philip as he preached good news about the kingdom of God and the name of Jesus Christ, they were baptized, both men and women. (13) Even Simon himself believed, and after having been baptized he continued with Philip. And seeing signs and great miracles performed, he was amazed.*
> (14) *Now when the apostles at Jerusalem heard that Samaria had*

*received the word of God, they sent to them Peter and John, (15) who went down there and prayed for them that they might receive the Holy Spirit. (16) For until then the Spirit had not fallen on any of them, but they had only been baptized in the name of the Lord Jesus. (17) Then they laid their hands on them and they received the Holy Spirit.* (18) Now when Simon saw that the Spirit was given through the laying on of the apostles' hands, he offered them money, (19) saying, "Give me also this power, that any one I lay my hands on may receive the Holy Spirit." (20) But Peter said to him, "May your silver perish with you, because you thought that you could obtain the gift of God with money! (21) You have no share nor rights in this, for your heart is not right before God. (22) Repent therefore of this wickedness of yours, and pray to the Lord that, if possible, the thought of your heart may be forgiven you. (23) For I see that you are in bondage to bitterness and enslaved by sin." (24) And Simon answered, "Pray for me to the Lord, that nothing of what you have said may come upon me."

(25) *And so, after giving their testimony and speaking the word of the Lord, they returned to Jerusalem, preaching the gospel to many villages of the Samaritans.*

*Outline*

Verse 4: Generalized note about the travel and preaching of the expelled Hellenists

Verses 5–8: The success of Philip's preaching in Samaria

Verses 9–13: Simon Magus is defeated by Philip
    9-11: The previous history: Simon's activity in Samaria
    12-13: The success of Philip's mission; Simon's conversion and
        baptism

Verses 14–24: Peter and John in Samaria
    14-17: The Holy Spirit bestowed through Peter and John
    18-24: Simon repudiated by Peter

Verse 25: Return of Peter and John to Jerusalem

## LUKE'S INTENTION

*Verse 4:* This verse is a Lukan transitional note. It has a close parallel in 11:19 (on this see below, p. 279).

*Verses 5–8:* These verses—based on tradition but shaped by Lukan language—are a summary account of Philip's preaching success in Samaria.

*Verses 9–13:* The first sub-section (verses 9–11) refers to the time before Philip's arrival and depicts the prehistory of Simon's activity in Samaria, which we need to know in order to understand what comes next. Luke's redactional hand (identified in the translation by italics) is more than clear in language and style. The second subsection (verses 12–13) depicts the superiority of the Christian miracle worker and preacher Philip to Simon. Verse 12 is a link to verses 5–8.

*Verses 14–24:* Verses 14–17 depict the bestowal of the Holy Spirit on the Christians in Samaria, thereby securing the endorsement of the Samaria mission by the Jerusalem apostles. To this end Peter and John are "smuggled into" the story of Philip. The separation of baptism and the bestowal of the Holy Spirit is artificial and done for the sole purpose of getting the Jerusalem apostles into the story. Elsewhere in Luke-Acts baptism and bestowal of the Holy Spirit coincide (see Acts 2:38, etc.).

Verses 18–24 answer the other question raised by verses 5–13: whether the notorious Simon remained in the Christian community. Their redactional character emerges mainly from arguments relating to content and from the link between the episode and the context. The negative use of the theme of money finds an analogy in Acts 5:1–11 and 24:24–26. The idea that money does not secure salvation occurs, as in verses 18–19, in Peter's remark in Acts 3:6: "Silver and gold have I none, but what I have, I give to you: In the name of Jesus Christ the Nazarene, walk!" The whole thrust of verses 18–24 is to express the fact that the Holy Spirit is not to be bought but is a gift of grace (see further on this Acts 2:38; 10:45; 11:17). Simon Magus was a welcome example which Luke could use to impress these ideas on his readers.

*Verse 25:* This verse is part of the Lukan framework and takes

Peter and John back to Jerusalem. On their way back they preach the word of the Lord (cf. 4:29; 6:2) to the people of Samaria. This fulfils the second part of 1:8 where the Twelve were told that they would be the witnesses of Jesus not only in Jerusalem and in Judea but also in Samaria. Since in Luke's opinion the mission of the Hellenist Philip was not fully valid, two of the Jerusalem apostles had to carry out a mission in Samaria.

## THE TRADITION REWORKED BY LUKE

*Verses 5–8:* The foundation of this is a written account of, or oral traditions about the spirit-filled activity of the preacher Philip, one of the seven Hellenists, in Samaria.

*Verses 9–13:* Here Luke has summarized a tradition which was an ingredient of the early Christian tradition about Simon Magus, a gnostic teacher who as early as the second century was regarded as the first heretic. In addition, I suggest that the tradition of Simon Magus underlying verses 9–13 is part of a written or oral tradition from Hellenist circles reporting the clash between the supporters of Simonian and Christian religions. Whether it was an individual tradition, and what form it may have taken, can no longer be decided with any certainty because of its fragmentary character, but an attractive hypothesis is that its basis was a cycle of stories about Philip. It is important to realize that the Hellenists were, as the story shows, confronted with other competing religions almost from the start and were doubtless exposed to all sorts of religious ideas, doctrines, and symbols.

*Verses 14–24:* Since this section is entirely redactional the search for any tradition can be omitted.

*Verse 25:* See on verses 14–24.

## HISTORICAL ELEMENTS

The mission in Samaria carried on by the Hellenist Philip is a historical fact. Chronologically, it took place in the 30s, after the expulsion of the Hellenists from Jerusalem on the occasion of the martyrdom of Stephen. However, it is not completely clear whether this took place among the Samarians (the Gentile population of Samaria) or the Samaritans (members of the religious community) who had their sanctuary on Mount Gerizim. As Simon Magus in all probability appeared among the Gentile population of Samaria and was worshipped there as an avatar of the God Zeus, it is likely that Philip also preached among the Gentile population of Samaria. However, this does not rule out a mission among the Samaritans. Similarly, the encounter of the Hellenists with followers of the Simonian religion in Samaria is likely to be an historical fact. Anyone who set foot there inevitably clashed with the followers of Simon, for in the middle of the second century Justin, who was born in Flavia Neapolis (Shechem) and probably knew the area, reports that almost all the members of his people worship Simon, the supreme God.[3] This sheds light on the question of the circumstances of the Hellenist mission in Samaria. The Hellenists had to clash with Simonians sooner or later. Therefore the tradition which Luke works on in Acts 8 is no doubt reliable in this detail.

*Acts 8:26–40:*

(26) Then an angel of the Lord said to Philip, "Rise and go south to the road that leads down *from Jerusalem to Gaza." This is a desert road.* (27) And he rose and went. Now it happened that an Ethiopian, a eunuch, a minister of Candace the queen of the Ethiopians, in charge of all her treasure, had come to Jerusalem to worship (28) and *was returning;* seated in his **carriage,** *he was reading the prophet Isaiah.*

(29) And the Spirit said to Philip, "Go up and join the **carriage.**" (30) So Philip ran up to him, and heard him reading Isaiah the prophet and asked, "Do you understand what you are reading?" (31) And he said, "How can I, unless some one guides me?" And he invited Philip to come up and sit with him. (32) *The passage of the scripture he was reading was this: "As a sheep led to the slaughter or a lamb before its shearer is dumb, so he opens not his mouth. (33) In his humiliation justice was denied to him. Who will ever talk about his descendants? For his life is taken up from the earth." (34) And the eunuch said to Philip, "Tell me, please, who is it that the prophet is speaking about*

here, himself or someone else?" (35) Then Philip opened his mouth, and
starting with this passage, he told him the good news of Jesus.

(36) As they went along the road they came to some water, and
the eunuch said, "Look, here is water! What is to prevent my being
baptized?" (37—an ancient gloss, omitted by the best texts) (38)
And he ordered the carriage to stop, and they both descended into
the water, Philip and the eunuch, and he baptized him.

(39) And when they came up out of the water, the Spirit of the
Lord snatched Philip away; and the eunuch saw him no more, for
he went on his way rejoicing.

(40) But Philip was found at Azotus, and passing on he preached in
all the towns until he reached Caesarea.

## Outline

Verses 26–28: Dual exposition: command of the angel to Philip to
travel along the road from Jerusalem to Gaza; return of
the Ethiopian eunuch from Jerusalem and his reading
from Isaiah

Verses 29–35: Encounter of Philip with the eunuch and preaching
of the gospel, based on Isa. 53:7–8

Verses 36 and 38: Baptism of the eunuch by Philip

Verse 39: Transportation of Philip after performing the baptism;
joyful return of the eunuch

Verse 40: Philip in Azotus (Ashdod). After preaching the gospel,
Philip arrives in Caesarea

*Verses 26–28:* The angel motif in verse 26 is redactional: Luke often
has angels appearing and giving commands to people in direct speech
(Luke 1:11–25, 26–28; 2:8–20; Acts 5:19f.; 12:6–17). The phrase "from
Jerusalem to Gaza" fits Luke's concept of mission; after Samaria in the
north has been missionized, the message now turns southwards: in
Luke's perspective Jerusalem once again becomes the starting point of
the gospel. "This is a desert road" (verse 26) is a redactional explanation (cf. 16:12b; 17:21; 23:8) which refers to the road between Jerusalem
and Gaza. The reference to the prophet Isaiah as well as the later
reported quotation (verses 32–33) comes from Luke (cf. Luke 4:17–18).

*Verses 29–35:* Verses 32–34 are completely redactional and, like

Luke 4:18–19, are Isaiah testimonies interpreted christologically. By contrast the narrative in the tradition which Luke redacted is about Philip's *proclamation* of Jesus, as verse 35 shows.

*Verses 36–38:* For the phrase in verse 36, "What is to prevent my being baptized?" see the almost identical redactional phrase in Acts 10:47 (cf. 11:17). Verse 37 does not belong to the original text, but was added later by the scribe of an ancient codex in order to make a dogmatic point. (The text runs as follows: "And Philip said, 'If you believe with all your heart, you may.' And he replied, 'I believe that Jesus Christ is the Son of God.'")

*Verse 39:* The sentence "for he (the eunuch) went on his way rejoicing" (verse 39d) does not fit well as the reason why he no longer saw Philip. The tension with the preceding sentence, and the linguistic evidence that "went on" and "rejoice" are favorite Lukan words, demonstrate that verse 39d is redactional and verse 39a–c is an element of the source material.

*Verse 40:* This verse is a pragmatic addition by Luke and tells the reader where Philip will be later, in Caesarea (Acts 21:8).


## THE TRADITION REWORKED BY LUKE

If we extract the certainly redactional features from the text we then get the following elements of tradition:

> "An Ethiopian, a eunuch" (verse 27b); "and they both descended into
> the water, Philip and the eunuch, and he baptized him" (verse 38);
> "now when they came up out of the water the Spirit of the Lord
> snatched Philip away, and the eunuch saw him no more" (verse 39).

Though we may have doubts about the exact length of the tradition, the evidence is enough for a form-critical classification: the tradition used by Luke is a conversion story, which probably had paradigmatic significance for the mission to the Gentiles in Hellenist circles. Luke has deliberately left the religious status of the eunuch in the air. Apparently he ventured to describe him as a proselyte because of what he found in his sources, but he could not let him appear as a Gentile because the full Gentile mission under the leadership of Peter really begins in Acts 10. Yet the tradition not only presupposes that he was a Gentile but also reports that the Gentile was a eunuch. That further emphasizes the statement that the gospel had gone beyond the bounds of Judaism. Perhaps in these circles the story was seen as the fulfillment of Isa. 56:3b–5:

> (3b) Let no eunuch say, "I am nothing but a barren tree." (4) For thus says the Lord: "To the eunuchs who keep my sabbaths, who choose the things that please me and hold fast my covenant, (5) I will give in my house and within my walls a monument and a name better than sons and daughters; I will give them an everlasting name that shall never be effaced.

The story gives the impression of being a very old one. It is probably part of a cycle of stories about Philip, two of which Luke worked into Acts 8 and from which he must have taken the report which is given later (21:8) about Philip and his prophesying virgin daughters. The style is legendary throughout, a mixture of the edifying, the personal, and the miraculous.

The legendary conversion story reflects the historical fact that the conversion of an Ethiopian eunuch was one of the missionary successes of the Hellenists and Philip. The possibility of this arises out of what is known about the Hellenists; the probability of such a verdict derives from the specific character of the tradition contained in Acts 8 (Ethiopian, eunuch) and the tension between this story and Acts 10. Chronologically we must think of the early 30s of the first century.

With this account Luke adds a second story about Philip to his narrative about the Hellenist mission outside Jerusalem. It should be noted that he does not report that the Spirit was bestowed on the eunuch, though as concerns verse 39 there is a secondary reading to that effect in an ancient codex the writer of which could not imagine that the eunuch did *not* receive the Holy Spirit. In this way Luke remained faithful to his principle, which became evident in the first story about Philip (8:5–25), not to connect the bestowing of the Spirit with the preaching of the Hellenists and to suppress reports to this effect.

That the possession of the Spirit is one of the main features of the

Hellenist tradition not only follows from the stories about Stephen and about Philip but can also be demonstrated on the basis of a later report in Acts about Philip's daughters.

*Acts 21:8–9:*

> (8) Next day we left and came to Caesarea; and we entered into the house of Philip the evangelist, who was one of the Seven, and stayed with him. (9) He had four unmarried daughters, who possessed the gift of prophecy.

This text is part of a source that narrated Paul's journey from Miletus to Jerusalem. It cannot be fiction because Luke does not invent stories, but transmits them on the basis of tradition while at the same time reworking them.

Paul's lodging at the house of Philip is also plausible because of his earlier contacts with the Hellenists (cf. also Paul's lodging in Mnason's house in Jerusalem, Acts 21:16). Remember that Paul's mother church was the Hellenist community of Antioch.

The account of the four prophetic virgin daughters of Philip is in all probability part of the tradition, since it fits in with the Hellenist traditions which report their spirit-filled activity, and is an interesting unbiased detail.

Polycrates of Ephesus reports on Philip and his three (!) virgin daughters in Hierapolis or Ephesus.[4] Although he includes Philip among the twelve apostles, the mention of the three prophetic daughters is likely to be evidence that the tradition originally meant the evangelist Philip. See also the narrative of bishop Papias of Hierapolis, about the stay of Philip with his daughters in Hierapolis.[5] However, he confuses the evangelist with the apostle Philip in the same way as Polycrates does.

*Acts 11:19–26c:*

> (19) *Now those who had been scattered because of the persecution that arose over Stephen traveled* as far as Phoenicia and Cyprus and Antioch, *proclaiming the word* to none except Jews. (20) But there

were some natives of Cyprus and Cyrene among them, and these, when they arrived at Antioch began to speak to the Greeks as well, *preaching the Lord Jesus. (21) And the hand of the Lord was with them, and a great number that believed turned to the Lord. (22) The news reached the ears of the church in Jerusalem, and they sent Barnabas to Antioch. (23) When he arrived and saw the divine grace at work, he rejoiced and exhorted them all to remain faithful to the Lord with steadfast purpose; (24) for he was a good man, full of the Holy Spirit and of faith. And a large company was added to the Lord.*

(25) So Barnabas went to Tarsus and looked for Saul; (26a–c) and when he had found him, he brought him to Antioch. For a whole year they met with the church, and taught a large company of people.

(26d) It was at Antioch that the disciples were for the first time called Christians.

*Outline*

> Verses 19–21: Spread of the preaching of the gospel to Antioch. *Notice of success* (verse 21)
> Verses 22–24: (After this event is noted by the Jerusalem community) sending of Barnabas to Antioch. *Notice of success* (verse 24b)
> Verses 25–26c: Barnabas brings Saul from Tarsus to Antioch. They work together there for a year
> Verse 26d: Passing remark about the origin of the name "Christians"

## LUKE'S INTENTION

*Verses 19–21:* Verse 19a corresponds word for word with Acts 8:4a, which in turn refers to 8:1. The verse is not a continuation of the interrupted statement 8:4a, but a redactional link to it. Luke wants to depict the continuation of the Hellenist mission, the external stimulus of which was the murder of Stephen in Acts 7:54–8:1a. In verse 19b–20 the phrases "proclaim the word" (cf. 4:29, 31; 8:25; 13:46; 14:25; 16:6, 32) and "preach the Lord Jesus" (cf. similarly 5:32) are redactional. Verse 19b brings out the fact that the mission of the Hellenists was originally only to Jews. That is in contrast to verse 20, according to which members of the Hellenists also preached to Gentiles. (Some important ancient texts read "Hellenists" instead of "Gentiles," but the context tells against this.) Also underlying verses 19–20 is the scheme "to the Jews first—then to the Gentiles" which also holds for Luke's Paul (cf. 13:5, 14; 14:1; 16:13; 17:1f., 10, 17). For the other redactional features in this section see the words and phrases printed in italics.

*Verses 22–24:* This section's derivation from Luke is evident from its language and content. Note that as in other cases the Jerusalem community intervenes when a decisive change is about to occur. This is especially true when 11:22–24 is compared with 8:14–24: Both passages are intended to show Jerusalem's sanction of the Hellenists' outreach and to attest the unity of the two groups within the earliest community. In fact, the danger of a split was very real, as is suggested by the suspicious independence with which the narratives about the Hellenists and Peter run side by side in Acts 6–12.

*Verses 25–26c:* Here Luke introduces the future hero and has him brought by Barnabas from Tarsus to Antioch.

*Verse 26d:* At this point where he gives a summary report, Luke introduces an interesting detail about the emergence of the name "Christian," albeit not within the narrative but at the author-reader level. It is obvious that the historical accuracy of the information in verse 26d at least in part depends on the trustworthiness of the narrative to which verse 26d belongs. Therefore we must carefully examine it by next asking whether there is any tradition contained in the account which so far we have analyzed at the redactional level.


## THE TRADITION REWORKED BY LUKE

Looking at Acts 11:19–26 as a whole we have to state that a relatively large number of facts are set side by side with little or no specific narrative context. This enhances our suspicion that Luke has condensed a large number of traditional pieces and added some redactional links to them.

*Verses 19–21, 22–23:* The report of the Hellenist mission to

Phoenicia, Cyprus, and Antioch is part of the tradition, since here we have concrete information without a bias. The sources about the mission on *Cyprus* were probably reports about Barnabas—himself a Greek-speaking Jewish Christian and active in the Antioch community (verse 22; cf. Acts 13:1)—which Luke used for his information in verse 19. Luke drew the majority of his material from *Antioch* (cf. later verse 26d and Acts 13:1–3; 15:1–2, etc.), so there certainly had to be a mention of Antioch here at the end, all the more since from 13:1 on Antioch will come into the foreground of the narrative.

The note about the mission to the Gentiles in verse 20 is tradition, since it does not fit into Luke's view of history. But by itself it means that the Hellenists were the first to inaugurate a Gentile mission, and not Peter through the conversion of Cornelius as Luke claims (Acts 10f.).

Underlying verses 22–23 is a tradition the content of which is the activity of Barnabas in the Antioch community (cf. Acts 13:1–2). We can also recognize that the link between Barnabas and Jerusalem (cf. earlier 4:36; 9:37) is a Lukan fiction: verse 24 seems to forget that according to verse 22b he was sent by the Jerusalem community and gives no reason for his stay in Antioch. This demonstrates the link in the tradition between Barnabas and Antioch.

*Verses 25–26c:* Tarsus as the place of Paul's stay is confirmed by Acts 11:30. The activity of Barnabas and Paul in Antioch for the period of a year is probably part of the tradition, since it is a specific unmotivated report in a context containing miscellaneous fragments of tradition.

*Verse 26d:* The information about the origin of the name "Christians" in Antioch is likely to go back to an isolated tradition which Luke has inserted here, or else it was part of the source that goes back to the Hellenists.

## HISTORICAL ELEMENTS

The traditions behind verses 19–26 are without doubt historical, namely that the Hellenists began the missions to the Gentiles on

Cyprus, Phoenicia, and Antioch. Their beginnings probably lie in the middle 30s.

The tradition that Paul and Barnabas worked together in the Antiochene mission for a period has a high degree of probability. We find Barnabas and Paul together at Antioch during the incident at Antioch (Gal. 2:11–14), Paul and Barnabas went together to Jerusalem (Gal. 2:1) when the Jerusalem Conference took place; and they were put in charge of the mission to the Gentiles (Gal. 2:9). Last but not least, 1 Cor. 9:6 adduces their previous partnership.

On the historical accuracy of verse 26d see above, p. 138.

## NOTES

1. For the following see my *Early Christianity according to the Traditions in Acts: A Commentary* (Minneapolis: Fortress Press, 1989), pp. 73–139.
2. See Philo *On the Special Laws* 1.54–57.
3. Justin *First Apology* 26.3.
4. Eusebius *Ecclesiastical History* 3.31.3.
5. Eusebius *Ecclesiastical History* 3.39.9.

# SELECT
# BIBLIOGRAPHY

Allison, Dale C., Jr. "The Pauline Epistles and the Synoptic Gospels: The Pattern of the Parallels." *New Testament Studies* 28 (1982): 1–32.

Baeck, Leo. *Judaism and Christianity*. Essays by Leo Baeck, translated with an introduction by Walter Kaufmann. Cleveland/New York: World Publishing Company and Philadelphia: Jewish Publication Society of America, Meredian Books, 1961.

Baur, Ferdinand Christian. *Paul, the Apostle of Jesus Christ*. 2 vols. London/Edinburgh: Williams & Norgate, 1875, 1876.

Betz, Hans Dieter. *Galatians: A Commentary on Paul's Letter to the Churches in Galatia*. Philadelphia: Fortress Press, 1979.

———. "Paul's Ideas about the Origins of Christianity." In Hans Dieter Betz, *Paulinische Studien*. Gesammelte Aufsätze III, pp. 272–88. Tübingen: J. C. B. Mohr (Paul Siebeck), 1994.

———. "The Birth of Christianity as a Hellenistic Religion: Three Theories of Origin." *Journal of Religion* 74 (1994): 1–25.

Bornkamm, Günther. *Paul*. New York: Harper & Row, 1971.

Bultmann, Rudolf. *Theology of the New Testament*. 2 vols. New York: Charles Scribner's Sons, 1951, 1955.

Chadwick, Henry, ed. Origen. *Contra Celsum*. Translated with an introduction and notes, reprinted with corrections. Cambridge: University Press, 1965.

Charlesworth, James H., ed. *The Old Testament Pseudepigrapha*. Vol. 1, *Apocalyptic Literature and Testaments*. New York: Doubleday & Company, 1983.

———. *The Old Testament Pseudepigrapha*. Vol. 2, *Expansions of the "Old Testament" and Legends, Wisdom and Philosophical Literature, Prayers, Psalms, and Odes, Fragments of Lost Judeo-Hellenistic Works*. New York: Doubleday & Company, 1985.

Collins, John J. *Between Athens and Jerusalem: Jewish Identity in the Hellenistic Diaspora*. New York: Crossroad, 1983.

Deissmann, Adolf. *Paul: A Study in Social and Religious History.* New York: Harper & Brothers, Torchbooks, 1957.

Dunn, James D. G. "Who Did Paul Think That He Was? A Study of Jewish-Christian Identity." *New Testament Studies* 45 (1999): 174–93.

Engberg-Pedersen, Troels, ed. *Paul in His Hellenistic Context.* Minneapolis: Fortress Press, 1995.

Fitzmyer, John A. *Romans: A New Translation with Introduction and Commentary.* Anchor Bible, vol. 33. New York: Doubleday, 1993.

———. *The Letter to Philemon: A New Translation with Introduction and Commentary.* Anchor Bible, vol. 34 C. New York: Doubleday, 2000.

Furnish, Victor Paul. *Theology and Ethics in Paul.* Nashville: Abingdon Press, 1968.

Harnack Adolf. *What Is Christianity?* New York: Harper & Row, Torchbooks, 1957.

———. *The Mission and Expansion of Christianity in the First Three Centuries.* 2 vols. New York: Harper & Row, Torchbooks, 1962.

Heininger, Bernhard. *Paulus als Visionär. Eine religionsgeschichtliche Studie.* Freiburg: Herder, 1996.

Hengel, Martin. *The Pre-Christian Paul.* Philadelphia: Trinity Press International, 1991.

Hengel, Martin, and Anna Maria Schwemer. *Paul between Damascus and Antioch: The Unknown Years.* Louisville: Westminster John Knox Press, 1997.

Hill, Craig. *Hellenists and Hebrews: Reappraising Divisions within the Early Church.* Minneapolis: Fortress Press, 1992.

Hock, Ronald F. *The Social Context of Paul's Ministry: Tentmaking and Apostleship.* Philadelphia: Fortress Press, 1980.

Hoffmann, R. Joseph, ed. *Porphyry's Against the Christians: The Literary Remains.* Edited and translated, with an introduction and epilogue. Amherst, N.Y.: Prometheus Books, 1994.

James, Montague Rhodes. *The Apocryphal New Testament Being the Apocryphal Gospels, Acts, Epistles, and Apocalypses.* Oxford: Clarendon Press, 1924.

Jewett, Robert. *A Chronology of Paul's Life.* Philadelphia: Fortress Press, 1982.

Jones, F. Stanley. *An Ancient Jewish Christian Source on the History of Christianity: Pseudo-Clementine Recognitions 1.27–71.* Atlanta: Scholars Press, 1995.

Kaufmann, Walter, ed. *The Portable Nietzsche.* Selected and translated, with an introduction, prefaces, and notes. New York: Viking Press, 1954.

Keck, Leander E. *Paul and His Letters.* 2d ed., rev. ed. Philadelphia: Fortress Press, 1988.

Klausner, Joseph. *From Jesus to Paul.* London: Allen & Unwinn, 1943.

Knox, John. *Philemon among the Letters of Paul: A New View of Its Place and Importance.* 2d ed. New York and Nashville: Abingdon Press, 1959.

———. *Chapters in a Life of Paul*. Revised by the author and edited, with introduction, by Douglas R. A. Hare. Macon: Mercer University Press, 1987.

Lieberman, Saul. *Hellenism in Jewish Palestine*. rev. ed. New York: Jewish Theological Seminary of America, 1962.

Loisy, Alfred. *The Gospel and the Church*. London: Ibister and Co., 1903.

Lüdemann, Gerd. *Paul, Apostle of the Gentiles: Studies in Chronology*. Philadelphia: Fortress Press, 1984.

———. *Opposition to Paul in Early Christianity*. Minneapolis: Fortress Press, 1989.

———. *Early Christianity according to the Traditions in Acts: A Commentary*. Minneapolis: Fortress Press, 1989.

———. *Heretics: The Other Side of Early Christianity*. Louisville: Westminster John Knox Press, 1996.

———. *Virgin Birth? The Real History of Mary and Her Son Jesus*. Harrisburg: Trinity Press International, 1998.

———. *Jesus After Two Thousand Years: What He Really Said and Did*. Amherst, N.Y.: Prometheus Books, 2001.

Maccoby, Hyam. *The Mythmaker: Paul and the Invention of Christianity*. New York: Harper & Row, 1986.

———. *Paul and Hellenism*. Philadelphia: Trinity Press International, 1991.

Malherbe, Abraham. *Moral Exhortation: A Greco-Roman Sourcebook*. Philadelphia: Westminster Press, 1986.

Mason, Steve N. *Flavius Josephus on the Pharisees: A Composition-Critical Study*. Leiden: E. J. Brill, 1991.

Meeks, Wayne A. *The Origins of Christian Morality: The First Two Centuries*. New Haven and London: Yale University Press, 1993.

Murphy-O'Connor, Jerome. *Paul: A Critical Life*. Oxford/New York: Oxford University Press, 1996.

Murray, Gilbert. *Four Stages of Greek Religion*. London: Watts & Company, 1935.

Neusner, Jacob. *Children of the Flesh, Children of the Promise: A Rabbi Talks with Paul*. Cleveland: Pilgrim Press, 1995.

Nock, Arthur Darby. *St. Paul*. New York and Evanston: Harper & Row, Torchbooks, 1963.

———. *Early Gentile Christianity and Its Hellenistic Background*. New York: Harper & Row, Torchbooks, 1964.

Petersen, Norman. *Rediscovering Paul: Philemon and the Sociology of Paul's Narrative World*. Philadelphia: Fortress Press, 1985.

Porter, Stanley E. *The Paul of Acts: Essays in Literary Criticism, Rhetoric, and Theology*. Tübingen: J. C. B. Mohr (Paul Siebeck), 1999.

Räisänen, Heikki. *Paul and the Law.* 2d ed., revised and enlarged. Tübingen: J. C. B. Mohr (Paul Siebeck), 1987.

Sanders, E. P. *Paul and Palestinian Judaism: A Comparison of Patterns of Religion.* Philadelphia: Fortress Press, 1977.

————. *Jewish Law from Jesus to the Mishnah.* Harrisburg: Trinity Press International, 1990.

————. *Paul.* Oxford/New York: Oxford University Press, 1991.

————. *Judaism: Practice and Belief 63 B.C.E.–66 C.E.* Philadelphia: Trinity Press International, 1992.

Schweitzer, Albert. *The Mysticism of Paul the Apostle.* New York: Seabury Press, 1968.

Segal, Alan F. *Paul the Convert: The Apostolate and Apostasy of Saul the Pharisee.* New Haven and London: Yale University Press, 1990.

Simon, Marcel. *St. Stephen and the Hellenists in the Primitive Church.* London/New York/Toronto: Longmans, Green and Co., 1958.

Stowers, Stanley K. *The Diatribe and Paul's Letter to the Romans.* Chico: Scholars Press, 1981.

Strack, Hermann L. *Introduction to the Talmud and Midrash.* New York: Jewish Publication Society of America, 1931.

Wedderburn, A. J. M., ed. *Paul and Jesus: Collected Essays.* Sheffield: Sheffield Academic Press, 1989.

Weiss, Johannes. *Earliest Christianity: A History of the Period A.D. 30–150.* English translation edited with a new introduction and bibliography by Frederick C. Grant. 2 vols. 1937. Reprint, Gloucester, Mass.: Peter Smith, 1970.

Wenham, David. *Paul: Follower of Jesus or Founder of Christianity?* Grand Rapids, Mich.: Wm. B. Eerdmans Publishing Co., 1995.

White John L. *Light from Ancient Letters.* Philadelphia: Fortress Press, 1986.

Wiles, Maurice. *The Divine Apostle: The Interpretation of St. Paul's Epistles in the Early Church.* Cambridge: University Press, 1967.

Wilson, A. N. *Paul: The Mind of the Apostle.* New York: W. W. Norton & Company, 1997.

Wrede, William. *Die Echtheit des zweiten Thessalonicherbriefs untersucht.* Leipzig: J. C. Hinrich'sche Buchhandlung, 1903.

Wright, N. T. *What Saint Paul Really Said: Was Paul of Tarsus the Real Founder of Christianity?* Grand Rapids, Mich.: Wm. B. Eerdmans Publishing Co., 1997.

# INDEX OF SELECT NEW TESTAMENT PASSAGES